Portugal, China and the
Macau Negotiations, 1986–1999

Royal Asiatic Society Hong Kong Studies Series

Royal Asiatic Society Hong Kong Studies Series is designed to make widely available important contributions on the local history, culture and society of Hong Kong and the surrounding region. Generous support from the Sir Lindsay and Lady May Ride Memorial Fund makes it possible to publish a series of high-quality works that will be of lasting appeal and value to all, both scholars and informed general readers, who share a deeper interest in and enthusiasm for the area.

Recent titles in the RAS Hong Kong Studies Series:
Hong Kong Internment, 1942–1945: Life in the Japanese Civilian Camp at Stanley
Geoffrey Charles Emerson

East River Column: Hong Kong Guerrillas in the Second World War and After
Chan Sui-jeung

Southern District Officer Reports: Islands and Villages in Rural Hong Kong, 1910–60
Edited by John Strickland

Cantonese Society in Hong Kong and Singapore: Gender, Religion, Medicine and Money
Essays by Marjorie Topley; edited and introduced by Jean DeBernardi

Early China Coast Meteorology: The Role of Hong Kong
P. Kevin MacKeown

Forgotten Souls: A Social History of the Hong Kong Cemetery
Patricia Lim

Ancestral Images: A Hong Kong Collection
Hugh Baker

Escape from Hong Kong: Admiral Chan Chak's Christmas Day Dash, 1941
Tim Luard

Governors, Politics and the Colonial Office: Public Policy in Hong Kong, 1918–58
Gavin Ure

Scottish Mandarin: The Life and Times of Sir Reginald Johnston
Shiona Airlie

Custom, Land and Livelihood in Rural South China: The Traditional Land Law of Hong Kong's New Territories, 1750–1950
Patrick H. Hase

Portugal, China and the Macau Negotiations, 1986–1999

Carmen Amado Mendes

HONG KONG UNIVERSITY PRESS

Hong Kong University Press
The University of Hong Kong
Pokfulam Road
Hong Kong
www.hkupress.org

© Hong Kong University Press 2013

ISBN 978-988-8139-00-2 (*Hardback*)

All rights reserved. No portion of this publication may be reproduced or transmitted in any form or by any means, electronic or mechanical, including photocopy, recording, or any information storage or retrieval system, without permission in writing from the publisher.

British Library Cataloguing-in-Publication Data
A catalogue record for this book is available from the British Library.

Digitally printed

Contents

List of Figures	vii
Acknowledgements	ix
List of Abbreviations	xi
Introduction	1

1 The Ambiguity over the Future of Macau 7
   The Political Background to the "Macau Question" 9
   Portuguese Withdrawal from Empire 18
   The Establishment of Sino-Portuguese Relations 25
   A Muddled and Multifaceted Process 33

2 Negotiations for the Sino-Portuguese Joint Declaration on Macau 37
   The Beginning 37
   The Hong Kong Model 39
   Getting Portugal to the Table 43
   The Search for a Formula 47
   Details of the Negotiations 50
   The Agreement 58
   All's Well that Ends Well? 61

3 The Transition Period and the Problems of "Localisation" 63
   Double Tutelage and Macau 64
   Portuguese Approaches for the Transition 68
   The Joint Liaison Group and the Land Group 72
   Localisation: Permanent Issues throughout the Transition Period 75
   The Impact of Portuguese Politics upon the Localisation Process 83

4 Other Delicate Transition Issues: Covenants, Construction and   85
   Possible Corruption
   The International Covenants   85
   The Macau International Airport   88
   The Orient Foundation   95
   Portugal, China, and the Transition Negotiations   100

5 A Final Assessment   103
   The Portuguese Strategy for the Macau Negotiations   104
   Portuguese Negotiating Advantages   107
   Negotiating Methods and Tactics   111
   Asymmetrical Bargaining   113

Notes   115

Bibliography   143

Index   153

Figures

Figure 1 Macau double tutelage system   65
Figure 2 The Portuguese decision-makers of the transition   66
          period

Acknowledgements

This book is based upon my dissertation, "Portugal and the Settlement of the Macau Question, 1984–1999; Pragmatism in International Negotiations" submitted to the School of Oriental and African Studies in the University of London. That research was made possible by a research scholarship from the Portuguese Ministry of Science and High Education—financed by the *Fundação para a Ciência e a Tecnologia* (FCT—Foundation for Science and Technology) and the European Social Fund, within the Third Community Support Framework—for which I am grateful. This book was published within the framework of the project, "Assessing the 'one country, two systems' Formula: The Role of Macau in China's Relations with the EU and Portuguese Speaking Countries", also generously funded by the FCT and by FEDER funds through COMPETE Programme (FCOMP-01-0124-FEDER-009198).

I owe a number of other debts. In the course of my thesis fieldwork in Portugal, a wide range of interviews were conducted in Lisbon, and I was granted access to a considerable amount of confidential documents. I am deeply indebted to various officials of the Portuguese and Macau governments for giving me so much of their time and offering many valuable comments and insights. I would also like to thank my dissertation supervisor, Dr. Phil Deans for his understanding and patience and insightful suggestions in my thesis, and Dr. Moisés Fernandes of the University of Lisbon, for his support and advice. In addition, I am very grateful to Professor Richard Louis Edmonds for his editing help in producing this book. While these people and many others have offered their support, I solely am responsible for any mistakes or misunderstandings.

Finally, I would like to thank my parents, Isabel and Mateus, and brother Miguel. The book would not have been possible without their help and encouragement over the years.

Abbreviations

BNU   National Overseas Bank (*Banco Nacional Ultramarino*)
CAM   Macau International Airport Company Limited (*Companhia do Aeroporto de Macau*)
CCP   Chinese Communist Party
CDS   Central Democratic Social Party (*Partido do Centro Democrático Social*)
CGA   Portugal's Retirement Fund (*Caixa Geral de Aposentações*)
EEC   European Economic Community
EU   European Union
GTJ   Legal Translation Bureau (*Gabinete para a Tradução Jurídica*)
HKSAR   Hong Kong Special Administrative Region
JLG   Joint Liaison Group
LG   Land Group
MP   Member of Parliament
MSAR   Macau Special Administrative Region
NATO   North Atlantic Treaty Organisation
NPC   National People's Congress
OAU   Organization of African Unity
PRC   People's Republic of China
PRD   Democratic Renewal Party (*Partido Renovador Democrático*)
PS   Socialist Party (*Partido Socialista*)
PSD   Social Democrat Party (*Partido Social Democrata*)
STDM   Macau's Tourism and Entertainment Company (*Sociedade de Turismo e Diversões de Macau*)
UK   United Kingdom
UN   United Nations
USA   United States of America
USSR   Union of Soviet Socialist Republics

Introduction

This book examines how the Portuguese government negotiated the question of Macau's retrocession with the People's Republic of China (PRC) in the 1980s and 1990s—primarily between 1986 and 1999. As negotiating partners interested in passive settlement, Portugal and China used Macau as a political showcase. In Portugal, the centre-right Social Democrat Party (PSD) in power (1985–1995), fierce opponent of the leftist Socialist Party (PS), was adamant to take advantage of the negotiations with the Chinese to leverage internal political support. The left's disorganised decolonisation in Africa and subsequent withdrawal from East Timor was the catalyst for the PSD's strategy. The 1974 Carnation Revolution, which marked the end of colonialism and authoritarian rule, was a bittersweet experience which the PSD sought to assuage. Meanwhile, the Chinese government saw Macau as part of a bigger plan for national reunification: a useful tool for summoning Taiwan to its "one country, two systems" formula.

Being a study of foreign policy set in a specific period, the focus is on inter-state relations during a negotiation process. The PRC's more powerful position was influential and a determinant in Portugal's behaviour and internal decision-making processes. The dynamics around the nature of the Sino-Portuguese negotiations on Macau's reversion thus were framed asymmetrically along the lines of small versus big, weak versus strong.

Relations between states are idealised to be symmetric but influential asymmetries between the parties often occur.[1] Studies on weak state-strong state negotiations, i.e. "negotiations in which the power resources and capabilities of the two actors are unequal" are relatively rare.[2] Besides, traditional theories of power assume that "power implies benefits in international bargaining", and that the stronger state wins over the weaker state.[3] This is not always the case, as strength may be a matter of perception and power is situational.[4] Power is not all in determining the outcome of negotiations: the weak negotiating with the strong may make some (even if minor) gain.[5]

In theory a stronger power prevails over a weaker power but a weak power may obtain certain concessions from a great power. It was generally expected that Portugal would struggle to achieve key objectives in the negotiations over Macau's reversion to China. This book argues that Portugal, a small and weak power, did manage to obtain some important concessions from the PRC. This demonstrates that small powers do have a certain influence on the outcome of negotiations and may obtain certain concessions from stronger powers. Then again the fact that Portugal has relatively little international influence does not mean that it is an insignificant state: it has privileged relations with Portuguese-speaking countries, for example.[6] Moreover, the Chinese leadership, although expecting to be treated with the respect of a great power, always professed a belief in equality and fair play in negotiations.[7]

This book argues that a weak power may obtain concessions from a strong power for two main reasons: the weaker power may have a veto power, and the stronger power may commit a *faux pas*. The Portuguese government had a veto that it could use during the negotiations with China—to threaten to abandon Macau and refuse to negotiate. If the Portuguese left Macau before the end of the negotiations and did not respect a date settled by the two countries, the Chinese Communist Party's policy of national reunification would have been seriously damaged and the application of the "one country, two systems" model to Taiwan would have become more problematic. The PRC wanted to avoid this at all costs and therefore, would make concessions to the Portuguese government because of this potential veto. Moreover, China committed an error of judgment by underestimating Portugal. Due to differences in power between the two countries, the PRC was convinced that after the Hong Kong reversion, Macau would be an easy negotiation. The Portuguese government, however, did not concede some of its positions, pushing China to more intermediate decisions and to some concessions.

The outcome of the negotiations included two major concessions by the Chinese. The first was the date of the Macau handover. The PRC wanted it to be simultaneous with the Hong Kong handover, whereas Portugal preferred to keep Macau until the twenty-first century, possibly to 2007, the date of the 450th anniversary of the Portuguese presence in Macau. The Portuguese government could not get all it hoped for; the PRC had committed itself to getting Macau back before the end of the twentieth century. Portugal, nevertheless, achieved its ultimate aim. The Hong Kong and Macau handovers were two and a half years apart, not simultaneous. China made another concession over the nationality issue. The PRC agreed to respect Portuguese passports carried by the residents of Macau—albeit described as "Portuguese travel documents".

The first chapter provides the political background for the Macau question. It begins with a discussion of Portuguese settlement in Macau from the sixteenth century until the establishment of Sino-Portuguese relations in 1979, noting that Macau was one of the obstacles that delayed the establishment of diplomatic relations between Portugal and the PRC. The 1979 agreement was very important as it established the principles for future negotiations: the two governments first defined their positions on Macau, agreeing to not unilaterally change the status quo and that the retrocession of Macau would only be settled through negotiation. We see that the Portuguese were very confused about how to deal with Macau—a small enclave without a sense of national identity—and did not develop a strategy for settlement of the question. When China put the Macau question on the table, Portuguese diplomats were confused and had no significant expertise on contemporary Macau, making it very difficult for the Portuguese government to delineate a coherent negotiating strategy.

The second chapter looks at the early period of the Sino-Portuguese negotiations for the settlement of the Macau question from 1986 to 1987. As previously noted, Macau's reversion to mainland China was highly influenced by the process occurring in the neighbouring colony of Hong Kong. On the one hand, Portugal was concerned that Macau got comparable treatment to that of Hong Kong but on the other hand, Portugal argued that Hong Kong and Macau were completely different cases because China had accepted a Portuguese presence in Macau over centuries and there was no formal time for the return of any part of Macau to China as was the case with the New Territories of Hong Kong in 1997.

The most contentious issues of the negotiations were the setting of the date for the transfer of Portuguese administration to the PRC and the future nationality of Macau's inhabitants. The Chinese government wanted a simultaneous handover for Hong Kong and Macau and would not accept a Macau transfer after the end of the twentieth century, whereas the Portuguese favoured a later date for the transfer as previously mentioned. The automatic imposition before the Chinese Communist Party (CCP) Central Committee of the end of the twentieth century as the date for reversion of the territory was a Chinese *faux pas*: knowing that China was under internal pressure to finish negotiations, Portugal put issues on the negotiating table that the Chinese had no time to manoeuvre against. A particularly problematic issue was the future nationality of Macau citizens holding Portuguese passports. The Portuguese government wanted them to have dual nationality whereas China wanted them to possess Chinese nationality only, as the Chinese Constitution does not recognise dual citizenship.

The next two chapters look at the Macau transition, which took place from the entry into force of the Sino-Portuguese Joint Declaration in 1988 to the Macau handover in late 1999. The Portuguese domestic context and the activities of the two joint commissions created in accordance with the Joint Declaration, the Sino-Portuguese Joint Liaison Group (JLG) and the Land Group (LG), are described in Chapter Three along with the three major permanent issues of the transition period: the localisation of language, civil service, and the law. The localisation of the civil service consisted of replacing Portuguese functionaries with local staff. This could not be done without the use of the Chinese language (essentially spoken Cantonese) in the civil service and at the legislative and judicial levels, as most local staff did not have a good command of Portuguese. The localisation of the law consisted in transforming Portuguese laws that were in force into an officially and practically local form for Macau.

Chapter Four discusses some sensitive issues of the transition period: the inclusion/exclusion in the Macau Basic Law of the provisions of the International Covenant on Civil and Political Rights as well as the International Covenant on Economic, Social and Cultural Rights, the construction of the Macau International Airport, and issues surrounding the future and the existing funds of the Orient Foundation. The Portuguese made several mistakes when negotiating these issues. They should have negotiated the extension of the covenants to Macau during the Joint Declaration negotiations, as the United Kingdom did with Hong Kong, instead of leaving the matter to be resolved in the transition period. In the case of the Orient Foundation, the delay in agreeing to discuss the issue in the JLG's meetings and in taking a stand led to a hardening of the Chinese position and a loss of Portugal's power. The Portuguese, however, were able to take advantage of reactions to the Tiananmen incident to better negotiate important concessions in the construction of the airport.

In sum, Portugal employed a low-key, non-confrontational strategy in the Macau negotiations, allowing China to control the pace of the talks. This consensual strategy was in part the result of Portugal's domestic political context. Divisions amongst political leaders and poorly prepared negotiators resulted in a lack of resolve to get the best benefits for Macau and for Portugal. Diplomats were poorly trained as a result of the institutional organization of the Ministry of Foreign Affairs: the shortage of human resources does not allow a permanent specialization on specific issues or regions and a serious preparation before the start of a new post. Diplomats usually move to a completely different country just when they are gathering expertise on their post. The result was the absence of experienced and prepared negotiators and the lack of a specialised department on Macau.

On the political side, the Portuguese took positions that limited the possibility for developing their own strategy for Macau upon China. The question over Macau's future status was greatly complicated by conflicts in Portugal over responsibility for negotiating with China. Due to the double tutelage system, negotiators received from the government contradictory orders to those given by the president to the governor. Basically Lisbon tried to ensure that Macau's treatment was not worse than that of Hong Kong. Despite this, Portugal managed to extract some concessions in the negotiation process based upon China's worries about their international image and Taiwan. After the withdrawal, Portugal generally expunged Macau from its political agenda, unlike the UK, which retained a presence in Hong Kong after handover of the colony in 1997.

1
The Ambiguity over the Future of Macau

Long before the negotiations about the future of Macau started, a cloud of precariousness hovered for a number of centuries over Portugal's presence in a small peninsula, offset by fluctuations in Chinese power. It was probably out of sheer short-sightedness that Portugal did not legitimise its presence in Macau, believing that the friendly relations it enjoyed with China would remain in the long run despite its fragile presence in the territory. In more recent times, a notion of historical shared sovereignty[1] and the vaguely worded Sino-Portuguese Joint Declaration of 1987 meant that Portugal and the PRC accepted the principle that both had jurisdictional rights in Macau.[2] This scenario served to reinforce Portugal's undetermined position in Macau.

The Portuguese established themselves in Macau during the sixteenth century and remained there for four centuries through shared sovereignty.[3] From the first Portuguese settlement until the signature of the Sino-Portuguese Joint Declaration in 1987, Portugal conformed to the rules imposed by China with a few exceptions. One occurred in 1783 when Portugal declared the right of sovereignty over Macau with both countries sharing equal sovereignty over the territory. Then in 1849, Governor Ferreira do Amaral succeeded imposing *de facto* Portuguese sovereignty over the territory, leaving China with limited powers. However, the 1862 Treaty of Friendship and Trade that appeared to shift the balance of power in Portugal's favour faltered. It was never ratified. Macau legally was not considered Portuguese territory. Territorial legitimacy was based on a loose system of values, riding on interests of economic and political significance.

In 1887 the two countries signed the Lisbon Protocol and the Treaty of Friendship and Trade, giving Portugal the same privileges and immunities that a number of other foreign countries enjoyed within China. This remained the status until 1949, the year that marked the termination of diplomatic relations with establishment of the PRC. The Portuguese right-wing regime refused to recognise the legitimacy of the PRC. This situation was bypassed through the establishment of unofficial channels bridged by Macau Chinese acting as *de facto* intermediaries.[4] It was not until 1976 that the Portuguese Constitution and the *Estatuto Orgânico de Macau* (Macau Organic Law) made decisive changes to Macau's legal status, defining it as territory under Portuguese administration. At the same time, China regained some of its powers of sovereignty over Macau. During the transition period (1988–1999) the two countries shared again a degree of sovereignty over Macau.[5]

After the establishment of the PRC in 1949, Portugal and China were bound by mutual interests that both enjoyed in Macau. For the Portuguese, Macau had symbolic meaning, strategically aligned to myths of imperial prominence and cultural largesse. Portuguese colonialism was sustained on these grounds. The status quo in Macau subsisted to pay lip service to Portugal's past world-leading role. On the other hand, rational China, keen to keep the status quo in Macau at that time, sought to undermine Portugal's administration of the enclave to facilitate its subservience to the PRC's will.

Historically Macau served as a gateway of communication with the West; an important commercial hub serving as an outlet for Chinese goods and an invaluable source of foreign exchange.[6] For example, during the Korean War (1950–1953) the PRC used Macau as a bridge to break the blockade imposed on it by the West.[7] In fact, Macau was *de jure* administered by Portugal but *de facto* controlled by China,[8] giving the impression that Portugal had nominal status vis-à-vis mainland China.

Decolonisation of the African possessions in 1974 resulted in Portugal's political system undergoing significant change. By 1975 the new Portuguese regime had withdrawn entirely from Africa and East Timor, which had a bearing on how Portugal viewed its role in Macau: complacent and disinterested. In fact Portugal feared further embarrassment by keeping Macau, in the context of the decolonisation of its possessions in Africa. Portugal's nonchalant attitude annoyed the PRC as it intended to maintain the status quo in Macau—reasoning based on a number of considerations including the safeguarding of Hong Kong's stability and keeping both territories as pathways open to trade and contact with the West.[9]

Finally in 1979 a new leftist regime in Portugal re-established diplomatic relations with the PRC after a prolonged stalemate, by signing a secret agreement in which Portugal agreed to accept China's sovereignty over Macau. This agreement, known as the *Acta Secreta* (Secret Memorandum), was signed simultaneously with the joint communiqué, establishing bilateral relations. In the *Acta Secreta*, Portugal accepted China's view of Macau as "territory under Portuguese administration". Portugal also gave China *carte blanche* to set an appropriate date for negotiations to settle the status of Macau.

Both Portugal and the PRC were aware that a negotiated settlement of Macau would have to happen eventually but for strategic, circumstantial and political reasons put it off. This state of denial would finally come to a halt with China's growing international predominance beginning in the late 1970s, and the simultaneous decline of Portugal enhanced by a decolonisation experience in Africa and ensuing economic crisis at home. This situation carved deep wounds in the Portuguese and later underpinned Portugal's modus operandi during the negotiation process of Macau. Portuguese negotiators knew that they were the weaker partner not just from a psychological perspective but also economically and politically, dampening their chances at a steadfast settlement, even though Portugal was determined to secure an honourable withdrawal from Macau.[10]

The Political Background to the "Macau Question"

The Chinese and Portuguese both hail back to historical greatness in constructing their world views. We need to learn how a degree of ambiguity came to exist around the status of the territory, beginning with the arrival of the Portuguese, and how this status was partially resolved in the late nineteenth century. We also must remember that the status of Macau remained unclear when compared to neighbouring Hong Kong vis-à-vis powers of administration conferred on the UK. Moreover, both Macau and Hong Kong were cases of retrocession, and not decolonization. Conceptually, by retrocession we mean situations in which the administering power withdraws but the enclave does not have the right to self-determination, while citizens of decolonized territories can decide upon their future through vote. This section will present other cases of retrocession experienced by China, providing an historical context to understand the case of Macau.

The year 1513 most likely marked the arrival of Portuguese sailors at the Zhu (Pearl) River estuary, and the beginning of a system of fruitful exchanges with the mainland. After a period of defiance faced by a Portuguese mission who aspired to meet the Chinese emperor, a meeting was eventually allowed. Occurring in Beijing in 1520, the meeting was doomed at the outset due to the emperor's sense of indignation, arising from a letter written by the Portuguese king, interpreted as discourteous due to its assumption of equal treatment. According to the Chinese emperor, the Portuguese king could by no means be considered an "equal". From his standpoint there could be no other authority superior than the emperor himself. In 1522, another attempt on the part of the Portuguese to establish relations with China failed. A number of attacks on the Portuguese fleet followed. The Portuguese king immediately suspended official missions to China, even though on the ground the reality was different. Trade relations between Portuguese and Chinese merchants flourished unabated.[11]

When the Ming dynasty cut off trade with Japan in 1523, the traffic of smuggled goods grew with Portuguese sailors acting as middlemen between Chinese and Japanese traders. The Portuguese acted as middlemen in most business interactions, where Chinese silk and Japanese copper and silver were concerned, which they sold interchangeably between the two countries. These transactions were highly lucrative for the Portuguese as well as Chinese and Japanese merchants. Chinese authorities turned a blind eye to this well-established illegal maritime trade.[12]

At first, these commercial transactions occurred at sea, but with the permanent growing settlement of Portuguese merchants in a number of locations in the Zhu (Pearl) River delta, business exchanges moved inland, fostering trade and tenure. Due to its strategic position, Macau gradually gained favour with the Portuguese merchants who occupied the enclave. In 1553, the mandarin of Macau authorised the Portuguese to build provisory tents in order to facilitate business activities. Until then it was customary for the Portuguese to put up the tents only to secure temporary residence until merchants set sail at the end of every trading season between the months of November and May. From 1557 onwards the traders erected wooden and stone houses, instituting Portuguese permanent settlement in Macau.[13] Macau evolved rapidly from a small community of traders to a politically organised society. By 1583, the enclave had a municipal government with a distinctive administrative model, the Senate Council, later called the Loyal Senate (*Leal Senado*).[14] Administratively Macau was organised differently from other Portuguese regions, in that the Senate did not pay *foro do chão* (ground-rent) to the Portuguese king but to the local Chinese authorities. Apparently, since 1573 a number of inhabitants in Macau had resorted to the use of bribes to pay annual rent to Chinese officials, valued at 500 taels (Chinese silver weight) and custom duties, worth 20,000 taels.[15]

In order to control its borders, China later built the *Porta do Cerco* (Barrier Gate), a garrisoned wall along the isthmus, from where Chinese troops controlled the trans-border flow of people and goods.[16] The annual payments of rent and all boundary delimitations showed both the Portuguese subsidiary position to the Ming dynasty and China's tacit acceptance of Macau's *de facto* foreign occupation.

In 1688, the Chinese built a customhouse in Macau. This structure was intended to limit the powers of the Portuguese governor in the enclave.[17] Throughout this period, Portuguese settlers were recognised as informal residents but were not considered legal permanent residents by the Ming dynasty. This situation persisted until 1783. At that time, the Portuguese administration began to find the non-permanent status of the Portuguese in the enclave objectionable. This sentiment deepened after apparent Chinese overtures in Macau. In counter-defence the *Providências Régias* (Regal Providences) claimed that the Portuguese had equal or a greater stake in the sovereignty of Macau. This was done to reinforce Portugal's jurisdiction in the territory and hopefully immobilise Chinese advances. The governor used his position of authority in the Senate to reinforce his powers and to push Chinese advances back. Later in 1822, Macau was given the status of constituent of Portuguese territory under the Portuguese Constitution.[18]

From the second half of the nineteenth century, foreign powers with interests in China pressurised the two sides to clarify Macau's political standing. China and Portugal, facing international decline at the time, were particularly impressionable to these external demands. The first "opium war" (1839–1842) broke China's unprecedented isolation, setting the tone for negotiations with foreign countries.[19] On the back of the Treaty of Nanjing (1842) and the cession of Hong Kong to the British Crown, China's grip was loosened in Hong Kong, facilitating the way for Governor Ferreira do Amaral to declare Portugal's *de facto* sovereignty over Macau in 1849. With this declaration, the Chinese mandarin of Macau lost important functions and later abandoned the enclave. Subsequently, Macau was declared a free port. The customhouse of 1688, which was for the Portuguese a symbol of China's disparate predominance in the area, was abolished.[20]

In 1862, Portugal signed the first Treaty of Friendship and Trade with China, an unprecedented attempt to moderate political tensions between the two sides through the promotion of financial and economic aspects of their relationship. The Treaty also defined Macau's political and juridical statute, although it did not mention the issue of Portuguese sovereignty.[21] Moreover, China did not ratify it. For the Portuguese, having a non-ratified treaty represented a kind of "blessing in disguise". Without an official endorsement, the Portuguese could buy time to explore other options and prepare a more favourable alternative agreement. Pushed by Britain, China negotiated with Portugal Macau's cooperation to control the smuggling of opium in the region. Portugal interpreted this as a relaxation of China's grip on the enclave. In the face of this apparent weakness, Portugal launched new demands on China to push it into a new treaty where recognition of Portugal's limited sovereignty over Macau would be sought.[22]

China recognised the "perpetual occupation and government of Macau and its dependencies by Portugal" in Article 2 of the Lisbon Protocol of March 1887 and reiterated it in Article 2 of the Treaty of

Friendship and Trade signed in Beijing in December 1887 and finally ratified in April 1888. Portugal also stood to win from a number of privileges conferred on countries to which mainland China gave preferential treatment. But the definition of Macau's borders remained unresolved.[23]

The beginning of the twentieth century marked a new dawn for Portugal and China, with the establishment of republican regimes in both countries. The Portuguese Republic was founded in 1910, while the Republic of China followed one year later. This new dawn also brought with it changes in the context of their relations over Macau. A growing nationalist movement in China voiced disapproval over the 1887 Treaty of Friendship and Trade, questioning its validity. This served to strengthen the original position that the mandarins in Beijing and Guangzhou had on the issue of Macau's sovereignty, stating vehemently that Macau was Chinese territory under Portuguese occupation.[24]

These contentions manifested themselves in the unresolved topic of Macau's borders. From China's perspective Portugal's extraterritorial ambitions had to be abated whilst Portugal, intent on sustaining the status quo, had concerns about enhancing its position in the territory.[25] After the 1928 Treaty of Nanjing, abolishing Portuguese consular jurisdiction in Chinese territory, it looked as if China had at last the upper hand in Macau. China believed that it was closer than ever to realising its aims for Macau.[26]

From the 1920s through the 1930s, after a prolonged period of granting territory to foreign powers, China enjoyed renewed confidence with the retrocession of some of these concessions. A number of "unequal treaties"[27] to which China had been subjected in the past compelled it to lease a significant number of territorial concessions to Britain, France, Germany, Russia and Japan as well as other countries, enabling them to enjoy privileged positions in China.[28] Britain led the pack in number and influence. During the First World War, the UK had added the Crown colony of Hong Kong, as well as concessions in Xiamen, Jinjiang, Jiujiang, Hankou and Tianjin. Britain also dominated the International Settlement of Shanghai and the entire Yangzi valley.[29]

At the Versailles conference in 1919, following the end of the First World War, China's attempts failed at dissolving the system, which held its territories hostage to foreign control.[30] Between 1918 and 1920 China became a member of the wider "international society" (as understood by the "English School" of international relations), by accepting international rules and norms.[31] China had hoped to use its new status to leverage international support for its lost territories through a process of treaty revisions but came to realise that any amendment at this level required significant bilateral negotiation.[32] At home, Chinese sentiment for reversion grew on the back of an anti-imperialist Chinese nationalism (from 1923 to 1928) reinforcing these claims. Foreign perpetuators were given the label of "enemies of the Chinese people".[33] Having support internally was an important advantage psychologically but the Chinese would only reap rewards later.

Britain's role of international protagonist on the world stage appealed to China's hunger for power and need to "settle scores" with imperialist Britain. Anti-British agitation first broke out in Shanghai and the rest of the Chang (Yangzi) River Valley, followed by an organised strike in the foreign concession of Xiamen. Hong Kong had boycotts by local Chinese from July 1925 to October 1926. The movement aimed to put an end to foreign domination.[34] These occurrences had a determining effect in the future status quo of the foreign concessions, beginning with the peaceful retrocession of the Hankou concession to China.[35]

This wave of pro-Chinese nationalism also reached the British enclave of Weihaiwei in Shandong, in the 1920s. The Weihaiwei case not only provides an interesting background for the understanding of retrocession in China, but sheds some light in the importance of Hong Kong for the British, as it had been leased to Britain by China in 1898, along with the New Territories of Hong Kong.[36] Although the arrangements for the two leaseholds were practically identical, Britain was far more committed to the New Territories than it was to Weihaiwei. While the inhabitants of the New Territories were given British citizenship, the subjects of Weihaiwei remained Chinese citizens: it had been a conscious British decision to differentiate between the Crown colony of Hong Kong-New Territories and Weihaiwei along citizenship and benefit lines. In short Britain sought a better stature for the former and, after a protracted negotiation process, Weihaiwei was redeemed in 1930.[37] Fearing an anti-British backlash, the British were happy to leave the colony, a process that was simplified further as Weihaiwei had in effect lost much of its value for Britain.[38]

China snubbed the idea of differences between the various foreign concessions, on grounds that these were of equal importance irrespective of size, economic or financial stature. They argued that the treaties, into which China was coerced, were unequal and that the restoration of sovereignty over these foreign concessions was inevitable. Through progressive negotiation, China succeeded in recovering most concessions by the early 1930s.[39] Hong Kong and Macau would continue under foreign administration. However, with the capitulation of Japan in 1945, China took a decisive step forward, requesting that Portugal end consular extraterritoriality in Macau. This meant:

> the extension of the jurisdiction of a state behind its borders, implying the existence of certain rights, privileges and immunities enjoyed by the citizens or subjects of a state within the limits of

other state, exempt from local jurisdiction and exclusively subjected to the laws and judicial administration of the respective state.[40]

In 1947 Portugal and China held a meeting to discuss Portugal's relinquishment of consular jurisdiction. The minutes of the meeting shaped the content of the notes that resulted in "Portugal renouncing its rights relating to consular jurisdiction in China".[41] Those notes were meant to mark the culmination of the end of extraterritoriality in China already experienced by foreign countries.[42] During the negotiations both sides resorted to a process of "give and take". China decided to abandon a clause relating to the Macau question in order to lure Portugal to agree with another clause in the agreement that "Portuguese citizens are subject to the law and jurisdiction of Chinese courts". Thus, the notes did not mention the status of sovereignty.[43] By the mid-1940s, against the background of a tenuous civil war on home ground between the Chinese Nationalists and Communists, China abandoned its claims on Macau for the time being.[44]

The CCP proclaimed the PRC on 1 October 1949. For the next couple of years, China's focus would remain internal. The PRC sought to maintain the status quo of Macau and Hong Kong.[45] The decision was based on pragmatism induced primarily by economic motives: it was fundamental to keep the two enclaves as they stood, i.e. neutral territories, as leverage to break the blockade imposed by the West while concurrently keeping the Soviet Union at arm's length.[46] It was not until the mid-1970s that the pending issue of Hong Kong assumed relevance once more. Naturally Macau assumed relevance in tandem with Hong Kong.

The Chinese Communist regime did not seek to remain completely isolated from international affairs, although it sought to retain some distance from imperialist and fascist nations. At some point the mainland would be required to resolve the issue of the remaining foreign concessions. With this in mind, the PRC developed a strategy, as a "warm up" exercise. To gauge Portuguese receptivity, the PRC made two attempts to establish diplomatic relations with Portugal: October 1949 and 1954 (after the Geneva Conference), but António Oliveira Salazar's regime opposed China's overtures. This had a decisive impact on the manner in which the mainland broached the Portuguese in impending dealings. In 1950 the PRC started to break away slowly from its erstwhile international isolation, reinforced by the recognition of four North Atlantic Treaty Organisation (NATO) members: the UK, Norway, Denmark and the Netherlands. This recognition set the tone for initiating a paradigm shift in the West, but the stubbornness of the Portuguese dictator allied with strong pressures within the regime and from the United States prevented this from happening.[47]

In spite of Portugal's stance, the PRC did not apply strong pressure to establish relations with Portugal because the Chinese recognized that they had *de facto* control over Macau. The PRC relied increasingly on the traditional associations in the enclave with which it maintained strong links and through which it exerted influence. An example of this tacit approach was the use of Macau to obtain Western military equipment during the blockade on China during the Korean War and to teach Portuguese language and culture to Chinese officials sent to influence the liberation movements in the Portuguese Africa.[48]

Throughout the 1940s and 1950s Portugal and the PRC did not have *de jure* relations, although they seemingly had good *de facto* relations. This had a positive overall impact on Macau. Before the formalisation of diplomatic relations in 1979, the Chinese elite in the enclave *de facto* managed affairs. On the other hand, the Portuguese government used political co-option to attract local elements to the administrative structure, as emissaries. These envoys, responsible for the exchange of information between Portugal and China, were the most influential political actors in Macau.[49]

Despite satisfactory Sino-Portuguese *de facto* relations, China considered the Portuguese presence in Macau illegitimate and ambiguous. The Chinese official position on Macau at the time was that: the Lisbon Protocol of 1887 had been an unequal treaty that had lost its validity; Macau's territorial status was one of "perpetual occupation" differing from "situations of annexation, concession or lease"; and it was a "question pending" inherited from the past, which "should be settled peacefully through negotiations and that, pending a settlement, the status quo should be maintained".[50]

Portugal's presence in the enclave grew in prominence, against the backdrop of rising internal discontentment. In 1952 a number of confrontations between the Portuguese and Chinese troops on guard[51] at the *Porta do Cerco* broke out, suggesting it was the dawn of resolving the question of Macau's administrative future. Later in 1955, through the use of a "stick" in stark contrast to the familiar "carrot" approach, the PRC prevented the Portuguese authorities from organising the fourth centenary celebrations of Portuguese presence in the territory. At the time, the PRC made the first public declaration on Macau, warning the Portuguese authorities that it would not accept much longer the occupation of the enclave.[52]

With the Cultural Revolution in the 1960s, the Portuguese obtained a respite from Chinese attempts to bring about a swift conclusion to the question of Macau. The social unrest in Macau coincided with instability in the mainland, peaking with the "1, 2, 3" incident. It was given that name as it had taken place on 3 December (in Chinese 12, 3). The

Portuguese refused to issue permission for the building of a "patriotic" (communist) school on Taipa Island, which led to a violent confrontation between the Macau police and Maoists, resulting in martial law being declared in the territory.[53] Internationally the press concluded that in effect the Portuguese government was beginning to show signs of lassitude in Macau and that they would surrender next. The reality was somewhat different.

Surrendering Macau was not an option for Salazar. Keeping Macau was considered less humiliating. Governor Nobre de Carvalho set out to undertake damage control and agreed to a "twofold agreement" with two parties, underestimating the consequences they carried for Portugal. Agreements were signed with the "people of Macau" and the Guangdong authorities. The agreements turned out to be extremely humiliating for the Portuguese, setting strict limits on the powers of the governor while the representatives of Beijing gained greater control of the territory.[54] Portugal's discomfort in the enclave became more apparent as one of the conditions that China imposed was the exhaustive fulfilment of a note that the government of Macau had published in the press in 1963 in which it:

> will not tolerate subversive activities towards China based from Macau. Anyone found implicated in these activities will be prosecuted and handed over to the Chinese People's Republic authorities.[55]

In the end the "1, 2, 3" episode had irrevocable consequences for Macau: Portugal recognised *de facto* Macau as a Chinese territory, marking the end of the Portuguese power over it.[56] It is arguable that the Portuguese government could have threatened to leave Macau and get a better deal with China, as Mao's regime intended to maintain the *status quo*: soon after "1, 2, 3", China declared that Taiwan was the priority, and only after recovering Taiwan would the PRC claim Macau and Hong Kong.[57]

At this point in time, we see a lack of finesse on the part of the Portuguese. The Portuguese government could have threatened to leave or simply left and in doing so could have pushed China into an advantageous deal for the Portuguese in Macau. The time factor was an important one that Portugal undervalued. Given that the retrocession of Macau was inevitable, Portugal could have used its trump cards at decisive moments, as in this case. It could have benefitted by drawing upon Mao's intentions to keep the status quo even after "1, 2, 3", which culminated with the declaration that Taiwan and not Hong Kong or Macau was a priority for the mainland (and only after recovering Taiwan did the PRC intend to take over Macau and Hong Kong).

The Chinese continued support for the liberation movements in Portuguese colonies, except, ironically, Macau, led them to make public declarations against Portuguese colonialism.[58] By 1971, after replacing Taiwan as the representative of China in the United Nations (UN), the PRC declared that the settlement of the question of Macau and Hong Kong was "entirely within China's sovereignty rights" and justifiable by the inequity of treaties that in effect bestowed rights and guarantees on Portugal to the detriment of China. The PRC argued that these enclaves did not "fall within the ordinary category of 'colonial territories'" requesting that they be removed from the UN list of colonised territories. The request was granted during the meeting of the Special Committee on Decolonization on 17 May 1972.[59]

The PRC could gain from UN entry both doctrinally and pragmatically in relation to their position on Macau. The PRC was able to validate internationally its position on why it viewed the treaties related to Macau as unequal. It argued that: the guarantees provided by the perpetual occupation of Portugal in Macau, instituted in the 1887 Protocol, was the result of an unequal imposition of imperialism, and therefore null and void; Macau was "Chinese territory 'occupied' by Portuguese authorities"; and that China had the right to exercise full sovereignty over Macau as the Portuguese retained their presence exclusively at the will of China. At the same time, the mainland attempted to contain the censuring voices of countries, such as the Union of Soviet Socialist Republics (USSR), that questioned China's contradictory behaviour on the world stage. On one hand China supported liberation movements in the Third World. On the other hand it approved of existing autonomous regions that bordered on illegitimate/authoritarian governance in Hong Kong and Macau.[60]

From a pragmatic viewpoint, the PRC took the decision to prepare the groundwork for the eventual re-integration of the two enclaves into China, seeking to deprive them of the means to self-determination. By avoiding a potential process of internationalisation from transpiring in the two enclaves, China believed that it could restrict the issue to Sino-British and Sino-Portuguese bilateral relations, curtailing interference from third parties within the traditional preference for bilaterality rather than multilaterality. In the end, the PRC succeeded at sustaining the status quo of Hong Kong and Macau until settlement was sorted through bilateral channels. Bilateral negotiations began when the PRC felt that the time was ripe.[61]

In Portugal the sentiment was similar to that of the Chinese in that the Portuguese felt the Macau question should not be settled within the UN. They agreed also with the Chinese that the UN should not list Macau as a colonial territory. They may have agreed in essence with one another but the motives were very different, demarcating stark contrasts in definition and strategy. The two countries regarded Macau as an extended territory: for the Portuguese it was an Overseas Province; for the Chinese it was a part of China. Under international law, both countries recognised that the UN could not intervene in Macau, as Macau fell under the territorial legitimacy of internationally recognised nation states.[62]

Portuguese Withdrawal from Empire

The rapid return of the majority of Portuguese from a number of colonies was a harrowing experience, a bleeding wound which had a profound impact on the country's domestic and foreign consciousness. These events brought with them a cloud of destitution that hovered in the country for some time to come. The decolonisation experience was psychologically and politically traumatic for Portugal. It is against this background that the Portuguese leaders conducted negotiations with China over Macau. The far-reaching effects of the abrupt withdrawal from empire were felt at every stage of the negotiations, mapping the way forward—uneventful and lacklustre. The Portuguese right (who kick-started the negotiation process) developed a strategy for the negotiations on the basis of fear, preventing at all costs another traumatic experience. Under this constraining environment Portugal gained less and lost more. The fear factor was counterproductive and self-destructive, constricting Portugal to calculated and risk-free moves. On the contrary China attempted to make significant use of Portugal's fragilities, which gave it in effect the upper hand in the negotiations.

By the mid-twentieth century, Portugal was arguably the oldest European empire, dating to the fifteenth century. The commercial empire it had in the Orient collapsed at the beginning of the seventeenth century but ambitious politicians and colonial ideologues longed for a return of Portugal's greatness, rooted in successful expeditions that opened exotic lands and sources of wealth. The motivation to keep this memory alive sustained Portugal's desire for India, Timor and Macau, regions in which it had a presence.

The second imperial construction had been in Brazil, lasting until 1822, even though Portugal exerted a level of influence there until the economic recession of the 1930s. The third imperial epicentre had been in Africa—Angola, Mozambique, Guinea-Bissau, Cape Verde, São Tomé and Príncipe. Although well into decline by the nineteenth century, Portugal managed to revive its claims in Africa during the European scramble for the continent at the end of the century.[63]

The colony or victim of a dominant power co-existed in a relationship of *colonised* host versus *colonising* parasite. By definition a colony is "a domination imposed by an external political power . . . with a tendency to subordinate the resources and institutions of the dependent region to the interests of the political power and the ethnic or cultural dominant group",[64] whilst decolonisation refers to the "measures intended eventually to terminate formal political control over colonial territories and to replace it by some new relationship".[65] European powers, including Portugal, claimed it a European responsibility to aid 'inferior' peoples to achieve higher levels of development.

Between the First and Second World Wars, there were two basic models of colonialism. European colonial powers more or less followed either the British model of autonomy or the French model of assimilation.[66] *Assimilation* derived from the common belief in France that the "natives" would assimilate French culture and language until they became French citizens, ultimately represented in the French parliament.[67] France claimed to have a special *mission civilisatrice*: a mission to civilise the indigenous peoples widely believed too primitive to rule themselves but capable of being uplifted.[68]

Britain conceived its empire along devolution lines. It sought non-interference in local affairs, while France was more interventionist, which resulted in a greater predisposition to fight for its colonies.[69] The French government believed in principles of equality and equity, although it gravitated towards a centralised administration. British counterparts preferred decentralised rule, equipping the locals for the task of governance. Unlike France, Britain understood that empire had a temporal limit: independence was inevitable, a component part of its anatomy.[70] The intention to transform the colonial subjects into British citizens was virtually non-existent, focussing more on developing capabilities for self-rule.[71]

Portugal was influenced heavily by the French model, a reality that peaked with the arrival of António Oliveira Salazar as the new Portuguese prime minister in July 1932. The *Estado Novo* (New State), the ideology of Salazar's rule, set out to establish new rules and objectives on which overseas policy was based, emulating the French colonial model as the prototype for its colonial policy at the beginning of the twentieth century.[72] The Portuguese colonial system was characteristically centralised, administratively autonomous and culturally assimilative,[73] with the exception of Macau and Timor. Through a kind of cross-pollination approach, the Portuguese nominally foresaw the beginning of a new civilisation for its colonies with native characteristics, composed of Portuguese citizens with equal duties and rights of other citizens.[74]

Like the French, the Portuguese government declared its relationship with its colonies special and the government of the empire was in essence authoritarian, centralising the administrative apparatus in the metropolis.[75] The *Acto Colonial* (Colonial Act), published in 1930, masked this reality, seeking to unify the colonial administration under centralised rule with "moderate autonomy".[76]

After the Second World War, European powers faced semi-forced removal from their colonies, officially bringing imperialism to an abrupt end on the African continent, with Portugal essentially remaining the odd one out.[77] Scholars found different reasons for this transformation, ranging from allegations around European declining military power to the impact of public opinion on domestic policy in most colonial powers, calling for more pro-activity in the development policies of colonial regions.[78] At the same time, new normative values rose up around the world, questioning the viability and validity of colonialism, underlining the exploitative and oppressive aspects of the system.[79]

By 1960 anti-colonialism had become the new catchword, encapsulated in the UN General Assembly Declaration on the Granting of Independence to Colonial Countries and Peoples. The right of all people in colonial dependencies to self-determination was claimed, condemning at the same time every kind of pretext that delayed the independence movements.[80]

These calls were ignored by the Portuguese, resolute on keeping its colonies that nominally were considered Portuguese provinces. Lisbon also played its neutrality trump card, rejecting the transformations internationally as products of the post-Second World War period. Portugal's attitude was one of general apathy with which it regarded these worldly events, facilitated by a number of existing situations. The combination of a number of factors, i.e. the invitation to participate in the Marshall plan, the Portuguese-British alliance, and Portugal's admittance into NATO (thanks to the use of the Azores as an air base by the Allies during and after the war), assured the Portuguese government international recognition.[81] This in effect carried forward the Portuguese colonial system in the African continent without Portugal feeling the pressure to initiate decolonisation.

There are a number of explanations for Portugal's rebuffing of the idea to consider decolonisation seriously. Some authors consider that, as a poor capitalist country, Portugal's need for external markets and foreign exchange (to fight the balance of payments crisis) superseded the inescapable necessity to decolonise sooner rather than later. Considering that the Portuguese colonies carried significant economic weight and that it was not only about prestige, they argue that the colonies were preferential markets and sources of cheap raw materials, allowing Portugal to create and save foreign exchange.[82] According to this argument, Lisbon had a lot to gain from exploitation of the colonies natural resources. At the time it would not make economic or financial sense to embark on neo-colonialism.[83]

Other theorists think that the idea that supports notions of Portugal's backwardness in relation to colonies is nonsensical. For example, it could be that the costs of maintaining colonial administrations led some imperial powers to get out of formal colonialism. Franco Nogueira, Portuguese foreign minister at the time, mentioned the emergence of a new type of colonialism with economic or ideological basis that dominated growing areas in Africa after the chaos. After all, one could take down the flag, reduce administrative costs and still largely exploit a former colony through control of local elites.[84] The reasoning behind this idea would be the belief that had Portugal decolonised in the 1950s, it would have had the means to exercise neo-colonial influence and more to gain in its former formal colonies.[85] This argument deduced that the colonies sustained economically the metropolis and not the other way around.

From the 1950s onwards the international economic environment showed signs of undergoing transformation, spilling into a number of domestic settings, agitating the foundations of this theory. By the 1960s Portugal had started to invest more in Europe. France and the United States and not Africa became attractive destinations for the escaping Portuguese émigré.[86] The outflow of people had a parallel effect on the commercial arrangements Portugal enjoyed with Africa, perceived to be beneficial and affluent. In reality the empire showed signs of financial fatigue; the colonies, it turned out, had become a burden to the metropolis' public finances and an obstacle to Portuguese integration in Europe. By the early 1970s, the trade balance between Portugal and the world tilted in Europe's favour, whilst the colonies constituted a smaller share in the overall balance, and African colonies were no longer exclusive resources of foreign currency, surpassed by the exponential growth of the tourism sector in Portugal and emigrant remittances.[87]

For Portugal, the colonies held the importance of an award, holding subdued prestige and political status and not necessarily economic value. The colonial war had seemingly been fought "to preserve the regime rather than to save the economy".[88] It is widely believed in Portugal that the *Estado Novo* commitment to the empire was more political than economic and that the psychological repercussions of a Portuguese withdrawal would surpass the costs involved in sustaining a diminishing empire.[89] The importance of this symbolical and psychological dimension later framed Portugal's approach regarding withdrawal from Macau, perceived by Portuguese politicians as a sensitive issue in their domestic political agenda.

Salazar used nationalism and myths of imperial greatness to harness social support with social and political homogeneity, factors which had given him initially the reins of power.[90] Salazar intelligently used these props to reinforce his position domestically, consolidating further his grip on power. The Portuguese bought into the ideals of a "single Portugal" composed of a mainland and colonies. It was not until the end of the 1960s that opposition to Salazar's policies began to be felt at home.

Salazar also appeared to consolidate his power internationally, namely in the UN. The *Estado Novo* argued that Portugal's reasons for colonialism stood apart from the economically motivated British and the Belgians. The Portuguese government argued that Portugal was driven by a universal mission[91] that aimed at civilising the natives in Lusophone Africa. Unmotivated by issues of control and power struggles over matters of territory, its concern was one of a humanitarian order, a duty towards the colonial people which the international community should consider earnestly.[92] According to Franco Nogueira:

> ... without the support of an European united Portugal, without strong bonds connecting the whole nation, it was difficult to maintain in Africa a multi-racial society and any of its ethnic groups should expect to subsist in peace and progress after breaking those bonds.... And when we are told that we have no techniques, no means, no instruments, we reply that our provinces in Africa are more progressive and developed in all domains than any other recently independent African territory in Sub-Saharan Africa.[93]

The *Estado Novo* used the "lusotropic" theories of the Brazilian sociologist, Gilberto Freyre's to seize the moment. Freyre argued:

> ... no other European was ever so intense and symbiotic in its constancies in different tropical areas"; The Portuguese people have a "deeper, more intimate, more constant, more emphatic" experience and knowledge of the tropics than any other European coloniser of the warm lands.[94]

Lusotropicology was meant to explain how the efforts on the part of the Portuguese served to integrate colonised peoples in Brazil, through a process of cross-pollination,[95] resulting in the creation of a new civilization in the form of *mestiços* (people of mixed race). It was applied to Portuguese-speaking Africa but not to Timor and Macau—these territories were not even included in Freyre's visit to Portuguese colonies in August 1951, organized by the *Estado Novo*.[96]

Demographic results attempting to prove this loose theory, which could almost have as easily applied to Spanish colonial America, were inconclusive, failing to demonstrate that this "racially blind" doctrine had ever taken place.⁹⁷ Further Portuguese claims of racial toleration and miscegenation in the tropics were flawed, failing to prevent discrimination from occurring on the ground.⁹⁸ However, the idea that Portugal had nobler intentions than Britain, for example, and that Portuguese people are less racist than other Europeans, are still part of domestic politics and public culture; even "anti-colonial" Portuguese believe in lusotropicalism.⁹⁹

The *Acto Colonial* of 1951 gave birth to the nominal expression "overseas provinces", putting an end to the term "colonial empire" as to avoid the negative repercussions of growing international antipathy towards colonial empires, from permeating the domestic front. The idea the Portuguese had was that the overseas empire would remain indefinitely a part of Portuguese reality.¹⁰⁰ So when Portugal faced disapproval at the United Nations in 1956 for its continued presence in Africa, the candid reply given by the Portuguese government was that Portugal "does not administer Territories which fall under the category indicated by Article 73"¹⁰¹ of the Declaration Regarding Non-Self Governing Territories which bound colonial powers to develop "self-government" and "free political institutions" in the colonies.¹⁰² In short the Portuguese government considered Chapter XI inapplicable to its circumstances and resultantly not bound by it as: "[Portugal] is, and always has been, a unitary state, regardless of the relative geographic situation of its various provinces".¹⁰³

Notwithstanding, social instability, which emerged in the mid-1950s and increased with the colonial war since early 1960s, had peaked in Portugal's African colonies by early 1970s,¹⁰⁴ exacerbated by the Nationalist agitation in Asia and other parts of Africa in spite of efforts by the *Estado Novo* to isolate these incidents. The belief that Portugal was protected from such incidents, which the expression "overseas territories" skilfully defended, paralysed the regime politically. Portugal had by every criterion the means to decolonise, hold democratic elections or negotiate with leaders of the liberation movements in time to prevent a catastrophic withdrawal in Africa.¹⁰⁵ By the time Marcelo Caetano took over from Salazar in 1968 it was already too late.

If Portugal had accepted the inevitability of decolonisation, negotiated a withdrawal or prepared the colonies for self-rule earlier, it could have mitigated the side effects of decolonisation. From an economic and social point of view, the return of several hundreds of thousands of Portuguese from the colonies, due to the abrupt change in the political situation and living conditions, had a devastating impact, not just on the regime but also in the people and nation of Portugal. The reintegration in the Portuguese society of those "returnees" (*retornados*) that left all their possessions in Africa represented a huge burden to the economy.

Had the withdrawal been prepared, many of those families would have stayed in the colonies. From a political point of view, the conservative part of the society continued thinking that the Empire was part of the Portuguese territory, blaming the left-wing for the withdrawal.

By 1975, Lusophone Africa had started to enjoy the benefits of its new-found freedom with independence established and East Timor faced invasion of the Indonesian military under the pretext of anti-colonialism. Exhausted by external developments, Lisbon started to show little interest in Macau. The enclave alone would not sustain the myth of Portuguese imperialism. Beginning with the withdrawal of all Portuguese military forces known as the Independent Territorial Command (approximately one thousand soldiers) and leaving the task of domestic security in the hands of the local police, Portugal demonstrated a paced policy approach to detachment from the enclave. Under the pretext of "lesson learnt", Lisbon would seek restitution from its dismal performance in Africa by avoiding the same fate for Macau.[106]

In October 1974 Portuguese Minister of Inter-territorial Coordination Almeida Santos paid an official visit to Macau, and the Chinese local elite "stated publicly the specificity of the Macau status, which was to be solved in due time by the two governments".[107] In 1975 (1 April) *The New York Times* stated that "Portugal's ruling Armed Forces Movement tried to give Macao back to China . . . but Peking said it did not wish to alter the status of the territory."[108] Articles like "China Does Not Want Macau", published in *The Star — Hong Kong*, would continue to appear quite often in the international press, saying that Hong Kong and Macau "were much more valuable to China as sources of information, trade and hard currency from the West than they would be as annexed territories". However, this news was strongly denied by Portuguese politicians in Lisbon and Governor Garcia Leandro classified it as "absolutely untrue": "The Macau Government regrets the issue of this sensationalistic and unethical type of information, on account of the serious repercussions on the future of both Macau and Hong Kong."[109] In his recent book he explained that:

> Since the beginning of the decolonization process some journalists frequently claimed in their articles that Portugal proposed the return of Macau to China. As governor I denied this statement whenever I had opportunity. After my return to Lisbon, when that happened, I always contacted the person responsible for that writing or tried to seek the source of this initiative, but I did never get a concrete answer. It was, they told me, a mere repetition of something that they read, but that they have not investigated . . .[110]

Nevertheless, researchers that have worked on the topic widely conclude that, at least, Lisbon was prepared to let Macau go, as there was relatively little Portuguese activity in the economic, financial, cultural and political spheres at the time.[111] Most of them argue that Lisbon offered to return Macau to China but Beijing declined those offers.[112] In any case, Lisbon's indifference, framed by the context of decolonisation in Portugal and the irrelevance of Macau to its economy, had a determining influence over the Portuguese later approach adopted during the negotiations over Macau.

In China, Portugal seemingly found an obliging ally. The PRC would pace its advances on Macau in accordance with Portugal's step by step process, although, in the mid-1970s it was in China's interest to maintain the status quo in the enclave. There were three reasons for this. First, the PRC was wrapped in internal social and political uncertainty. Mao Zedong and Zhou Enlai were seriously ill, resulting in a sense of insecurity around China's future. It seemed wisest to concentrate efforts internally and not towards Macau or Hong Kong. Second, the PRC maintained its closed door policy but understood the significance of utilising Hong Kong and Macau as intermediaries and gateways to the world. Both were important sources of investment and foreign currency that kept it in Beijing's interest to maintain their status quo. Third, attempts to recover Macau at that time were considered inappropriate, only serving to marginalise the British and jeopardise international and local confidence in Hong Kong. China feared damaging its relations and reputation, the reunification with Taiwan being the priority.[113] In the late 1970s, CCP rhetoric was like a two-edged sword: on the one side revolutionary and ardently anti-colonialist; on the other, and when it suited Beijing, pragmatic, bouncing between favouring and/or criticising Portugal's decolonisation in Africa and asserting the Portuguese administration in Macau.

The Establishment of Sino-Portuguese Relations

Soon after the founding of the PRC in 1949, there were several attempts by China to establish diplomatic relations with Portugal. Throughout the 1950s and 1960s, these efforts remained inconclusive. Salazar refused to recognise the PRC. Under a new political regime after 1974, Lisbon became willing to establish contacts with China and to discuss Macau's future. The first sign was an official press release by the Portuguese Ministry of Foreign Affairs, on 6 January 1975, declaring intentions to establish relations with all countries, including China.

In two separate declarations, Portugal demonstrated a positive position towards China, stating that it regarded the PRC as "the sole legitimate representative of the Chinese people", and that Taiwan was "an integral part" of Chinese territory. Portugal surprised sceptical onlookers on the question of Macau by declaring that it "could be negotiated when both Governments considered appropriate" and until then the Portuguese government would uphold "the rights of the Chinese citizens of Macau".[114] In short, Lisbon suggested that it saw Macau as an opportunity to forge political ties with China and not as an obstacle to achieving its foreign policy goals. On the other side, Portugal was also beginning to make preparations to distance itself from Taiwan, which had a Legation in Lisbon and a Consulate in Timor; this was a pre-requisite to resuming diplomatic relations with the mainland.[115]

In an unexpected reaction, the Chinese demonstrated a degree of indifference to the Portuguese declarations. Even though the Chinese Foreign Ministry welcomed the communication with optimistic caution, its response on 13 January 1975 revealed that on the " . . . question of Macau there is still some distance between the attitude of the Portuguese Government and the consistent position of the Chinese Government".[116] The Chinese position on the Macau question was non-negotiable. Macau could not be the object of negotiations with a foreign power as it was Chinese territory and not the territorial possession of a third party. The PRC described the eventual termination of Portuguese rule in Macau as a "transfer of administration".

Shortly after the 6 January 1975 note, the Chinese ambassador in Budapest communicated in confidence with the Portuguese ambassador that the Chinese were considering seriously the resumption of diplomatic relations with Lisbon. Later, the chargé d'affaires of the Yugoslav Embassy in Lisbon informed the Portuguese Ministry of Foreign Affairs that, despite divergences regarding Macau as a (non-)negotiable question, the Chinese government was content with the Portuguese declarations but that the resumption of relations would be shaped by responses from the Organization of African Unity (OAU) concerning the interdiction imposed on African countries to establish relations with Portugal.[117] This official Chinese narrative also spread to other European capitals, such as Paris and Rome, in preparation for Chinese willingness to engage the Portuguese bilaterally.[118]

The argument of waiting for the OAU to free up African countries, and countries supportive of the OAU such as China, to resume relations with Portugal, allowed China to gain time. The PRC opted to concentrate on domestic problems, in spite of dissatisfaction and the weakness of Portugal's rule in Macau, following demonstrations there in 1966. Having to focus on domestic issues was only one reason that China did not rush to establish diplomatic relations with Portugal: the Chinese leaders feared a Portuguese reversal to colonialism. The PRC was waiting for the accomplishment of the conclusion of the Portuguese decolonisation process and the definition of country's political re-alignment on the international stage.[119]

China's hard line softened when reassured that the new regime in Portugal post-1975 was ending the era of colonialism, was not under Soviet influence, and thus was not regarded as an enemy of China.[120] Portugal's submission to the European Economic Community (EEC) in 1977 served to tranquilize China, reassuring it of Portugal's integration into Western Europe. China's fears of Soviet influence were reduced further in 1979, by the formation of the new political party, the *Aliança Democrática* (Democratic Alliance), offering a viable political alternative to the communists.[121] By the late 1970s China appeared more willing to embrace the likelihood of welcoming a new juncture in Sino-Portuguese relations.

In August 1975, informal talks between Portugal and China began in earnest in Paris. The French capital had become a privileged European platform for negotiations with China since 1964, following General De Gaulle's recognition of China.[122] Given the trend, it was only a matter of time until Portugal followed suit. After establishing cordial relations, involving Zeng Tao (representing China) and Coimbra Martins (representing Portugal), talks began with a slow start but they included discussion of Macau.

At the same time, the final version of the Macau Organic Law was approved by the Council of the Revolution in Lisbon on the 6 January 1976 and came into force on 17 February of the same year, after a period of intense debate.[123] The Organic Law stipulated that the new political system of Macau gave a high degree of legislative, administrative, economic and financial autonomy to the territory and delegated all the powers in the governor and Legislative Assembly.[124] Similarly to the note published on 6 January 1975, the Organic Law avoided addressing the sovereignty of Macau.

As will be discussed later, Portugal has a semi-presidential system where the president has certain functions while the prime minister has sole responsibility over the Ministry of Foreign Affairs and foreign policy. Under normal circumstances this meant that the Ministry of Foreign Affairs managed Sino-Portuguese bilateral relations but, in the special case of Macau, the territory fell under the tutelage of the president as well. The Macau Organic Law was approved at a time of political difficulties in Portugal: governments changed very often and this instability would not be beneficial to Macau.[125] As a result, the Organic Law bestowed certain political powers upon the governor of Macau. The governor was appointed by the president and not by the government or prime minister as such.[126] The governors nominated, who were sometimes friends or political allies of the president,[127] were politically accountable to him.[128]

The same situation applied to the appointment of the under-secretaries (*secretários-adjuntos*) of the Macau government who functioned as a sort of cabinet. The president of the Republic could dismiss all political appointments. In addition, the Portuguese president was in charge of Macau's external security. The president had powers to dissolve Macau's Legislative Assembly and to determine when the courts should have jurisdiction.[129] In short the Macau Organic Law gave greater powers over Macau to the Portuguese president while the prime minister and the government had negotiating authority over the territory with China. This division of powers would leave room for confusion and disagreement on the Portuguese side and was one important reason for Portugal's weakness at the negotiating table, especially during the transition period.[130]

In any event, the Portuguese Constitution of 25 April 1976 confirmed the paragraph about Macau's status in the Organic Law. The new Constitution categorized Macau as a "territory under Portuguese administration".[131] According to Governor Garcia Leandro (1974–1979), this designation facilitated relations with China as the debate on sovereignty was abandoned. Furthermore, within the Portuguese logic of decolonisation, it made sense to state that Macau was not a colony any more.[132] The Organic Law and the new Constitution gave some stability to Macau at what was a time of great uncertainty in Portugal. The Macau administration now had some autonomy, particularly the capacity to make investment decisions.[133]

While these changes reflected a sharp political turnaround for Portugal, the PRC faced similar challenges. Successive internal crises in the leadership inhibited China from having decided earlier to establish relations with Portugal. In the late 1970s, Deng Xiaoping emerged as the new political leader, bringing order and internal tranquillity to China after the Cultural Revolution. Deng chose to reinstall purged party leaders, marking the beginning of a new phase of Chinese pragmatism, pulling away from the radical ideology with which China had been associated for the past two decades.[134]

The rise of Deng Xiaoping meant China was now to strategize along nationalist and not Marxist or Maoist lines. In a period marked by intense political in-fighting among conservative and radicals groups, on either side of the political scale, Deng managed to instil political order at home whilst simultaneously beginning to look abroad with new foreign policy directives and objectives. Pragmatic Deng sought to distance himself from earlier political rhetoric, seeking ways to establish better relations with America and Europe, not only for political reasons but also on economic grounds. He believed that his internal reforms required significant engagement with the outside world. On the question of Macau, Deng had a longer-term view of the issue, preferring to think of reversion as part of China medium-to-long term priorities. As a strategist, the realisation of this objective required time and adequate planning.

In August 1976 the Portuguese prime minister, Mário Soares from the Socialist Party, presented plans in parliament to normalise relations with China.[135] The Portuguese, through Minister of Foreign Affairs Medeiros Ferreira, were beginning to sound out the Chinese for clues of their strategy for Macau, hoping to buy time but simultaneously preparing the groundwork for establishing bilateral relations. After questioning the Chinese ambassador in New York in 1976 and 1977, Medeiros Ferreira concluded that the Chinese leadership was not certain about their national or foreign strategy for reunification and the question of diplomatic relations with Portugal would be shaped through the definition of Beijing's strategy towards the future of Macau.[136]

It would take years and numerous informal meetings before China would finally agree to arrive at a date for resuming bilateral negotiations. In January 1978, formal negotiations began in Paris. This resulted in the establishment of the Xinhua delegation in Lisbon in March, under the directorship of the previous director of the Xinhua-New China News Agency in Beijing, Zeng Tao. Once bilateral relations were a reality the tone was set to broach the issue of Macau.[137]

China believed its rights to Macau's sovereignty outweighed any Portuguese position, although Portugal demanded acknowledgment of the weight of history on which its national dignity and self-respect rested.[138] Both sides were pragmatic and open to compromise. They agreed mutually that Macau was "a problem left over from history". At the outset of the negotiations, it seemed that Portugal did not oppose the Chinese sovereignty principle and China acknowledged the importance of Portugal's history in Macau. They were committed unilaterally to maintain the status quo for the time being, seeking settlement of the question through negotiation.[139]

From January to June 1978, formal conversations proceeded without significant hitches, concluding the last leg of negotiations to resume bilateral relations. The Chinese ambassador in Paris, Han Kehua, made a formal visit to the Portuguese embassy to celebrate Portugal's National Day, 10 June. This was extremely significant, as in the past Chinese ambassadors agreed to meet with Portuguese diplomats in secret, when there were no representatives of other countries present.[140] However, the signature of the much-anticipated joint communiqué was cancelled at the last minute and delayed for more than seven months as a result of internal issues on the Portuguese side. During a coalition government cabinet meeting in Lisbon on 14 July, Minister Basílio Horta objected on patriotic grounds to the agreement on Macau as it stood.[141] Horta belonged to the Central Democratic Social Party, a right-wing party representing a group of politicians who were against "giving away the empire", as it was understood. In the end, Cabinet approved a secret political directive, highlighting specific instructions to be undertaken by Ambassador Coimbra Martins:

> [T]he Portuguese Constitution does not include Macau in the Portuguese territory; it merely considers it under Portuguese administration. The Portuguese Government considers that the end of the Portuguese administration of the territory of Macau could be an object of negotiations between the People's Republic of China and Portugal, when both Governments consider it appropriate. Meanwhile, the Portuguese Government assumes the responsibility for the rigorous respect of the rights of the Chinese citizens residents in Macau. The Portuguese Government also assures the Chinese Government that it will not allow the use of this territory under its administration for the practice of acts hostile to the People's Republic of China.[142]

However, the opportunity to establish diplomatic relations was delayed as the coalition cabinet collapsed and Portugal's internal political crisis led to three different governments in one year: the first provisional government was led by Mário Soares, the second by Alfredo Nobre da Costa and the third, Carlos Mota Pinto. Coimbra Martins waited in Paris for the Portuguese position on how to proceed with resuming diplomatic relations with the PRC. When Mota Pinto took over as the new prime minister the negotiations finally began in earnest.[143]

A new set of conversations around bilateral relations commenced between Coimbra Martins and Han Kehua, resulting in the signature of the joint communiqué. It was agreed that the signing of the accord take place at the Portuguese embassy in Paris on 10 January 1979. The Portuguese Foreign Affairs Ministry, however, considered that the agreement required minor changes on the subject of Macau, postponing the ceremony to a later date.[144] The reasons the Portuguese provided for the alterations to the text were pretexts to delay the negotiations, arguably revealing the position of the prime minister, Mota Pinto, who feared a negative reaction in Portugal to an agreement on Macau.[145] Since a number of political leaders such as Basílio Horta relied on political manipulation through the use of nationalistic jargon to reinforce existing fears rooted in the decolonisation process, the prime minister was cautious about adopting assertive positions on Macau. The period was marked by political in-fighting as political parties in Portugal altered positions continuously, reflecting the lack of a common strategy on

Macau in Portugal which would persist throughout the negotiations process.

On 8 February 1979, the joint communiqué on the establishment of diplomatic relations between China and Portugal was finally signed. The two sides agreed to exchange ambassadors within three months and to hold diplomatic relations according to "the principles of mutual respect for the sovereignty and territorial integrity, of mutual non-intervention in internal affairs, of equality and reciprocal affairs". Portugal recognised the government of the PRC as "the only legal Government of China, and Taiwan as an integral part of the People's Republic of China".[146]

The official joint communiqué made little reference to Macau other than mentioning the principle of "sovereignty and territorial integrity".[147] A number of declarations around Macau's future in a memorandum signed between Coimbra Martins and Han Kehua along with the joint communiqué were initially kept secret, allegedly to protect the stability of Hong Kong but by Portuguese suggestion these were omitted from the joint communiqué. Throughout this period Prime Minister Mota Pinto kept the negotiation details on Macau away from public scrutiny, insisting continuously that Macau's status remained unchanged in spite of allegations suggesting that both sides would need to prepare for the eventual retrocession of Macau to China.[148] On the Chinese side, Foreign Minister Wu Xueqian reported on what the joint communiqué had achieved at the Fifth National People's Congress:

> While negotiating the establishment of diplomatic ties, the two Governments reached a mutual understanding on the Macau issue, confirming that Macau was Chinese territory and deciding that the time and details for returning Macau to China would be settled between the two Governments at an appropriate time.[149]

Portuguese government officials were extremely careful not to upset the Chinese, seeking almost at all costs to keep the negotiations behind closed doors. This was one of the reasons behind the political decision to wait ten years before making parts of the content of the *Acta Secreta* (Secret Memorandum) public in 1987, referred to as *Acta das Conversações* (Minutes of Conversations).

The *Acta Secreta* constituted a mutual agreement establishing reciprocal obligations and rights, although by having picked the word "memorandum" instead of "agreement", it demonstrated a general unimportance with which both parties viewed the content material of the *Acta*.[150] There were moments in the negotiation process when claims were made about the legitimacy of this *Acta* with some political figures stating that they had no prior knowledge of its existence. Notwithstanding, the *Acta* had been written up on the basis of Portuguese cabinet instructions on 14

June 1978,[151] consisting of two paragraphs. The first represented the Portuguese position via a statement by Coimbra Martins, while the other gave China voice on the matter through Han Kehua. The Portuguese government stressed agreement with the position of the Chinese government on Macau, as follows:

> 1- Macau is part of Chinese territory and will be returned to China. The question of the date and the modalities of the reversion can be solved through negotiations in the future, when both Governments consider appropriate. 2- Before the reversion, the Portuguese authorities of Macau must respect and protect the rights and legitimate interests of the Chinese inhabitants, without allowing the Soviet Union, Taiwan's authorities or other political forces to use Macau to hold activities prejudicial to the People's Republic of China.[152]

This official reference to the Soviet Union or Taiwan was behind the decision of keeping the *Acta* secret, as it could lead to misinterpretation and potentially damaging for continued Sino-Portuguese talks. However, it remained Portugal's official stance even after the PRC had ceased to regard the Soviet Union as "the most dangerous superpower and the first enemy of the peoples".[153]

While China's posture towards Portugal remained one of relative irreverence, having it appeared to welcome the Portuguese declarations as a pre-condition for proceeding with formal negotiations, China's apparent unexpected interest in discussing Macau was a reflection of the changing climate in the Chinese and Portuguese domestic environments.

In Portugal, the trauma experienced in the mid-1970s from the decolonisation process in Africa resulted in demands from the Portuguese public to ensure a more dignifying withdrawal from Macau. Many Portuguese resent the left for abandoning the African colonies in the aftermath of the 1974 democratic revolution and, even amongst those that stood against the colonial war, there is the feeling that decolonization should have been handled differently to avoid negative impact in the economy and the society. Being part of the decision-making process regarding the "decolonisation" of Macau, as it was domestically perceived, centrist and right-wing politicians were not in favour of adopting unpopular measures that could lead to public finger-pointing. Even if Macau was never a hot topic, public opinion in Portugal is very critical about the "loss" of empire.

During the 1986–1987 Sino-Portuguese negotiations the *Acta* became a source of embarrassment among the governing classes. After a number of politicians declared never having seen it and doubting its existence, eyebrows were raised among the political elite about the credibility of the negotiations. For example, in 1986 and early 1987, Macau Governor Pinto Machado referred frequently to the *Acta* in the press, declaring that he had no previous knowledge of it.[154] Adriano Moreira was the first member of parliament (MP) to raise the question of the *Acta*,[155] seeking its complete public disclosure, during a parliamentary discussion on 20 October 1986 nearly four months after the Portuguese-Chinese negotiations had begun.[156] The Central Democratic Social Party MPs made similar requests only to have these fall on deaf ears.[157] Ramalho Eanes, Portuguese president in 1976–1986, in a decisive move, explained that the *Acta* remained in the archives of the office of the prime minister,[158] Aníbal Cavaco Silva from the Social Democrat Party (PSD), which succeeded Mário Soares and Mota Pinto of the Central Block (PS and PSD). Prime Minister Cavaco Silva stated that the *Acta* had been misplaced,[159] adding another layer of mystery to the debacle. These inconsistencies triggered an angry response from President Eanes, given that the *Acta* served as "the negotiation base of all the process of the transfer of the Portuguese administration of the territory of Macau to the People's Republic of China".[160]

The *Acta* was finally found at the Ministry of Foreign Affairs. The prime minister took the decision to read the contents at the State Council meeting on 6 January 1987. Two days later, the Cabinet released a communiqué, providing a background explanation to Portugal's policy towards China over Macau. Around the same time, Cavaco Silva had begun to show discontent about accepting the responsibilities of negotiating Macau's future left by the previous government. After having consulted Mário Soares, which succeeded Eanes as Portuguese president in 1986, Cavaco Silva agreed to publish the communiqué.[161] For the first time since 1979, the content of the *Acta* was made public, to the relief of sceptical political onlookers.[162]

A Muddled and Multifaceted Process

As we have seen, Portugal lacked a national strategy for negotiations with China over Macau. The Portuguese were reduced to this passive strategy because of their precarious presence in Macau and the fatigue felt from the African decolonisation process and withdrawal from East Timor. From the Portuguese settlement in Macau in the sixteenth century to the establishment of diplomatic relations with the PRC in 1979, Portugal had shared sovereignty over Macau with China. Sino-Portuguese relations evolved through different stages and the fragility of the Portuguese presence in Macau fluctuated with China's levels of political stability and power. For example, events associated with the Cultural Revolution during 1966–1967 led to Portugal losing *de facto* sovereignty over Macau.

Portugal's diminished legitimacy in the enclave remained superimposed as an idealistic aspiration of prominence—the only way to sustain the Portuguese administration in the territory.

For China, Macau never ceased to be a part of its national territory. The government, however, only began to contemplate retrocession when it was advantageous. Macau had an important role to play in Chinese national reunification. The PRC wanted to use it and Hong Kong as showcases for Taiwan. In 1972, soon after China became a member of the United Nations, Macau was removed from the UN list of colonial territories, paving the way for the re-integration of Macau into China, depriving it of the possibility of self-determination. The PRC had a bipolar political policy, playing the revolutionary or the pragmatic card depending on the question at hand. This was the case with the support it gave to Third World movements against colonialism whilst interested in maintaining the status quo in Macau, even though for them Macau was Chinese territory.

After the 25 April 1974 revolution in Portugal, due to the prevailing indifference regarding Macau explained in the previous section, and eager to gain international recognition, the new regime was more interested in developing diplomatic relations with the PRC than in maintaining (arguably recovering) sovereignty over Macau. The process for the establishment of Sino-Portuguese diplomatic relations was onerous. The new Portuguese regime publicly announced on 6 January 1975 that it considered the PRC the sole representative of the Chinese people with Taiwan an integral part of China, and Macau would be the object of negotiations when both governments considered it appropriate.

These unilateral concessions reflected the Portuguese attempt at cooperation with China through which it hoped to obtain significant concessions from the Chinese, even if it meant Portugal renouncing many important positions.[163] Recognizing Taiwan as part of China, although as a concession, was not harmful for the Portuguese interests. However, accepting that the Macau question would be solved through Sino-Portuguese negotiations acknowledged the Chinese sovereignty over the territory: Macau would not be offered the right to self-determination or a seat at the negotiation table. By 8 February 1979, with the Sino-Portuguese bilateral relations firmly in place, Portugal reinforced its concessions in the *Acta Secreta* signed in Paris along with the joint communiqué for the establishment of diplomatic relations to which both swore secrecy. Later, these negotiations proved to be very advantageous for the PRC.

While negotiating the *Acta Secreta*, the Portuguese government could have obtained noteworthy political returns in exchange for the maintenance of the status quo as it had been China and not Portugal, who had demonstrated approval at Portugal's continued administration in Macau. In the context of withdrawal from Empire and lack of interest regarding Macau, the new regime did not take advantage of these exceptional circumstances. A close analysis of the process suggests that the *Acta* had in fact limited negotiating space for the Portuguese government during the 1986–1987 talks: there was not much left to negotiate if Portugal had already promised to hand Macau over to China. Once the Chinese leaders considered that the time was ripe for negotiating the Macau question, they fell back on the agreement endorsed by Portugal. At that time, the Portuguese leaders were uncoordinated and lacked a concise strategy for going forward. It was a period of controversy and uncertainty, reinforced by the amplified mystery under which the negotiations advanced.

2
Negotiations for the Sino-Portuguese Joint Declaration on Macau

The Beginning

The first signs that Beijing was considering seriously the settlement question came in June 1982, when Deng Xiaoping made a public declaration of China's sovereignty over Hong Kong and Macau stating that these territories would be re-integrated into China within a few years, under the banner of "one country, two systems". In 1983, the Chinese ambassador in Lisbon claimed that the Macau statute had already been discussed in the *Acta Secreta*; this could be understood as a sign that China was open to embark on negotiations.[1]

For political reasons China chose to draw parallels between Hong Kong and Macau, centring on common threads that seemingly bound them to a similar end. The historical differences, resultant from differing administrative experiences, were immaterial, as both territories had been "lost" to foreign rule and were bound to revert through historical association with the mainland. The peoples of both territories were denied the right to self-determination and excluded from the negotiations. China wished to combine the retrocession of Hong Kong and Macau under the formula "one country, two systems" as a yardstick against which the reintegration of Taiwan would be set. China was cautious to conduct the negotiations in both cases on the basis of a common strategy, evident in the similar accords into which it entered with both Portugal and the UK, comparable in form and substance with a few striking exceptions.[2]

Still a number of historical and legal differences were detectible, which resulted in Britain and Portugal having divergent positions on Beijing's claims of legitimacy. For China, Hong Kong was a result of the era of unequal treaties. Three Hong Kong treaties had provided Britain with greater bargaining power, fortified under international law. A segment of land understood to be Chinese territory had been given to the British crown under internationally recognised decree. The Portuguese government did not have comparable status over Macau. Incapable of negotiating on similar grounds to that of its British counterparts, the Portuguese had to work through a haze of ambiguity around Macau's status. Without having the necessary legal underpinnings, Portugal had little with which to negotiate a position of sovereignty. Portugal and China had *de facto* shared sovereignty, an arrangement that had developed out of a special understanding and correlations of interests.[3]

Macau and Hong Kong also had different colonial experiences. While the British set about delivering economic results in Hong Kong through the creation of a hub of securities and investments along with prosperous industrial and banking sectors, the Portuguese only could use Macau as a touristic reminder of Portugal's past power. Portugal did not even invest in the promotion of use of Portuguese, which spite of being the official language, was not encouraged and was rarely spoken by the Chinese population.

Hong Kong was held with greater esteem and importance by the UK than Macau by Portugal, resulting in the former experiencing greater anxiety with the retrocession. Being a financial centre of international renown, Hong Kong had elevated to international status and the negotiation was more vulnerable than Macau to greater international pressure. The nature of the relations between Portugal and China differed significantly from those enjoyed by the UK and China. There was relatively greater asymmetry of power between the former than the latter. Beijing regarded the UK as more developed than China and laudable of an equal (or higher) international status.[4]

As a consequence, the strategies adopted by the parties to the negotiations were also different. Perceiving itself to be a great power, the UK adopted a defensive strategy and certified that it controlled the pace of the negotiations with China, taking provocative steps at times to change Hong Kong political structures which annoyed the Chinese.[5] The Portuguese negotiated from a position of submission, given their country's minor international importance at the time. They conferred certain privileges upon Beijing including setting the agenda for the negotiations. Lisbon believed that in avoiding contesting sensitive issues that could be misinterpreted by Beijing, it would be better placed to extract important concessions from China during the retrocession negotiations.[6]

Formal Sino-Portuguese negotiations took place from 1986 to 1987. The most sensitive subjects that were tabled during the negotiation process were the date for the transfer of the Portuguese administration to China and the nationality issue of the Macau's residents within the future Special Administrative Region. Both topics were contentious, reflecting the differing preconceptions. While the Chinese sought to apply the Sino-British accord from Hong Kong to Macau, favouring a simultaneous handover, the Portuguese argued that the Hong Kong model should be shaped in conformity with Macau's requirements, drawing on the experience in Hong Kong. The Portuguese were not pinned down by a predetermined date as in the case with the UK in Hong Kong's New Territories with a lease that was to expire in 1997. The Portuguese envisioned a broader transition period with which to work, in spite of the non-negotiable cut off point stipulated by China as the end of twentieth century. By mutual concession it was finally agreed that 19 December 1999 would be the last remaining option for the handover. The Portuguese leaders sighed relief, perceiving China's decision as a sign of flexibility and major concession, which they should not underestimate.[7]

The nationality issue consisted of finding a way to assimilate Macau residents holding Portuguese passports into a future autonomous region under Chinese rule. Portuguese leaders felt that such people should continue to have dual nationality. Chinese Nationality Law makes no provisions for dual nationality. Chinese leaders felt that ethnic Chinese citizens in Macau should renounce Portuguese nationality and maintain Chinese nationality alone. Over the course of the negotiations, the two countries bickered continuously without reaching a consensus. Divergent opinions were annexed to the Joint Declaration in two different memoranda. The nationality issue was passed on to the Joint Liaison Group, to resolve after the signing of the agreement.

The Hong Kong Model

After a ruinous defeat in the Opium War, China was obliged to agree to the terms of the Treaty of Nanjing (Nanking) on 29 August 1842, surrendering the island of Hong Kong to Britain, opening five other treaty ports, and foreigners were granted extraterritoriality exempting them from Chinese law. After ratification of the Treaty of Humen on 26 June 1843, Hong Kong was declared a crown colony.[8] The Convention of Peace and Friendship, signed in Beijing on 24 October 1860 after the second Anglo-Chinese war, ratified the Treaty of Tianjin signed in 1857, opening up eleven new treaty ports, allowed foreigners to travel anywhere in China with a passport,[9] and resulted in the Kowloon Peninsula being added to the colony. The "Convention Respecting an Extension of the Hong Kong Territory", signed in Beijing on the 9 June 1898, added another 350 square miles of the mainland and 235 islands to the colony of Hong Kong by means of a 99-year lease, which is known as the New Territories.[10]

The British favoured the leasing system over a permanent cession of territory from China to avoid accusations of being responsible for its territorial break up.[11] Hoping to minimize their losses, the Chinese quickly agreed that the New Territories should be leased for an exact period. The "walled city of Kowloon", a previous Chinese military fort, would remain under Chinese jurisdiction. Britain did not perceive Chinese continued presence in an enclave within the colony as harmful to its interests.[12]

By Royal Order in Council of 20 October 1898, the newly leased territories were declared to be "part and parcel of Her Majesty's Colony of Hong Kong", ignoring claims that these were bound by a leasing agreement.[13] Thereafter the British authorities behaved in a manner that suggested they believed they had been granted the equal rights to govern concurrently the New Territories and Hong Kong. When China sought support to end territorial leases at the Washington Conference from 1921–1922, in an attempt to weaken China's assertions, Britain suggested, unsuccessfully, that the New Territories and Hong Kong did not have the status of leaseholds.[14]

From 1941 to 1945, Hong Kong was occupied by Japan. After Japan's defeat, China had hoped to take over Hong Kong but it was Britain that accepted Japan's surrender, restoring the enclave as a Crown colony in 1946. Despite mounting internal pressure from Chinese Nationalists for the recovery of Hong Kong, Nanjing favoured settling the Hong Kong issue at a later stage through friendly negotiations with the UK. With the establishment of the PRC in 1949, China's Hong Kong policy remained unchanged. In the early 1950s, at the height of the Korean War the enclave assumed greater geopolitical importance for China; through which it sought to divide Britain from the United States and break the embargoes imposed on China by the US. This strategy also could ensure that China acquire important strategic materials and foreign exchange.[15]

By the late 1970s, investors in Hong Kong were beginning to contemplate how the deadline for the New Territories lease on 30 June 1997 would impact on their future.[16] Many reservoirs and utilities of Hong Kong were located in the New Territories, which represented 92 per cent of the total area of Hong Kong and thus was absolutely vital for the functioning of the colony. It was widely believed that without the UK having a say over the management of the New Territories lease, Hong Kong Island and Kowloon would be unviable and lose significant economic prominence. The British understood that a fractious confrontation with China over Hong Kong was not the solution. Taking that route meant facing the inevitability of recoil from the mainland in the form of food and water embargoes, an influx of refugees from China and a growing Chinese military presence in the region.[17]

The Hong Kong model was also influenced by the evolution of the Macau question. The *Acta Secreta* of 8 February 1979 gave concerns to the British Foreign Office of the likely impact that the formula "territory under Portuguese administration" would have on the New Territories.[18] The British governor, Sir Murray MacLehose, would attempt to unravel the enigma during a state visit to Beijing in March 1979. He was reassured by the Chinese leader, Deng Xiaoping, that the capitalist system would remain unaltered in Hong Kong, and that "investors should put their hearts at ease", although Deng did not make known what political solution would be adopted. Chinese leaders demonstrated they were not prepared to talk about Hong Kong's future at that juncture, concentrating instead on Taiwan. The extent of the mainland's preoccupation with the Republic of China on Taiwan found expression in a nine-point plan in September 1981 that envisaged the reunification of Taiwan with the mainland under a special administrative region (where it would enjoy a high degree of autonomy). Under that plan, Taiwan would maintain its original economic and social systems.[19]

Later it became apparent to Deng that reunification with Taiwan could not be achieved in the short term due to Taiwan's hostility to the mainland and to the lack of American support for merger. China decided to delay its reunification policy until a more propitious time, shifting its attention to Hong Kong where reunification with the mainland appeared both inevitable and easier to achieve, with the deadline for the end of the New Territories lease near, with the added benefit of having the potential to serve as a template on which to build an effective reunification strategy for Taiwan.

Beijing soon after broke the "silence" over the Hong Kong issue, seeking to bring the British to a point where discussions would be held around the retrocession of Hong Kong. China intended to have sovereignty by 1997 without endangering the prosperity and international prestige Hong Kong enjoyed.[20] In June 1982, Chinese aspirations became clearer during an official address to an audience representing twelve personalities from Hong Kong and Macau:

> (1) Both territories belonged to China and were subject to Chinese sovereignty; (2) China did not recognise any validity to the unequal treaties of the past; (3) the reunification of the two territories would be made soon under the concept one country, two systems, which allowed them to maintain their economic systems.[21]

The Chinese government argued that, at the time of signing the Treaty of Nanjing of 1842, the Convention of Peace and Friendship of 1860, and the Second Convention of Beijing of 1898, Britain and China were not on equal bargaining terms. On these grounds China declared that it would not accept the validity of these treaties, calling them unequal. The Chinese felt that states only were bound by treaties founded on principles of equality.[22] Notwithstanding, Beijing realised that for the UK these were valid treaties and that they were subject to honour the terms under which they were negotiated, including the 1997 deadline for the retrocession of Hong Kong, unless there were exclusions arising from precipitated negotiation.[23] In fact, Britain's attitude was to honour the Sino-British treaties as valid and recognised[24] by international law where a treaty could not be considered invalid on grounds of discrimination or unfairness.[25] In accordance with international law, treaties cannot be classified "according to the equality in the bargaining power of the parties and the benefits and burdens created by the treaty itself". [26]

The Falklands War brought a new dimension to British perceptions, but it did not meet the reality.[27] Some argue that Britain's victory in the Falklands resulted in Prime Minister Margaret Thatcher creating an illusion of British dominance on the world stage, a position from which London set out to negotiate the terms of Hong Kong's retrocession with China.[28] However, the Chinese made clear that there was nothing to negotiate: the United Kingdom was left with the role of "cooperating" with the resumption of Chinese sovereignty and administration over the all enclave.[29] In the end, it was by mutual consent that the negotiations would take place in an environment of diplomacy.[30]

By July 1983 the British and Chinese had already done a lot of negotiating before getting to a point of consensus, finally deciding on the date for initiating roundtable talks.[31] On 26 September 1984, after twenty-two plenary meetings, the Sino-British Joint Declaration on the Question of Hong Kong was signed in Beijing by the British ambassador Sir Richard Evans and by the Chinese vice foreign minister Zhou Nan.[32] On 19 December the British and Chinese prime ministers, Margaret Thatcher and Zhao Ziyang, signed the document at Beijing's Great Hall of the People.[33]

The Sino-British retrocession negotiations together with the Sino-British Joint Declaration had a bearing on speculation about the future of Macau. In October 1984, Deng had sought to moderate its impact indicating that the Macau question could "be kept aside for up to eight years". He insisted that Beijing's primary objective was the economic and social sustainability of both Macau and Hong Kong.[34] In an atmosphere of speculation and Beijing's apparent quiet about Macau, Portuguese elites paced softly around the main issues. While simultaneously some suspected that China would take the necessary steps to recover Macau quickly, others thought China would want to keep Macau as an open door to the West. Such uncertainty in the end added to the disinterest manifest among officials of the Portuguese Foreign Ministry, seemingly incapable of drawing up a strategy in aid of effective negotiations with the mainland.

Getting Portugal to the Table

After the negotiations around Hong Kong's reversion had been concluded it was apparent that Macau, and not Taiwan, was next in China's priorities for reunification. Despite Deng's declarations to the press, during the final stages of the Sino-British negotiations Chinese leaders had demonstrated growing predisposition to engage the Portuguese over the future of Macau,[35] highlighted by the Chinese president Li Xiannian's visit to Lisbon in November 1984.

The visit started with references at the *Acta Secreta* by the foreign minister, Wu Xueqian, who reminded the Portuguese that, at the time of the establishment of formal relations in 1979, Portugal had recognised Macau as Chinese territory.[36] The *Acta Secreta* had also given the two sides flexibility for beginning discussions around Macau's retrocession on grounds of mutual consent. President Li's visit was timely in that it provided the Chinese the means with which to showcase Beijing's willingness to initiate talks with Lisbon on Macau.

A second reference to the *Acta Secreta* was made in a February 1985 meeting between Li Xiannian and the Macau governor, Vasco Almeida e Costa. Li suggested that a Macau solution should be based upon peaceful negotiations under the principles of the agreement of 1979 to which each side was mutually bound. In March 1985, the Hong Kong newspaper, *Guangjiaojing* (*Wide Angle*), published information of an apparent Chinese provisional plan for the reunification of Macau. This plan stressed the seriousness with which Beijing desired a "simultaneous solution" for the return of Hong Kong and Macau in 1997. The newspaper article announced that the mainland planned to discuss this matter with President Ramalho Eanes during a state visit to Beijing in May.[37]

The Chinese were careful about how they presented official concerns: an indirect approach was a preferred modus operandi. Before Ramalho Eanes' arrival in Beijing on 21 May 1985, the Portuguese delegation suspected that the Chinese would attempt delicately to push the issue of Macau, and were not surprised to have it raised.[38] The Portuguese had contemplated cancelling the visit, feeling a degree of ineptitude resulting from a lack of preparedness on how to communicate effectively with the Chinese. A number of sceptics towards the visit argued that the president was at the end of his mandate and the outputs of the visit could be problematic for his successor. Internal opinions around the state visit split between those who favoured settling the Macau question quickly and those who preferred to stretch the matter out as long as possible.

Portugal's sense of trepidation paralysed their team from asserting a strong position in the negotiations and prevented them from seeking viable alternatives. At the same time the delegation wanted to ensure that Portugal's integrity internationally was not severely compromised and that the solution for Macau would not vary greatly from that reached for Hong Kong. In the end Portugal failed to negotiate effectively with the Chinese. Knowing all too well the problems of inconsistency on the Portuguese side, the Chinese stood as a united front and consistently played on the fears of the Portuguese, thus neutralizing their bargaining power.

The Chinese strategy was built around disarming the other side by means of contradictory messages. During the preparation for the Ramalho Eanes' visit to Beijing, the Chinese embassy in Lisbon announced that Macau would not be on the agenda, indicating instead a generic topic for the visit focussing primarily on Sino-Portuguese bilateral relations. As a matter of fact, during an informal dinner which took place on the eve of the arrival of Ramalho Eanes, the ambassador of Portugal in Beijing was informed by a vice foreign minister that the Macau question would be raised at the talks with the president of Portugal. But the president himself, who at this time had already initiated his trip, only could learn this development after his arrival in China.[39] In the end, Beijing's move to out-manoeuvre the Portuguese reassured China that the Portuguese president would neither cancel the visit nor return to Portugal without accepting the terms of the joint communiqué, settling for an indefinite period the question of the future of Macau.

In the meeting that was held on 22 May 1985 with the Chinese prime minister Zhao Ziyang, replacing President Li Xianian who was ill on that date, the Portuguese were informed "that the time for settling the Macau issue was ripe".[40] Ramalho Eanes showed receptivity to later initiate talks with China on Macau, as long as the interests of China, Portugal and Macau were guaranteed; Portugal would respect the 1979 agreement on Macau regardless of the results in the upcoming presidential election planned for March 1986.[41] Ramalho Eanes sought to draw benefits from raising the issue on his terms, safeguarding some important principles for Portugal.[42]

Receptiveness on the Portuguese side, evident during President Ramalho Eanes' visit to Beijing, was reassuring for the Chinese. With the Portuguese seemingly on board, Zhao Ziyang suggested a plan for Macau's reversion using the same formula of the "one country, two systems" as envisaged for Hong Kong, and emphasising "to be desirable to observe the pertinent model defined in the ambit of the accord on Hong Kong, in the same manner as to emphasise that the stability of Macau had everything to gain with the acceptance of the concomitance of the deadlines established there". China envisaged the date for the hand over "could happen simultaneously with the date anticipated for the recovery of sovereignty over Hong Kong".[43]

The day after the presidential meeting, Portuguese Foreign Minister Jaime Gama and Chinese Foreign Minister Wu Xueqian published a joint communiqué in which "both sides agreed in starting, in the near future, talks through diplomatic channels for the settlement of the Macau question".[44] During a press conference, Ramalho Eanes stated that since 1979, China and Portugal shared an exemplary relationship and that they were on the same page with regard to the future of Macau, driven by a mutual desire to guarantee the territorial stability and development of the enclave. The Portuguese president admitted the Macau issue had been tabled by the Chinese, although, anticipated beforehand by the Portuguese prior to Li Xiannian's visit to Lisbon.[45]

Upon his return to Portugal, Ramalho Eanes was criticised for initiating the process of retrocession of Macau during the first visit of a Portuguese head of state to China. Within the already mentioned negative perception for the loss of Empire, it was tempting for Portuguese leaders and parties to use Macau for criticising political opponents. In Macau, the Macanese (*Macaenses*—people of mixed Portuguese, Chinese, and in some cases colonial Portuguese ancestry) felt betrayed and had expected to be consulted, strongly criticising the Portuguese president in the press. In any event, had Ramalho Eanes refused Beijing's invitation to visit China, it would for all effects and purposes have annoyed the Chinese which was a risk that the president could not afford in light of the circumstances. Ramalho Eanes initiated a process of self-defence. On 7 June 1985, during an address to the State Council, Eanes set out to quiet critics such as to Prime Minister Mário Soares, explaining that Soares had been involved in talks on the process of Macau's retrocession.[46] The president showed how in 1975, Soares, then foreign minister, had published a note in which he had agreed to the establishment of diplomatic relations. The *Acta Secreta*, signed in 1979, had been negotiated when Soares was prime minister, in 1978. The joint communiqué for the settlement of the Macau question, signed in May 1985, was negotiated by Jaime Gama, the foreign minister in Mário Soares' government.

In September 1985, the Portuguese and Chinese ministers of foreign affairs mutually agreed to meet at the UN General Assembly to hold in-depth discussions about Macau soon after Portugal's legislative elections in October. The elections brought the Social Democrat Party to power led by Prime Minister Aníbal Cavaco Silva. As soon as Cavaco Silva took up office he got to work settling a number of pending issues but demonstrated a readiness to "start preliminary talks with the PRC about the future of the territory". In January 1986, the Chinese leadership informed the Portuguese ambassador in Beijing that China was equally ready to start negotiations.[47]

Negotiations did not start before the Portuguese presidential election in March 1986 for constitutional reasons. According to the Portuguese Constitution, Macau's administration depended upon a balancing act of two co-existing political forces i.e. the government and the president. This is called the double tutelage system which will be discussed in more detail in Chapter Three. When Mário Soares took the office of president in the elections, Chinese government representatives were invited to the ceremony and tried to push the Portuguese to begin negotiations, but to no avail. Such had been Chinese preparedness that they had already identified a team leader to head up the negotiations: Vice Foreign Minister Zhou Nan, head of the Chinese delegation during the Sino-British negotiations over Hong Kong.

Zhou Nan warned Cavaco Silva during the inaugural ceremony that: "the Macau question affects the national feelings of the Chinese people and is very sensitive to China". Cavaco Silva appeared forthcoming, indicating that his government required a period of two months to analyse these concerns. They decided that late May was an appropriate time to start negotiations over Macau.[48] Seemingly prepared to take on the task but distracted by the presidential election, in March 1986, the negotiations were felt to be a minor concern for Portugal.[49] Cavaco Silva, however, did not wish to disclose the extent of Portugal's apparent lack of concern. Later, one of Beijing's most favoured intermediaries transmitted China's intentions on the question of Macau to Cavaco Silva in the following message:

> (1) the Chinese community in Macau did not want Portuguese party conflicts to affect the territory; (2) Ma Man Kei and himself [Roque Choi] are loyal people and are available to bring messages to the Chinese authorities if the Portuguese Government finds it convenient; (3) they will tell China that the Macau question should be settled through negotiations on equal terms and not through impositions, because both Portugal and China's dignity should be respected; (4) unlike the United Kingdom regarding Hong Kong, Portugal did not have strong material interests in Macau and the end of a leasing of territories was not under discussion.[50]

After the meeting, Cavaco Silva resolved that Portugal should be prepared to embrace negotiations with the Chinese and together with the Minister of Foreign Affairs, Pires de Miranda, concluded that Portugal's aims for the negotiations should be:

> to assure an ordered transfer of the administration and to safeguard the stability and economic and social development of Macau; to

protect the rights and guarantees of the residents in the territory; to preserve the Portuguese cultural presence; to develop relations of friendship and cooperation with the PRC and strengthen Portugal's projection in the Far East.[51]

Portugal seemed closer to implementing an action plan. In the first round of negotiations, the Portuguese objectives included seeking to avoid Beijing as the predominant location for formal talks; respect for the principle of non-discrimination; equal benefits for Macau as those gained for Hong Kong; transparency; and the Chinese to reveal political intentions and positions so as to enable the Portuguese to plan counter-strategies as and when required.[52] The latter was one of Cavaco Silva's greatest concerns as he planned to encourage the Portuguese negotiators to entice the Chinese to gently "reveal, formally or informally, the totality of its proposals without assuming any commitment".[53]

Unfortunately Cavaco Silva's approach for the negotiations fell short. The Portuguese delegation arrived at the Sino-Portuguese talks without a comprehensive strategy when it thought the first meeting would be mainly a methodological discussion around preparing the groundwork against which the future negotiations would be set.[54] In contrast, a far better prepared Chinese team announced its official policy on the negotiations going forward, one month before formal talks began.[55] However, the Portuguese were aware that they had a strong veto power of threatening unilateral withdrawal from Macau before concluding negotiations, and this was a strong negotiation card. In August 1985, Governor Almeida e Costa is quoted as having said:

> Must we go to the negotiating table to take Chinese orders because China is such a powerful country? After 500 years of colonial rule, we are tired. Maybe we cannot wait for 12 years. We can leave within one or two years.[56]

The Search for a Formula

The first Sino-Portuguese plenary meeting, to discuss practical details of the talks, took place in Beijing on 30 June and 1 July 1986. Ambassador Rui Medina, an experienced diplomat who had led the Portuguese delegation at the United Nations, headed the Portuguese delegation. The delegation included Portuguese consul-general in Hong Kong Nuno Lorena, previous Macau under-secretary for the economy José Henriques de Jesus, presidential adviser to Mário Soares—Carlos Gaspar, a diplomat and member of the inter-ministerial commission on Macau at the Ministry of Foreign Affairs in Lisbon João de Deus Ramos, and administrative member of staff to the Portuguese Mission at the

United Nations João Ascensão. The Portuguese ambassador to Beijing, Octávio Neto Valério, participated in an advisory capacity.[57] Portugal had expected a delegate representing Macau at the negotiations but, since it was considered Chinese territory, China refused to accept a representative. The ambiguous status of Macau and the positions adopted by Portugal in the 6 January 1975 note and the 1979 *Acta Secreta* guarded the Chinese against further discussion on this topic. A decade later, the domestic context was very different and the will of the Macau people was now part of the equation, but Lisbon was forced to honour decisions taken by the previous government.

Chinese Deputy Foreign Minister Zhou Nan led the Chinese delegation. Zhou Nan and Rui Medina were familiar with each other from their days at the United Nations. Other members included: Ke Zhengping, a National People's Congress delegate; Shao Tianren a judicial adviser in the Foreign Ministry; Director Ke Zhaisuo of the Hong Kong and Macau Office in the Foreign Ministry; Department Director Zhu Hua of the Hong Kong and Macau Office in the State Council; and Deputy Director Zhao Jihua of the Hong Kong and Macau Office in the Foreign Ministry.[58]

One of the first steps taken by the Chinese early in the negotiations was to present in writing the official position of China spelling out a number of the basic policies visualised for Macau. The Chinese believed the Hong Kong agreement would serve as a model, mapping out the way forward in the negotiation stages for the settlement. Understanding the merits of the agreement in the course of the negotiations, the Portuguese were aware also of the disadvantages of the Hong Kong precedent. They were particularly concerned by the limitations of the agreement and its ability to inhibit widening the scope in search of more desirable alternatives for Macau. However the Portuguese felt they might be able to extract further concessions if pushed into using the Hong Kong template as the basis for negotiations.[59] After the Portuguese had used Hong Kong as a yardstick for negotiating Macau's basic conditions in the first round, they tried instead to get concessions in the second and third rounds based upon Macau's specific conditions. The Portuguese delegates played this specificity card to obtain negotiating advantages.

The second plenary meeting took place on 9 and 10 September 1986. It was marked by a wave of divergent opinions around the date for the handover and the sensitive nationality clause. The Chinese delegates presented a draft of the Joint Declaration consisting of two annexes, one dealing with China's basic policies for Macau, and the other with the functions of two joint working groups for the transitional period.[60] The Chinese did not foresee a stalemate, expecting the Portuguese to agree wholeheartedly with them, and they were annoyed when Portugal rejected the proposal, presenting a counterproposal at the third plenary meeting on 21 and 22 October 1986. The Portuguese counterproposal, agreed to by two previous disparate political figures, Prime Minister Aníbal Cavaco Silva (PSD) and President Mário Soares (PS), accepted the general outline proposed by the Chinese, but made suggestions and comments on the Chinese joint declaration draft and the first annex as well as commenting on various details.[61]

The third round of talks was evidently abrasive, culminating in a deadlock over several issues, the handover date and the nationality of the Macau people being the most sensitive ones. A joint working group, consisting of three representatives from both sides, was set up to solve the impasse. The Portuguese team leader was João de Deus Ramos along with Carlos Gaspar and José Henriques de Jesus. Zhao Jihua, deputy director of the Hong Kong and Macau Office in the Ministry of Foreign Affairs, headed the Chinese team.[62] The working group was tasked "to discuss and revise all draft agreements and documents that had been worked out during the talks"; it also was expected "to discuss and revise all draft agreements and documents that had been worked out during the talks".[63] The approach, through which a solution was sought, however, was inherently flawed by two starkly different frames of reference on either side.

The Chinese leaders, aiming at a quick-fix solution for Macau, desired to push for ratification of the agreement in the National People's Congress in April, before the Thirteenth Chinese Communist Party Congress in September 1987.[64] The Chinese were motivated by internal considerations. It was widely believed that the signing of the Joint Declaration would corroborate Deng's "one country, two systems" formula and open-door policy, at a critical juncture in the country's internal affairs. China was feeling a rise in instability at home. Political validation through association with external affairs would consolidate the Chinese leaders' leadership, having a domestic sedative effect. The Portuguese were unconcerned about negative undercurrents on the home front. They were in disagreement with rushing negotiations and critical of drawing up a potentially bad agreement for Macau.[65]

Compared to Portugal, the Chinese favoured a faster paced negotiation process. China sought quick, fast-tracked solutions to meet the demands of the deadline for the plenary meeting of the two delegations in Beijing. The Chinese exerted pressure on the Portuguese to pick up the pace. This motivated Zhou Nan's visit to Portugal from 17 to 22 November 1986, accompanied by Zhao Jihua and Han Zhaokang, representatives of the Chinese Ministry of Foreign Affairs. Appearing to be a courtesy call or diplomatic compensation for the lack of negotiation rounds in Lisbon, the visit was politically loaded and integral to the negotiation process.[66]

The Portuguese leaders perceived this visit as a victory, given that during the Hong Kong negotiations the Chinese had made it a requirement of the negotiations to hold all meetings in Beijing.[67] Lisbon seized the opportunity to boost its negotiating position, beginning with making hasty changes to the programme of the visit.[68] Instead of putting the more important and sensitive issues on the negotiating table during the third plenary meeting in October, the Portuguese approach was to confront Zhou Nan with those issues during his visit to Lisbon.

Details of the Negotiations

Zhou Nan's November 1986 visit was marked by discussions around a number of sensitive issues: the date for signing the Joint Declaration, the functions and place of residence for the Joint Liaison Group, the date for the return of Macau to China, and the question of nationality for the 80,000 Macau Chinese with Portuguese nationality. Two central themes dominated the Portuguese agenda: fear of Chinese interference in the administration of Macau during the transition period and safeguarding citizens of Chinese origin living in Macau with Portuguese nationality.[69]

The date for the transfer of Portuguese administration to China was arguably the most contentious issue. Prime Minister Zhao Ziyang informed President Ramalho Eanes during a meeting on 22 May 1985 of China's intentions of linking the retrocession of Macau with that of Hong Kong. The Chinese wanted to use whichever tools in reach to push the Portuguese into accepting this precondition.

A favourite Chinese pressure tactic applied throughout the Sino-Portuguese negotiations was the use of the media to make known intentions or disagreements. By not confronting the Portuguese directly, Beijing was in effect seeking to restrain Lisbon's negotiating position by attempting to humiliate or manipulate them. This could be seen as one of the reasons for the decision to publicise a provisional plan in *Guangjiaojing* on 16 March 1985 which the Chinese described as a "simultaneous solution" for Hong Kong and Macau in 1997.[70]

The Portuguese government strongly objected to Chinese suggestions of a simultaneous British-Portuguese withdrawal and the integration of Macau with Hong Kong into one special administrative region or with the adjacent Zhuhai Special Economic Zone. They argued Macau and Hong Kong were different cases as were Macau and Zhuhai with the dates for the retrocessions reflecting the unique characteristics of each. A different special administrative region should be created separately for Hong Kong and for Macau, taking into consideration different levels of development, both social and economic.[71]

The Portuguese intention was to derail Chinese efforts. They proved effective at times with Zhou Nan's visit to Lisbon serving as an example. Cavaco Silva, Pires de Miranda and Mário Soares concentrated their strengths, vowing that the Chinese representative would not return to Beijing with an endorsement from Portugal on "simultaneous solution". Instead they carefully probed the Chinese for an indication of what they would regard as the last acceptable deadline for the handover.[72] The process unravelled in stages, beginning with Pires de Miranda who gauged Zhou Nan for a consensus on the date for the retrocession without success. Then Cavaco Silva advanced a later transition date, which widened the gap between the two sides to the surprise of Zhou. Zhou Nan reminded the Portuguese prime minister that China had superpower status. Cavaco Silva, on the other hand, recalled the importance of friendship and cooperation in the negotiations and asked Zhou to take into consideration the impact of a longer transitional period on the stability of Macau. An extended period of transition would secure a peaceful transfer after all infrastructural projects in progress at the time were concluded. Later, Zhou Nan met with Mário Soares as a last effort to obtain consensus on the date but the talks continued to evolve in an atmosphere of rigidity and intransigence.[73]

In the end a wrestling match ensued with the Portuguese claiming responsibilities on the one hand and the Chinese rights on the other. Negotiations would remain in deadlock until an agreement on the date was reached. The end of the century appeared as the cut-off date for the retrocession and a more acceptable point from which to re-commence negotiations.[74] A sense of acquiescence followed the threats of the Chinese side.[75] The press speculated about the state of the negotiations, suggesting that Zhou Nan had threatened to annex Macau if Portugal did not accept to hand the territory over before the year 2000, though a spokesman from the Portuguese Ministry of Foreign Affairs denied Portugal having received any threats.[76] In his autobiography, Prime Minister Cavaco Silva admitted Zhou Nan's visit had been tough. When Portugal did not succumb to China's "good intentions", Zhou threatened to unilaterally seek a solution for Macau. The Portuguese were encouraged to take the threat seriously or confront greater inflexibility from the Chinese at other stages in the negotiation process.[77]

Zhou Nan toured the north of Portugal with Macau Governor Pinto Machado, avoiding the press.[78] Later in a television interview, Zhou explained that the Portuguese government should understand the reasons for the importance with which China viewed the date for reunification before the end of the twentieth century:[79] this was an important goal of the national reunification policy and had had already been announced. The Chinese were vigilant about exerting as much pressure as the Portuguese could handle. Yet China had to circumvent confrontations with Portugal in order to avoid endangering the ultimate goal—Taiwan.

After Zhou Nan's visit to Portugal, the Sino-Portuguese working group, created during the third plenary meeting, met on 8 December 1986 but did not achieve a breakthrough on the issue of the retrocession date. The meeting remained deadlocked as the Chinese refused to negotiate on other matters until agreement was reached on the date.[80] The Chinese remained adamant that the 2000 cut-off date for the retrocession was non-negotiable.[81] In addition, they suggested that interference from suspected Portuguese partisans who were not party to the negotiations would not be tolerated. Chinese leaders were extremely annoyed on hearing about an article in the *Diário de Notícias* on 28 December, written by a socialist member of parliament, António Barreto, one of Mário Soares' closest advisors, in which he suggested that an acceptable date for the handover could range between the years 2007 or 2057. The Portuguese preferred a much later date past the end of the century so that the handover might match the 450th or 500th anniversary of the Portuguese presence in Macau.[82] The Chinese lashed out through an article in *Aomen Ribao*, a pro-PRC Macau paper:

> This kind of interference in the process of negotiation is a huge impudence. If they think that the consideration that China has for Portugal's interests is a demonstration of weakness . . . they are deeply wrong.[83]

Despite the Portuguese attempts, the Chinese apparently did not recognise that Barreto's article in the *Diário de Notícias* expressed a personal rather than an official government opinion.[84] In a formal diplomatic communication which resulted from Barreto's article, the Chinese repeated that "it was a determinant and firm position of the Chinese government and its people to recover Macau before the year 2000".[85] At this juncture, moving forward depended upon the level of effectiveness of how the Portuguese conducted damage control and the next stages of the talks.

The Portuguese negotiators realised that insisting on pressing the Chinese to accept a date for the handover beyond 2000 was dangerous and nonsensical.[86] Although this rule found favour with the prime minister Cavaco Silva, in contrast it did not with President Mário Soares. Soares appeared more interested in insisting on the symbolic dates of 2003 or 2007[87] as the dates for the handover of Macau to mark the 450th anniversary of the Portuguese settlement. This insistence, however, appeared out of context given the tensions of the time and was masking an underlining interest of some politicians in Portugal, politically connected to the Macau administration, to keep Macau until the expiry of the STDM (*Sociedade de Turismo e Diversões de Macau*, Macau's Tourism and Entertainment Company) gambling contract in 2002. This would guarantee that the percentage of the gambling profits that the STDM was bound to give to the Macau government until the end of the contract would be received by the Portuguese. The role of personal interests involved on this topic is better understood in the Orient Foundation section, one of the delicate transition issues analysed later in this book.

Soares found a supporter in Carlos Monjardino, a fellow member of the Socialist Party and the Macau under-secretary for economics, finance, and tourism who was appointed by the president as acting governor during the governor's absence from Macau. On 25 September 1986, aware of the veto power that Portugal had in the negotiations, Monjardino threatened unilateral withdrawal from Macau, which worried the Chinese:

> We will withdraw early if we are not happy about the way things go. We have nothing to lose, and we don't want to lose face . . . like the British kicked out of Hong Kong.[88]

There were a number of other considerations riding on the adoption of a more flexible approach by Portugal, crucial to safeguard other interests such as obtaining rights for the Portuguese *Banco Nacional Ultramarino* (BNU) to continue issuing Macau's banknotes (Pataca); the preservation of the statute of the Catholic Church in Macau; and the location for Joint Liaison Group's meetings. The venue for the meetings was a contentious issue during the negotiations that required significant skill to overcome. The Portuguese would have to find ingenious ways to persuade the Chinese into believing that rotating meetings around (between Lisbon and Beijing too) could be potentially more advantageous than having them situated only in Macau. The Chinese found safety in having the meetings in Macau for reasons of better access and control. But Lisbon favoured independence and revolving meetings in effect to compensate for Beijing's mounting political weight in the negotiations and also to keep the Macau administration free of Chinese pressure.[89]

There was agreement on the subject of the Joint Liaison Group during Zhou Nan's visit to Lisbon. China accepted the Portuguese position: the group would revolve between Beijing, Lisbon and Macau, and finally would reside in Macau one year after the signature of the agreement. The other two issues, however, failed to come to a consensus and remained sources of intense dissension.

For almost a year President Soares and Prime Minister Cavaco Silva stayed locked in disagreement over the date for the retrocession but they assembled along with Foreign Minister Pires de Miranda on 3 January 1987.[90] Three days later, the president evoked the State Council meeting on the negotiations that was characterised by a strong disagreement between Ramalho Eanes and Prime Minister Cavaco Silva on the subject of the *Acta Secreta*.[91] These disagreements deserved some consideration in the section of this book that analysed the *Acta* in detail, as they help to explain the difficulties that the Portuguese leaders had in presenting a united front, although it seems that the Chinese did not react significantly to this controversy.

Meanwhile the conflict between the president and the prime minister paved the way for a complaint from an opposition party, declaring the bilateral relations with China invalid. The reason was that the 1979 agreement consolidating Sino-Portuguese relations never was ratified in parliament. Neither the Portuguese Parliament nor the Macau Legislative Assembly was consulted regarding the signature of the *Acta Secreta*, violating the Portuguese Constitution and the Macau Organic Law.[92] Cavaco Silva intervened, explaining that the *Acta* was a memorandum of understanding, not a treaty agreement, and thus did not require ratification. The debate spilt over into the public domain and became potentially explosive.

Thus, Cavaco Silva set out to present documents to support the legality of Sino-Portuguese relations during the State Council meeting. These included documents from the negotiations in Paris for the establishment of diplomatic relations with China in 1979, such as the joint communiqué on the resumption of diplomatic relations, together with the proposal submitted by the then prime minister Mota Pinto, consisting of four amendments to the agreement of which the Chinese had accepted three.[93]

A communiqué released shortly afterwards reviewed Sino-Portuguese relations post-1974 and quoted the most relevant documents, namely the unilateral statement of the Portuguese Ministry of Foreign Affairs sent to the press on 6 January 1975 revealing a growing interest to establish diplomatic relations with China; the secret political directive approved on 14 June 1978 by the Portuguese Cabinet giving Ambassador Coimbra Martins specific instructions on how to negotiate with China; and a portion of the first paragraph dealing with the *Acta Secreta*.[94]

The communiqué also documented Ramalho Eanes' responsibility in the negotiations, quoting the 1985 Beijing joint communiqué in which both countries "agreed to enter into talks through diplomatic channels, in the near future, to settle the question of Macau".[95] The Cabinet also recalled that although the government was in charge of foreign policy, in the case of Macau and Timor "the Constitution points to a co-responsibility of the President and the government".[96] Cavaco Silva made this public release of information because he did not want to be accused of acts that were the responsibilities assumed by the previous governments.[97]

By 6 January 1986 a consensus was finally reached between Soares and Cavaco Silva on the date for the transfer. A specific date was not given although many supported the idea that retrocession should occur after the Hong Kong handover. The Portuguese also seemed to bank on the benefits of having a well-structured strategy with which to engage the Chinese. They decided to discard previous unworkable methods, opting to nominate a special envoy who would be responsible for communicating relevant Portuguese positions to the Chinese instead of the head of the Portuguese delegation or Portuguese ambassador in Beijing, as "a sign of the importance that Portugal attached to the relations with China".[98] In January 1987, the Portuguese secretary of state for foreign affairs and cooperation Azevedo Soares was dispatched to Beijing as the new special envoy tasked to communicate the Portuguese position on the date for Macau's transition.[99] Azevedo Soares would endeavour to extend the transition period as much as possible but was aware that the Chinese had already made known that they would not negotiate a date beyond 1999.

On his return to Lisbon, Azevedo Soares stated that a fourth plenary meeting would take place and that many issues remained open, including the date for the handover.[100] Foreign Minister Pires de Miranda confirmed that "all the questions would only be resolved with the signature of the agreement".[101] Nevertheless, Prime Minister Cavaco Silva considered that there was a significant progress on talks and Portugal even got some advantages over China's initial position.[102] The joint working group held several meetings to finish the texts of the agreement and on 14 March the Portuguese and Chinese Ministries of Foreign Affairs issued a joint communiqué announcing the decision that the fourth plenary meeting would take place in Beijing from 18 to 23 March 1987.

With the date for the retrocession on hold until the other issues were set, the nationality clause assumed priority in the discussions, although the second round had anticipated the importance of taking steps to resolve this concern in advance of other less contentious matters[103] and the negotiations hit another stumbling block. For the Chinese, nationality was implicitly about ethnicity—*jus sanguinis*, while the meaning for the Portuguese was defined by the place of birth—*jus solis*.[104] These differences of opinion were problematic, but Portugal felt responsible for the ethnic Chinese of Macau who were holders of Portuguese passports, and Lisbon determined to uphold their rights. According to the

Chinese, nationality was a procedural problem and not a political one. They found it humiliating to witness the Macanese preference for the Portuguese nationality instead the Chinese nationality or to keep both nationalities. However, China did "not recognise dual nationality to any Chinese national",[105] although it appeared as the best solution for many in Macau.

The articulation of these two divergent positions would result in a proposal of dual Portuguese and Chinese nationality to a large sector of the Macau inhabitants. The Chinese proposed "that those with Portuguese and Chinese nationality where the Portuguese nationality was grounded in the *jus soli*—on the fact that the person was born in Portuguese territory and not in consanguinity—should have the right of choice.[106] This suggestion was strongly rejected by the Portuguese who already had one definition for nationality and did not want to make a distinction for Macau. The aspect of the right to choose presented a problem for the Portuguese, fearing that it would lead to social instability, thereby possibly resulting in an influx of newly registered ethnic Chinese as Portuguese nationals.[107]

The Portuguese adopted a counter-proposal, suggesting that carriers of dual nationalities could renounce one. Alternatively Chinese citizens of Macau could keep Portuguese and Chinese passports, on the condition that the Portuguese passport was obtained prior to the final date of the retrocession.[108] According to Prime Minister Cavaco Silva, this appeared to be the best way to safeguard Macau's stability, as a very restrictive approach could have resulted in an outflow of people, abandoning Macau in search of better opportunities elsewhere, endangering efforts to preserve Portuguese heritage in the new special administrative region.[109]

The British government did not appreciate the Portuguese 'permissiveness' that could lead to the immigration of ethnic Chinese from Macau to the UK, under European Union law. Besides applying pressure at the bilateral level, the UK raised the issue in the European Economic Community, complaining that the Portuguese were raising the number of citizens with right of entry and free transit within the EEC.[110] Portugal had no advantage to multi-lateralise the issue: the Portuguese Nationality Law was particularly generous, resulting in millions of citizens with dual nationality spread around the world, namely in Africa, allowed to enter the EEC.

The Portuguese negotiators also faced pressure from the British government at the bilateral level, who was concerned that Portugal might obtain a more advantageous statute for Macau Chinese holding Portuguese passports than they had obtained for the Hong Kong Chinese holding British citizenship. In Hong Kong, the inhabitants that in the British Nationality Act of 30 October 1981 had the status of "British Dependent Territories Citizenship" changed to become merely holders of the "British Overseas Citizenship". They obtained passports with less status and international recognition,[111] as they only give access to "British consular services and protection in third countries", and did not grant the right of entry and abode in the UK.[112] As the Chinese Hong Kong inhabitants did not hold a full UK passport, the British did not worry about the nationality issue after the handover.[113]

The Portuguese negotiators were not interested in this arrangement. They could not deny Portuguese nationality to those who already had it, and could not accept anything that was illegal under the Portuguese Nationality Law. These different approaches arguably reveal that the British government feared that a large amount of citizens from Hong Kong (and even Macau) decided to move to the UK, while the Portuguese did not expect that a significant percentage of Macau ethnic Chinese would chose to live in Portugal. Even if this was the case, the number of Chinese with Portuguese passports was much lower than the British passport holders, so this type of migration would have a completely different impact for Portugal and for the UK.

As the Portuguese and Chinese delegations struggled to reach a consensus on the issues around nationality and Lisbon continued to propose a system of dual nationality for those eligible in Macau while acknowledging that Beijing could not sign dual nationality treaties, a solution was found. With authorisation to use Portuguese passports settled by the Foreign Ministry and by the Joint Liaison Group during the final stages of Cavaco Silva's rule, called "Portuguese travel documents" by the Chinese, residents of Macau could travel outside China and Macau on their Portuguese passport. Having a Portuguese passport was a guarantee to the option of leaving Macau in the event of domestic instability, avoiding a "pre-emptive" exodus.[114] This ambiguous solution was acceptable to both parties and was possible to implement in practice.[115] For China, it was not dual nationality: in Chinese territory "Portuguese travel documents" would be ignored. For Portugal it was a dual nationality system: outside China, those citizens could be treated either as Chinese or as Portuguese.[116]

The last round of the negotiations took place from the 18 to 23 March 1987. Negotiators discussed freedom of religion and the status of the Catholic Church in Macau, protection of Macau's cultural relics, the production of Macau's banknotes by the *Banco Nacional Ultramarino*, and the nationality and pensions fund that will be examined in detail in the next chapter.[117]

With the plenary meeting underway in Beijing, the Portuguese State Council assembled on 21 March 1987 to analyse the terms and approve the final version of the Joint Declaration including the clause relating to Portuguese passports. The Portuguese Communist Party raised concerns over the apparent need to protect ethnic Chinese Macau citizens. In anticipation of a massive emigration to Portugal, on what grounds could this be justified? In providing an evasive answer, the prime minister suggested that offering Portuguese consular protection in Macau was a plausible way to avoid an exodus from Macau to Portugal. Furthermore, Cavaco Silva explained that through the retrocession process residents and citizens of Macau would enjoy a number of privileges, rights, guarantees and responsibilities. A Special Administrative Region would be set up with a high degree of autonomy and independent executive consisting of legislative and judicial powers, while Portuguese language would remain an official language.[118]

The final communiqué of the fourth plenary meeting declared that the Sino-Portuguese Joint Declaration would be initialled on 26 March 1987. On that day, Rui Medina and Zhou Nan, initialled in Beijing the "Joint Declaration of the Government of the People's Republic of China and the Government of the Republic of Portugal on the Question of Macau" and two annexes: "Elaboration by the Government of the People's Republic of China of its basic policies regarding Macau" and "Arrangements for the transitional period". While initialling the accord, the Portuguese and Chinese governments also exchanged memoranda on the question of passports for the Portuguese citizens of Macau.[119]

The Portuguese and Chinese prime ministers signed the Joint Declaration on 13 April 1987 in an environment described by Cavaco Silva as "solemn and very honourable". Chinese, Portuguese and Hong Kong entities were present but the Macanese were left out,[120] triggering considerable resentment. This act of exclusion was not a one-off affair but arose from perceptions of exclusivity, upheld by China and to a degree Portugal, who saw Macau as marginal to the two negotiating powers. Although the Portuguese could have insisted on Macanese representation at the talks, the negotiating process was a balancing act of give and take and the Portuguese feared that by giving into moral codes of equal representation by all stakeholders to the process they could be endangering their desire for non-confrontational negotiations, which they deemed necessary to get their own concessions.

The Agreement

Despite their virtual exclusion from the negotiation process, the Sino-Portuguese Joint Declaration did bestow rights and guarantees upon the people of Macau. Among these were rights to territorial autonomy as well as some socio-cultural and economic liberties and freedoms.[121]

Prior to the entry into force of the Sino-Portuguese Joint Declaration, Cavaco Silva made a public address in Lisbon about "Macau's future". He evoked images of an encounter between East and West, appealing to national feelings of past prominence and Macau's historical significance. Cavaco Silva took the public through a process of recollections, ending with the reversion of Macau to the mainland. He stated that the negotiations had been "long and sometimes hard" but triumphant considering the circumstances and aims of the negotiations: "to assure an ordered transfer of the territory and to safeguard, in the medium and long term, the legitimate interests and expectations of the citizens of Macau"; "to reinforce the Portuguese presence in the region"; and "to develop its relations with China".[122]

According to the Prime Minister, on the major issues, Portugal achieved its objectives. It was granted the right to stay in Macau almost to the year 2000. The administrative system would remain in force until 2050 and Portugal's relations with East Asia could continue to be developed via Macau. Cavaco Silva ended by stressing the determining role that agreement between the prime minister and president had on the negotiations and safeguarding of Portuguese interests.[123]

Cavaco Silva's public address had an immediate effect. Prior to the Prime Minister's public address, there had been an attempt by an opposition party, the Democratic Renewal Party (*Partido Renovador Democrático* or PRD) headed by former president Ramalho Eanes, to cause a political confrontation in parliament via a censure motion.[124] Cavaco Silva ignored this and stated that he would sign the Joint Declaration, in Beijing in April.[125] On 3 April 1987, after parliament accepted the censure motion, the government was dismissed. The political crisis in Portugal, however, did not affect the negotiations with China. Soon after the censure, President Mário Soares authorised Cavaco Silva to fly to Beijing thus avoiding further setbacks to the signing of the Joint Declaration.[126]

Public opinion in Portugal was generally impressed by the consensus that the agreement had achieved and it appeared that the Macau question had been treated with a rare sense of state. Treating Macau as a national issue, the prime minister and the president sought advice from the State Council and consulted the political parties that were not represented there.[127] Portuguese public opinion generally accepted the secrecy of the negotiations as "justifiable".[128] However, the press criticised the absence of a parliamentary debate in Lisbon[129] and the lack of consultation of the Macanese.[130]

The Portuguese expressed support for the negotiations and satisfaction overall. There was some discontent with the hasty manner in which Macau's future was seemingly negotiated in comparison with Hong

Kong. Negotiations took place over a two-year period in the case of Hong Kong compared with nine months for Macau, which raised questions about the planning and adequate preparation.[131] Some also wondered if a thirteen-year transition was "enough time for the creation of structures able to safeguard the interests of the Macanese and to preserve Portuguese culture in that region of the Far East".[132] Portuguese negotiators, however, declared the Sino-Portuguese Joint Declaration "very positive"—more so than the Hong Kong agreement.[133] They regarded the terms of the agreement for Macau as rendering greater benefits when compared with the Sino-British accord: Macau had greater religious freedoms and residents of Macau could possess a proper Portuguese passport in contrast to what the UK offered the people of Hong Kong.

A couple of days after the signing of the Joint Declaration in Beijing on 13 April 1987, Cavaco Silva undertook the first visit ever by a Portuguese prime minister to Macau. One of the purposes of the visit was to have an opportunity to discuss the contents of the Declaration. Cavaco Silva left Macau feeling that the Joint Declaration had been widely accepted. Residents of Macau of Portuguese origin could remain in Macau as Portuguese citizens post-1999. Civil servants could keep their posts and retirees would be able to access pension funds. Foreign Minister Pires de Miranda also stated that Portugal had achieved the proposed objectives and the Joint Declaration was a worthy agreement without parallel in post-1974 Portuguese history, an example of:

> how the superior national interests are efficaciously served on the external front when there is sense of state, collaboration between the sovereignty organs, clear political definition of the ends to attain and operational capacity on the side of the diplomatic agents.[134]

The Joint Declaration was also applauded in China. Chinese Vice Foreign Minister Zhou Nan stated that the resolution of the question of Macau was an important step towards the goal of completing national reunification before the end of the twentieth century.[135] The contentment and the presence of Deng Xiaoping and Li Xiannian in the signing ceremony for the Macau Joint Declaration confirmed his view.[136] Foreign Minister and State Councillor Wu Xueqian presented a report to the National People's Congress (NPC) on the Sino-Portuguese Joint Declaration briefing deputies on various aspects.[137] According to Wu's report, China's basic policies regarding Macau "which embody China's sovereignty over Macau, will be conducive to maintaining the long-term development and stability of Macau".[138] Deng guaranteed Cavaco Silva that China would fully respect the agreement and that the capitalist system would remain in Macau beyond the transition period.[139] Premier Zhao Ziyang pledged to delegates from Hong Kong and Macau attending the Fifth Session of the NPC that China would observe the Hong Kong and Macau Joint Declarations and their annexes.[140]

All's Well that Ends Well?

The negotiations over the future of Hong Kong served as a template for negotiations over Macau and stimulated China to seek a smooth settlement with the Portuguese. For its part, Portugal sought to maintain the rhythm of the negotiations while obtaining concessions from China for Macau that were comparable to those obtained by the British in their Hong Kong negotiations. Portugal's strategy for the talks was predominantly unstructured with a desire to negotiate along co-operative lines, which had an ameliorating effect on the Chinese negotiators. In the end, the Portuguese perceived the Joint Declaration on Macau as a "more advanced" agreement than the one on Hong Kong, namely regarding the electoral system of the Legislative Assembly (two-thirds of which elected and not chaired by the governor),[141] although this was not a direct result of the Sino-Portuguese negotiations.

Chinese negotiating patterns, combining charm with ambiguity, were evident throughout the negotiations: Portuguese officials identified the use of sightseeing trips and banquet talk to establish personal relationships and to entice them to accommodate to the Chinese position. The Portuguese presidential visit to Beijing in 1985 is a very good example of Beijing's negotiating tactics, regardless of existing preparedness on the part of the Portuguese president who seemed receptive to initiate negotiations. Portugal and China had a common purpose but were motivated for different reasons. They had a common vision of a peaceful transition for Macau but had different incentives. For the Portuguese it seemed important to honour earlier agreements such as the *Acta Secreta* whilst the principle of justice and saving face had greater symbolic value for the Chinese.

On the ground the negotiations underwent various stages. There had been disagreements amongst Portuguese leaders, especially on the subject of the date for the retrocession. The negotiations highlighted how charismatic leaders (such as Mário Soares) had a determining effect in the outcome. This will be discussed at greater length in the following chapter. In the end the negotiations appeared well-rounded, resulting in overall success for either side of the negotiating table. The next chapter will discuss Portugal's strategy for the so-called transition period (1988–1999).

3
The Transition Period and the Problems of "Localisation"

The Joint Declaration on Macau left many issues to be negotiated before the transfer of the Portuguese administration to China. The 1989 Tiananmen incident removed from power some of the Chinese leadership that had signed the Joint Declaration, most importantly the progressive Zhao Ziyang. The Chinese leadership had modified its philosophy, but maintained China's global strategy.

The transfer of Macau's administration to China was prepared during what came to be called the transition period that started on 15 January 1988, after the Sino-Portuguese Joint Declaration had entered into force, and ended with the handover on 19 December 1999. During this period, the Portuguese government had sole responsibility for the administration of Macau with powers unchanged, except for matters revolving around land leases made by the Macau government that would be in force after 1999.

Although the Joint Declaration gave Portugal exclusive administrative powers until the handover, it encouraged the Chinese government to cooperate in promoting development and stability. The agreement was a blueprint for providing continuity after the Portuguese had left and required cooperation in Macau's politics and economy from the two sides.

The transition process was complex as it required transparency and trust. It required the articulation of positions not only between the Portuguese and Chinese governments but also between Portugal's central authorities and their administration in Macau. The Portuguese were fearful that the process would falter under pressure from either side of their political spectrum, in full knowledge of the importance of continuously striving for consensus with China. Consensus was a safe way of avoiding public dissensions, allowing the Portuguese politicians to convey the image of a dignifying withdrawal amongst public opinion. As mentioned before, Lisbon's indifference regarding Macau and the trauma of decolonisation shaped the Portuguese leaders' approach to negotiations, using them for domestic political consumption. This realisation had consequences for the future as it functioned as a guarantee that adopted measures and positions remained in place over the long term.

The Joint Declaration defined the institutional framework against which the talks on the transition were set, highlighting the roles of the Sino-Portuguese Joint Liaison Group (JLG) and the Sino-Portuguese Land Group (LG). These groups were tasked to resolve matters on the ground and only as a last resort would the Portuguese and the Chinese political leaders step in. However, before each formal meeting of the Joint Liaison Group there were informal meetings between the Portuguese ambassador in Beijing and the deputy minister of the Hong Kong and Macau Office. The Portuguese ambassador in Beijing would then inform officially the Foreign Affairs Ministry in Lisbon and unofficially the governor in Macau about the Chinese position on the discussion topics of the JLG agenda.[1]

First we will look at the context in which Portugal conducted negotiations with China during the Macau transition period, exploring the domestic political environment for clues as to how Portuguese strategy was defined, examining the personalities and views of policy-makers responsible for formulating strategy in the years 1988–1999. Then we will analyse the three inter-related issues that were discussed in the JLG until the end of the transition period: the localisation of language, the localisation of the civil service, and the localisation of law.

Double Tutelage and Macau

Jurisdiction over the Macau question in Portugal was complicated by internal conflicts over who would represent the country in negotiations with China. The leaders' personal style played a predominant role in defining Portugal's strategy for the transition period. Strategy was grounded in the domestic political context, including political affiliation and the temperament of the leaders. Where there was a situation of political cohabitation with the president and prime minister from different parties, policy depended almost entirely on the leader of a party who would determine the merits of seeking cooperation with the other side over a specific matter.

As the Portuguese government remained in charge of the negotiations with China, the delegations to the Sino-Portuguese joint groups (explained later) received instructions from the foreign minister. Between the meetings of these groups, the Foreign Ministry would consult the prime minister, and not the president. Given that the governor of Macau received orders from the president and was not directly accountable to the prime minister, clashes could arise between the governor and the Portuguese members of the joint groups.[2] The situation worsened as the head of the Portuguese delegation resided in Portugal and only came to Macau for meetings.

Moreover, the administration of Governor Melancia (July 1987 to April 1991) created a post in charge of transition issues—the under-secretary for the transition.[3] Therefore, during the Melancia period, two different posts supervised the negotiations. One was the head of the JLG representing the Portuguese government while the other was the under-secretary for the transition representing the Macau governor.[4]

As illustrated in Figure 1 the president imparted his wishes for the Macau administration through the governor. If the president sensed the need to exert influence in a given direction during the negotiations, he could use the presidential representative of the Portuguese delegation in the JLG. The Portuguese delegation of the JLG had three diplomats—the head, the deputy head, and the counsellor of the Portuguese embassy in Beijing—and the other two members were personal choices of the president and the prime minister, although this was not officially stipulated.

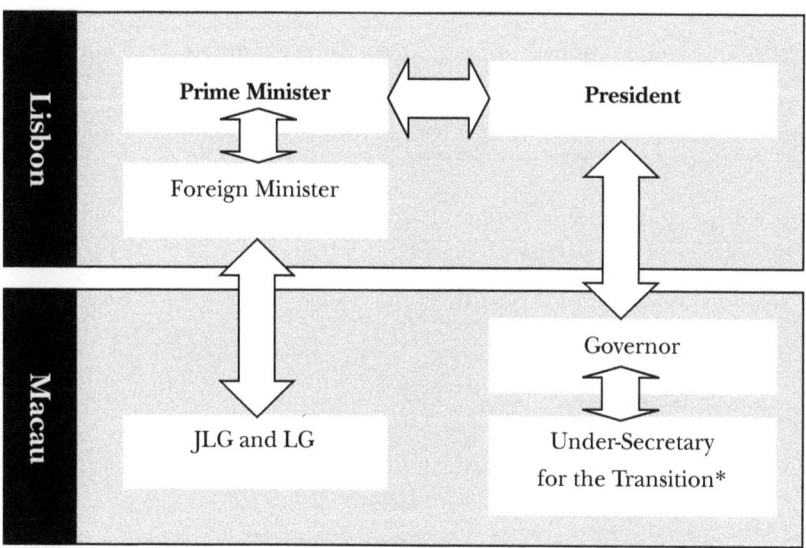

* Only during Governor Melancia's administration

Figure 1 Macau double tutelage system

In any event, the two-stream political system coming out of Lisbon resulted in inconsistencies in the negotiations. During cohabitation a political consensus was more difficult to achieve and individual or party interests could override the interests of the nation. The necessity to score domestic political points determined the extent to which consensus was sought or not. At times when the presidency and the government held conflicting views, they engaged in "parallel diplomacy", following different paths.[5] This is what happened at the time of deciding the date for the Macau handover during the final stages of the Sino-Portuguese negotiations, previously addressed. During the transition period, however, dissensions between the key leaders diminished Portugal's negotiating power.

Year	LG*	JLG*	Foreign Minister	PM	PR	Governor	
1988		Simões				Carlos Melancia (PS)	
1989		Coelho	Deus Pinheiro				
1990		Pedro	(PSD)	Cavaco	Mário		Cohabitation
1991		Catarino		Silva	Soares		
1992	Head of the principal base of the JLG		Durão Barroso	(PSD)	(PS)		
1993		Andresen					
1994		Guimarães	(PSD)			Rocha	
1995		Jorge Ritto				Vieira	
1996			Jaime Gama	António	Jorge	(PSD)	Cooperation
1997		Santana Carlos	(PS)	Guterres	Sampaio		
1998				(PS)	(PS)		
1999							

*Head of the Portuguese Delegation

Figure 2 The Portuguese decision-makers of the transition period (approximate dates)

As suggested from Figure 2, it is useful to divide the analysis of the transition into two major periods: the period of Social Democrat Party (PSD) and Socialist Party (PS) cohabitation, from 1988 to 1995, and the years of Socialist cooperation, from 1995 to 1999.

In the Portuguese system, the powers of the president are largely ceremonial, although they can be adapted in accordance to his personal style or preferences. Until 1995, the Portuguese domestic scenario was apparently the same as the 1986–1987 negotiating years with Prime Minister Aníbal Cavaco Silva and President Mário Soares from different political parties. After 1995/96 there was a turnaround in the political environment in Portugal: the new Prime Minister António Guterres and President Jorge Sampaio were from the same political party (PS).

As highlighted in Figure 2, Portuguese strategy during the PSD/PS cohabitation period (1988–1995) can be analysed in two phases: before and after 1991. From 1985 to 1995, Aníbal Cavaco Silva was the head of the Social Democrat Party (PSD). An economist with no experience in foreign policy, he perceived Macau as economically inconsequential for Portugal, showing an evident disinterest in the matter and passing it to the president's office. Mário Soares, president from 1986 to 1996, had experience in foreign policy and an interest in Macau.[6] Until 1991, Prime Minister Cavaco Silva and President Soares maintained broadly speaking the same approach towards Macau as adopted in 1986. While Soares had adopted an interventionist approach, Cavaco Silva assumed a low profile. As discussed in the previous chapter, President Soares played a crucial role during the early Sino-Portuguese negotiations and was a charismatic leader.

Thus, in the period 1988–1991, the strategy of the Portuguese administration in Macau reflected the ideas/interests of President Soares and was translated into action in Macau by Governor Carlos Melancia. Soon after, the Portuguese media accused the Melancia's administration of lacking probity and transparency. By the end of 1990, Macau's administration was under a blanket of political scandals, namely regarding the airport. Governor Melancia was allegedly implicated in a major corruption scheme leading to his dismissal although he was later absolved in Court. At the height of this scandal, the Chinese decided to seek clarity on the status of the Orient Foundation in the JLG's meetings as they suspected it was misusing funds derived from Macau coupled with other irregularities. The influence of double tutelage and different PS/PSD interests in dealing with this case will be discussed in detail later.

To avoid being implicated in any of the scandals, President Soares changed his strategy for Macau assuming a low profile. Soares' appointment of General Vasco Rocha Vieira as governor in 1991 was out of the norm. In contrast to the way governors had been selected in the past,

Rocha Vieira was not a personal preference but a convenient choice.[7] Convention had it that, being a general, the new governor was better prepared than anyone to restore order in Macau against the backdrop of the scandals. Moreover, as a Social Democrat, Rocha Vieira was close enough to Cavaco Silva to facilitate him taking charge of the Macau question and allowed the Socialist Soares to distance himself before any scandal affected him. Showing a lack of interest, Soares turned the Macau question over to the Foreign Ministry. This was problematic in light of the prime minister's above-mentioned disinterest in Macau and, when combined with Soares' estrangement, it gave significant space to the governor to assume greater power than traditionally was sanctioned.

From 1991–1995, it was the governor who defined the strategy of the Macau administration in consultation with the president, the prime minister, and the head of the JLG.[8] Governor Rocha Vieira lost dominance during the 1995–1999 period of Socialist cooperation[9] (note the darkened areas on Figure 2). This was because both Prime Minister António Guterres and President Jorge Sampaio belonged to the Socialist Party and worked more harmoniously than the previous leadership.

Jaime Gama, Socialist foreign minister (1983–1985 and 1995–2002), had long been involved in Macau affairs.[10] Until the handover, the foreign minister had a strong impact on Portuguese local strategy and did not approve of the decision-making power of the governor. President Sampaio tried to be proactive and claimed that Portuguese strategy was conceived in permanent articulation with the governor,[11] but he could not avoid the conflicts that this situation created between Gama and Vieira. Vieira was negative to what he saw as Gama's rush into agreement with the Chinese proposals. The desire growing in Lisbon to settle the Macau question also was a point of contention for the governor: he believed strongly that no agreement was better than a bad agreement. Nevertheless, he considers that he did not attempt to block the implementation of Foreign Minister Gama's policies.[12]

Portuguese Approaches for the Transition

As suggested from the previous discussion on the double tutelage system and highlighted in Figure 2, the most relevant personalities involved in the definition of the Portuguese approach during the transition era were: President Mário Soares from 1988 to 1991, Governor Vasco Rocha Vieira from 1991 to 1995, and Foreign Minister Jaime Gama from 1995 to 1999. At the beginning of the transition, the strategy adopted by the Macau administration was defined mainly by President Soares. According to the President, Macau was important because it was economically self-sufficient with economic conditions that could be explored by potential

Portuguese investors, it was crucial for Portuguese foreign policy in Asia, and it was a privileged centre for diffusion of Portuguese language and culture.[13]

Soares appointed governors that reflected the importance with which he viewed Macau. During the Joint Declaration negotiations, Governor Joaquim Pinto Machado, a former medical professor, was asked to promote the objective of preservation of Portuguese language and cultural heritage as well as implementation of the rule of law. In the beginning of the transition period, Governor Carlos Melancia, a civil engineer, had another priority: to implement Soares' new infrastructure-oriented approach in Macau.[14] In 1991, due to corruption scandals involving Melancia as well as the problems of the Orient Foundation, Soares' strategy changed dramatically and General Vasco Rocha Vieira was appointed to restore credibility.[15]

President Soares consistently spoke of the need for a "consensual" strategy in order to get national support for a policy on Macau. He attached importance to the inclusion of all decision-making bodies, political parties, social partners, universities, and interested persons in order to avoid unnecessary controversy. The Portuguese should see Macau as a "national question": "Nothing would be worse for Portugal than having the last years of our administration perturbed by issues between the Portuguese, around material interests lacking national dimension."[16]

President Soares made a state visit to Macau in March 1989 where he presented an official statement on Macau, stating that the territory should be regarded a "true national question . . . and should not be politicised or reducible to the interests of the groups that operate there".[17] The decision of inviting the deputy prime minister Eurico de Melo for the visit was also an attempt at seeking solidarity between the Presidency and the government on Macau, which demonstrated a shift from Soares' earlier political positions.

One year later, in a presentation to the *Missão de Macau* (Macau Mission—Macau's informal embassy) in Lisbon, Soares noted that the significance of Macau was a state priority similar to European integration, African cooperation, or Luso-Brazilian relations. Macau should be viewed from the perspective of a "new era" in Sino-Portuguese relations and not from a stereotypical colonial position. Through the use of an analogy Soares attempted seemingly to explain Portugal's new position in an evolving bilateral relationship rather than the end of the Portuguese colonial empire: "We are not closing a door: we are trying to switch on a light."[18]

In October 1993, President Soares made another official visit to Macau in the company of two members of the Portuguese Parliament, one representing the party in power and the other, the largest opposition party.[19] Mário Soares took advantage of the visit to reiterate the official Portuguese strategic orientation for Macau during the transition pledging to observe the spirit of the Joint Declaration and to maintain political and social stability. Portugal also envisaged creating a "strategically relevant reality" for post-1999 Macau, highlighting its geographical position in the Zhu (Pearl) River Estuary and its potential for enhancing the relations of China with the world.[20] The preservation of Portugal as a partner in East Asia depended upon achieving that objective. At this point, Portugal banked on securing "stability and progress" for Macau. Stability was essential for attracting investment for development. The president believed that Portugal's biggest card was delivering what it had promised in order to be able to demand China do the same.[21]

Portuguese policy underwent a significant shift in emphasis from politics to economics during the transition period. Soares' strategy for Macau was infrastructure-focused. The Macau administration developed a five-year economic plan in two phases. The plan wanted to reduce Macau's dependence on Hong Kong for transport and communication. Thus the first phase included developing a Macau International Airport, the Ká-Hó Port and a new Taipa Bridge. The second phase intended to maximize upon this infrastructural investment by diversifying Macau's financial resource base away from almost entire dependence on gambling towards a more diversified services sector.[22]

In spite of Portugal's awakening to the economic needs of Macau, Soares recognised a need to work through a number of constraints before this strategy could be implemented. Macau had significant structural vulnerabilities—there were no up-to-date communication channels with Portugal. The five years left before retrocession was a serious limitation to implementation, inadequate to make up for years of Portuguese neglect.

The responsibility for implementing Soares' development strategy fell to Governor Carlos Melancia. The plan did focus on infrastructural development projects, starting with the airport and the harbour. This development trajectory, shared by the Chinese, continued during Governor Rocha Vieira's administration—"continuity, future, autonomy"[23]—where it expanded to include four aspects:

> 1) to consolidate the political and judicial system, supporting political pluralism, the separation of powers and the Western concept of human rights; 2) to consolidate the conditions for Macau autonomy, giving the territory infrastructure and international connexions, namely with Europe, allowing it to have its own role in China's economic modernization process; 3) to develop a good relationship with China through the respect and implementation of the Joint Declaration; 4) to protect the interests of the Macau population.[24]

The Chinese and Portuguese generally agreed in principle on matters of substance if seen as advantageous but they remained divided by a distrust of each other's intentions. Rocha Vieira shared a fear common amongst Portuguese that Macau would lose economic advantage to other Chinese interests in the Zhu (Pearl) River estuary after the handover.[25] He thought Chinese distrust was mainly due to the ambiguity of the "one country, two systems" formula. On the one hand, the Chinese authorities wanted to show the world that they could accomplish this largely economic programme. On the other hand, they wanted to assert their authority and avoid any instability up to the end of the transition.[26]

The Chinese were suspicious of the Macau political and judicial system. The "one country, two systems" formula did not allow them to criticise it openly, but they expressed doubts about the judicial system to deputies of the Macau Legislature. The key question was the effectiveness of the Macau system of rights and guarantees. China argued that the "specific nature" of Macau did not assure the regular functioning of the judicial system. Governor Rocha Vieira had suggested that the Chinese authorities were promoting insecurity in Macau by their actions in order to be able to dismantle the territory's system of rights and guarantees in the post-1999 period.[27]

The development of a good working relationship was particularly sensitive because neither China nor Portugal wanted to appear responsible for any conflict or any deviation from the Joint Declaration. Rocha Vieira argued in a Portuguese State Council meeting on 15 April 1997 that the Portuguese strategy of developing a good relationship with China only made sense if Portugal had effective power to influence China's international image. A major Portuguese aim was thus to preserve some influential power in the negotiations. The bigger the Portuguese vulnerabilities to Chinese criticisms, the less influence Portugal would have.[28]

In 1996, Jorge Sampaio was elected president of the Republic and developed his own strategy for Macau. Sampaio wanted to project Macau's position as a modern city with its own stable institutions subordinated to the primacy of law, to settle its economy on solid foundations, and to guarantee the security and the well-being of its community with the respect to their rights, liberties and guarantees.[29] To do this, he adopted a broad vision for Macau based upon three objectives. The first was promoting Macau's development, economic prosperity and security, thus hoping to leave the enclave with the infrastructure to succeed as a centre of tourism and services. The second was to consolidate Macau's political and judicial institutions as a guarantee for the preservation of the territory's political autonomy as well as its identity as a place for the encounter of peoples for the ensuing fifty years. The third was to provide for Portuguese and Chinese as the official languages of the

Special Administrative Region with bilingualism in the administration, to localise administrative staff, and to establish full judicial autonomy.[30]

The Portuguese were aware that the transition period was too short to consolidate the territory's economic development and, although the airport would be built within the transition period, it could not offer Macau guarantees for wealth creation in the short run. Moreover, after 1997 the evolution of the Hong Kong transition would have a bigger impact on Macau then any policies of the Portuguese administration.

The Joint Liaison Group and the Land Group

The Sino-Portuguese Joint Liaison Group (JLG) and the Sino-Portuguese Land Group (LG) were formal institutions specified under the Joint Declaration for implementation of the agreement. The proceedings and the decisions of these Joint Commission meetings had legal force that both the Portuguese and the Chinese respected. However, the two countries often held different perceptions of how these groups should function which resulted in numerous conflicts during the meetings.

The Sino-Portuguese Joint Liaison Group was established on 15 January 1988 and continued its work until 1 January 2000. The Portuguese and Chinese JLG delegations each had five members, the leader being of ambassadorial rank. Experts and supporting staff were designated when required. According to the Joint Declaration, this Group functioned with four specific functions:

> 1) to conduct consultations on the implementation of the Joint Declaration and its Annexes; 2) to exchange information and conduct consultations on matters relating to the transfer of government of Macau in 1999; 3) to conduct consultations on actions to be taken by the two governments to enable the Macau Special Administrative Region to maintain and develop external economic, cultural and other relations; 4) and to exchange information and conduct consultations on other subjects as may be agreed by the two sides.[31]

The Portuguese used the JLG as a communication tool for clarifying positions, as an informative tool for specifying progress and achievements, and as a consensus tool seeking Chinese buy-in when an impasse seemed likely.[32]

The head of the Portuguese delegation was based in Lisbon, and the only Portuguese member of the JLG that resided in Macau was the deputy head who was also the head of the Portuguese delegation in the LG. In contrast, all the members of the Chinese delegation were based in Macau, with the exception of the counsellor of the Chinese embassy in Lisbon. Although the Chinese often insisted on a stronger

Portuguese presence in Macau to solve pending issues in between the JLG meetings, Portugal feared that this would lead the Chinese to put more pressure on the Macau administration. The Chinese tended to use the JLG to approve all the issues that had a possible impact on the future Administrative Region. They argued that all the issues that would have an impact after 1999 should be subject to prior consultation, otherwise China would not recognise them after the handover. The Portuguese did not accept this principle, arguing that according to the Joint Declaration, the JLG "shall not interfere in the administration of Macau nor shall it have any supervisory role over that administration".[33] The Portuguese stance was that it was responsible for the Macau administration until 1999 free from Chinese interference.[34]

Usually the JLG meetings were routine but on certain sensitive issues the meetings could become over-heated. The Chinese delegates did not have decision-making power and were forced to consult their superiors to know how to proceed. This deprived both teams of the ability to make decisions during the meetings, even regarding urgent matters. The Chinese analysed each issue very carefully and constantly reported to their superior officers.[35] The Portuguese side also had to report to the Ministry of Foreign Affairs in Lisbon, but had more control in what concerns the decision-making process during the meetings. Thus the Chinese were the ones to set the rhythm and the distance between the meetings.

When there were delays in communication, the Chinese rarely informed the Portuguese whose decision they were waiting for. If the delays were on the Portuguese side, the Chinese were told which stage in the decision-making process the Portuguese were discussing. One Portuguese negotiator commented that some members of the delegation were too friendly with the Chinese and told them too much. This probably was due to the lack of experience that the Portuguese delegates had in negotiating with the Chinese. The members of the Portuguese delegation were not well-prepared and were changed too often to gain expertise on Macau. In contrast, the Chinese delegation knew Macau well and was prepared.

The LG, with its principal base in Macau, was established and ceased functions at the same time as the JLG. Both delegations had three representatives each, although, the Portuguese team had one Portuguese (deputy of the JLG) along with two staff from the Macau administration proposed by the governor. The LG was another instrument that Beijing used to interfere in Macau during the transition process, namely in decisions concerning granting land leases. This interference was particularly noticeable regarding the construction of the Macau International

Airport, analysed in detail in the chapter dedicated to sensitive transition issues.

The Portuguese and Chinese also had different views of the LG's functions. The Joint Declaration had listed a number of functions for the LG which can be highlighted as follows: "an organ for handling land leases in Macau and related matters on behalf of the two governments."[36] In generic terms, the Joint Declaration appeared to transfer decision-making powers over the granting of leasing rights from former Portuguese authorities to the LG. As there were many aspects related to the contracts of granting land leases, this could mean that the LG was authorised to interfere in matters not related specifically to land. The Chinese argued that the LG had the right to be more than a monitoring body; it could act in matters relating to land lease conditions. The Portuguese argued that the Joint Declaration did not support China's view because the following generic paragraph was the only text that facilitated the Chinese position:[37]

> 1) to conduct consultations on the implementation of Section II of Annex II of the Joint Declaration; 2) to monitor the amount and terms of land granted; 3) to monitor the division and use of income from land granted; 4) to examine proposals of the Portuguese Macau Government drawing on the Macau Special Administrative Region Government's share of income from land; 5) to make recommendations to the Chinese side on these proposals for decision.[38]

The Portuguese argument was that the restrictive enumeration of the Joint Declaration was intended to enumerate specifically all the issues to be treated by the LG. The above paragraph began with "the functions of the Land Group shall be: . . . " meaning that its functions only were those stipulated and not others. Words such as "namely" or "especially" were not used. By stating that those were the functions of the LG and not using any word that could lead us to conclude that these are only some of its functions, the Joint Declaration indicated that the LG only had the above-mentioned functions. The Macau administration was solely authorised to make contract granting land leases and the LG could not replace the Macau authorities in deciding whether to grant land leases or not.

The Joint Declaration imposed limited restrictions on the Portuguese administration during the transition period on matters of land use. New leases were permitted until 19 December 2049 but limited to 20 hectares a year. Although restricted by the Chinese right to a veto, the LG had jurisdiction to examine and make alterations to this quota provided resulting incomes were received by the future administration of the Special Administrative Region.[39] The only card left for the Portuguese on this issue was to clarify the reasons behind the lease proposals and state the damage caused to Macau's development in cases of Chinese disproval.

Apart from the alteration of the limit of 20 hectares, the LG did not have any decision function. It had consultation and monitoring functions and could only make recommendations. Thus, the policy of the Portuguese was:

> to give all the explanations required by the Chinese side on the contracts celebrated by the Macau government, to refuse uncompromisingly the emission of statements in the Land Group aiming at conditioning the activity of the Macau government or that transform it into offender for the decisions taken.[40]

More political land issues were negotiated by the JLG, such as the discussion of the annual land concession plan and the construction of the Macau International Airport. These will be discussed in the next chapter along with other sensitive issues of the transition period.

Some of the other issues discussed in the JLG meetings included: Macau's participation in international organisations and agreements; the establishment of a Centre of Software of the United Nations University in Macau; direct cultural exchange between Macau and China; exchange of juridical entities between Macau and China; the value quotation of the Macau pataca within China; the regulation on entrance, permanence and settlement in Macau; new legislation on Macau identity cards; arrangements regarding the Portuguese Consulate in Macau after 1999; and the construction of a major port and industrial park. There also were prerogatives of the sovereignty of the two countries—similar to the revision of the Macau Organic Law and the elaboration of the Basic Law—that could not be issues of formal deliberations of the JLG or the LG, but were the object of informal exchange of views between the two delegations.[41]

Localisation: Permanent Issues throughout the Transition Period

Achieving progress on the most special issues in the transitional period—localisation of the civil service, language and law—was a strong pledge of both Portugal and China on the behalf of the good administration functioning after the handover and, despite different perspectives on what 'progress' meant, a joint working group, divided into three sub-groups, was created to deal with these questions. In the end, these three localisations tended to be considered as one since progress in one localisation implied and depended on development in the other two,[42] despite greater significance held to the civil service than to the others.

Localisation of the civil service tended to be conceived as Sinification by the Chinese authorities and Chinese population of Macau, who argue that "localisation should accurately reflect the ethnic composition of Macau's citizens". For the Macanese, localisation was identified as "Macanisation" or the conception that "promotion priority should be given to bilingual Macanese". The Portuguese claimed, on their part, localisation as a fair and just combination of Sinification and Macanisation: "recruitment and promotion of civil servants [which] should also be based on qualification and merit, regardless of race and nationality".[43]

Actually, the localisation of the civil service was regarded as a two-pronged process: on one hand, it would lead to an increase in the number of local civil servants in the Macau administration; on the other hand, to the reintegration of Portuguese expatriates into the Portuguese Republic. The perception on this was also very different for both sides. China believed that Chinese language would replace Portuguese in judicial matters, once ethnic Chinese had assumed the Macau administration high ranks[44] and the Portuguese expectation was, by contrast, to contain Chinese interference after the handover.[45]

The Macanese integration into post-1999 Macau's civil service was a Portuguese desire as the Macanese were regarded as local guardians of Portuguese's influence and culture. However, even though the Macanese could opt between Chinese and Portuguese nationality after 1999, "localisation" was to mean Sinification,[46] and they had to be aware of leadership-post exclusions if their first choice would be to remain Portuguese citizens. According to the Chinese JLG delegation, Chinese should occupy 97 per cent of middle and high-ranking positions in the future administration or at the very least something approaching the ethnic proportions of the population.[47] Notwithstanding, the Portuguese noticed the Sino-Portuguese Joint Declaration did not use the Chinese proportionality proposal to nominate Chinese nationals to middle and high-rank posts and argued that the local Chinese had low educational level and language proficiency[48] and local staff promotion should be based upon qualification:[49]

> After the establishment of the Macau Special Administrative Region, public servants, (including police) of Chinese nationality and Portuguese and other foreign nationalities previously serving in Macau may all remain in employment . . . The Macau Special Administrative Region may appoint Portuguese and other foreign nationals previously serving in the public service in Macau or currently holding Permanent Identity Cards of the Macau Special Administrative Region to public posts (except certain principal official posts) . . . The appointment and promotion of public servants shall be on the basis of qualifications, experience and ability.[50]

By contrast, during the early years of the transition, the increasing in number of civil service servants was continuously criticised by the Chinese delegation in the JLG,[51] seen as creation of positions for Portuguese friends' accommodation and overlapping services.[52] As happened with the leadership positions in the prior Portuguese Macau administration, political activities were usually filled by the civil service superior ranks. This led to few openings for the local Chinese or Macanese at the director level, to the absence of leadership training programmes for local civil servants, and to recruitment examinations only written in Portuguese for permanent staff.[53] The Portuguese delegates gave evidence that the rapid increase of administrative staff was rather a consequence of the integration of new (Chinese) local civil servants and would be counterbalanced by the integration of some (Portuguese) staff into Portugal's bureaucracy in 1999.[54]

The Chinese pressed for recognition of academic qualifications of local people who did not have a Portuguese education, along with the cut of educational requirements, namely proficiency in Portuguese.[55] In 1988, the Macau administration took over the University of Macau[56] and, to avoid local talent brain drain, reforms were implemented.[57] In 1993, educational qualifications obtained outside Macau were recognised as well as for unofficial education systems existing in Macau.[58]

Essentially, Chinese delegates wanted to know which civil servants would remain in Macau so they could find out which positions in the upper administrative ranks could be "localised".[59] Confronted with that issue, Portugal had to guarantee a place in their civil service to Portuguese functionaries that opted to stay in Macau after 1999 in case they later decided to be reintegrated in Portugal: despite being integrated into the permanent Macau civil service, those civil servants did not lose the right to their "original" job in Portugal. The Chinese position on this issue was that the Portuguese civil servants who chose to stay in Macau after the handover could not remain Portuguese civil servants as dual national status would not be accepted in the future Special Administrative Region government.[60]

The Portuguese wanted the Macau Special Administrative Region (MSAR) to pay the pensions of all Macau civil servants, except for those who were reintegrated into Portugal before 1999. There were several situations to be considered: civil servants that stayed in Macau after the handover; that integrated Portugal's bureaucracy before the handover; and that retired before the end of the Portuguese administration.[61] Consensus was reached without difficulty for the first two groups: the future MSAR was responsible for paying civil servants pensions that stayed in Macau, while the pensions of the civil servants reintegrated in Portugal were transferred to Portugal's Retirement Fund (*Caixa Geral de Aposentações*, CGA). The contentious were in the civil servants group that retired before the end of Portuguese administration. Portugal argued that their pensions should be paid by the MSAR, but that was not accepted by China.

In the end, the Portuguese government agreed to be responsible for the payment of the pensions for the civil servants who retired before 19 December 1999.[62] Before 24 May 1994, Macau civil servants could opt between joining Portugal's Civil Service after 1999, retiring with the transfer of pension responsibilities to the CGA, leaving the civil service with pecuniary compensation, or remaining in Macau's civil service on new SAR terms.[63] According to Governor Rocha Vieira:

> Those who had already retired from government service in Macau or who would retire meanwhile could choose between remaining linked to Macau or transferring to the Civil Service Pension Fund in Portugal. This process involved complex negotiations with the Government in Lisbon. Macau fulfilled its pledge to transfer the necessary amount for each employee to the Civil Service Pension fund so that the pensions would be paid by Portugal in the future.[64]

This was a heavy burden for Portugal's pension fund that possibly could have been alleviated if the Portuguese had created a pension fund with Macau money to pay transition-era Macau civil servants or negotiated cautiously this issue. Had this been considered a priority for the Portuguese government, it could probably have obtained China's approval against some concessions on questions that had small impact in Portugal, such as the date of the handover (during the Joint Declaration negotiations) or the Orient Foundation (during the transition period).

In what is referred to as the second localisation, China expected that the official status of their language would raise the number of Chinese in Macau's bureaucracy;[65] and Portugal, who had never succeeded in disseminating the Portuguese language, assumed that the best way to safeguard the language and culture in Macau after 1999[66] was turning the Chinese language official during the transition period—as Portuguese would remain official afterwards.

In April 1991, Portugal and China signed a Memorandum of Understanding on the Portuguese and Chinese languages status. The Portuguese decided to publish legislation conferring official status on Chinese before the end of the same year. In exchange, they wanted assurances that the Portuguese language would remain official in the Macau Basic Law after 1999.[67] At the execution level, it was up to Macau's government to guarantee that, "in conformity with the local reality, the official status of the Chinese language was gradually and progressively implemented in the administrative, legislative and judicial domains".[68]

Doing so, the Macau administration gradually adopted measures to extend the official use of Chinese,[69] to improve the quality of the interpreters-translators training, as well as to support Sino-Portuguese education.[70] As a result a team was created by the administration to assess the plans for the bilingualism and linguistic training generalization in the administration.[71]

The attribution of official status to the Portuguese language was also seen by Portugal as a statement of the Macau's juridical system stability beyond 1999 and a Portugal-Macau juridical cooperation safeguard.[72] However, it turned out to be a tactical mistake for Portugal accepting the vague Chinese declaration in the Joint Declaration: "In addition to Chinese, Portuguese may also be used in organs of government and in the legislature and the courts in the Macau Special Administrative Region."[73] As a result of the Macanese exit and the Chinese lack of interest in learning Portuguese, the number of civil servants that had a good or fair command of written Portuguese decreased almost 5 per cent between 1987 and 1995. In contrast, those who had a good or fair Mandarin command increased more than 15 per cent and bilingual civil servants (those who had a good or fair command of written Portuguese and Chinese) 5.8 per cent.[74]

Still, official recognition of Chinese had little practical influence on the use of Portuguese as the working language of the Macau administration. All official and legal documents were in Portuguese and due to the lack of translators only important policy announcements were translated and chief positions continued to be occupied by Portuguese and Macanese who could not read or write Chinese.[75]

Concerning the Chinese language recognition, the most delicate issues were in the legislative and judicial areas. The majority of jurists did not read Chinese and only a minority could speak Cantonese while just a small number of technical staff of Chinese origin had command of Portuguese. The population itself had a very poor understanding of the juridical organisation.[76] The need of official Chinese versions urged for an adequate number of competent translators, but the quality was still deficient.[77]

Before the entrance into force of the Macau Organic Law, the most part of the legislation was produced in Portugal and only laws that directly affected the Chinese community were translated. From 1976 to 1989, the legislation produced in Macau increased in comparison to that from Portugal, but there were still a limited number of legislative translations.[78] Thus with the Sino-Portuguese Joint Declaration signature in 1987, the translation of the laws became a priority assignment.[79]

In 1989, the publishing of a Chinese translation of all legislative and legal charters was declared obligatory by decree, though "in case of doubt, the text in the Portuguese language prevails upon the translation of the text in the Chinese language".[80] Lack of coordination of Chinese versions increased the speed of the translations but reduced the degree of trust so that the versions in Chinese could not be invoked with the identical authenticity to Portuguese versions.[81]

The implementation of Chinese as an official language involved attributing identical legal value to Portuguese and Chinese versions of legislative documents. The authenticity of both versions required fixed Chinese definitions for technical-juridical terms. There was also a need for prevision of rules in case of divergence between interpretations.[82] Although the localisation of the Chinese language in Macau's legislation was a rather consensual issue in the JLG meetings, it was a slow process that required much cooperation and coordination.

The slowest and most complex implementation process was at the judicial level. Priority was given to the bilingual jurists training, as well as to the translation of laws and to gradual use of Chinese in the courts.[83] The Legal Translation Bureau(*Gabinete para a Tradução Jurídica*, GTJ) strategy was to train translators who held knowledge of the law in force in Macau.[84] Priority was given to the recruitment of local personnel with higher education or some legal training,[85] and to the translation of the structural norms and diplomas of the Macau juridical system.[86]

The third special issue, localisation of the law, included the classification of laws in force and the legal reform itself, which consisted of revising, updating and adapting current Portuguese-imposed legislation to the local situation.

Up to 1988, Macau's judicial organization was largely the same as Portugal although there were two major sources of law: Portuguese and local.[87] The local legislation production increased after 1976 with the entrance into force of the Macau Organic Law. The Portuguese thought that, as stated in the Sino-Portuguese Joint Declaration, "the laws currently in force in Macau will remain basically unchanged"[88] and the existing laws would remain during the fifty-year transition. They wanted to keep the Portuguese juridical system, albeit in Chinese language, as a way of confirming Macau's autonomy from Zhuhai and Hong Kong[89] but, by 1989–1990, the Chinese authorities made it clear to the Macau government that only local laws would be respected.[90] In the JLG the Chinese suggested that all the "colonial" legislation, this is, legislation that had been made in Portugal and applied to its colonies, would become invalid after 1999. If the Portuguese wanted the MSAR to adopt those laws, they had to pass through a process to become Macau laws.

Initially, the Portuguese interpreted the Chinese position as a negotiating plan to accelerate Macau's legal reforms and to interfere in the legislative process. However, Chinese persistence led the Macau administration to consider the Hong Kong situation where the local authorities and the British had created a negative precedent by consenting changing their colonial institutions. In both Sino-Portuguese Joint Declaration on Macau and the Sino-British Joint Declaration on Hong Kong has been predetermined the permanence of the laws in force in the enclaves after the handover but the two agreements used different techniques to define the nature and origin of the laws that would remain in force. In the Sino-British Joint Declaration the acts to remain in force were limited and defined that non-localised laws would not be maintained. In the Sino-Portuguese Joint Declaration there was no restrictive enumeration of the normative acts thus for the Portuguese, the norms did not need localisation.[91]

There was no reference to the British Acts of Parliament in the Sino-British Joint Declaration extended to Hong Kong and there was no residual category for non-localised normative acts.[92] Thus, laws with origin in the UK would not remain in force in Hong Kong. In the Sino-British Joint Declaration, the principle of the localisation of laws emanating from British legislative bodies was accepted by the UK. The British were thus obliged to assume a vast programme of localisation, through informal talks with the Chinese.[93]

Portugal perceived the localisation of law as the main legacy that the country could leave in the territory.[94] The Annex I, Paragraph III, of the Sino-Portuguese Joint Declaration stipulated that:

> After the establishment of the Macau Special Administrative Region, the laws, decrees, administrative regulations and other normative acts previously in force in Macau shall be maintained save for whatever therein may contravene the Basic Law or subject to any amendment by the Macau Special Administrative Region legislature.

As an international treaty, the Sino-Portuguese Joint Declaration did not specify the obligations of localising law within Macau's legal structure,[95] but the Portuguese could claim that the Joint Declaration was clear enough on the lack of need for localising laws and that there was no ground for more discussion. Prevalence of a Chinese version of law could result in the loss of the most significant part of Portuguese Macau's legal structure, damage the interests and rights of Macau's citizens, and end any possibilities of preserving a legal structure of Portuguese origin. Macau's market economy and social stability were meaningless if not translated into local laws that guaranteed the rights and liberties of the residents after 1999. Thus it was absolutely necessary to make sure the rights, liberties and guarantees recognised in the Macau Organic Law were put into local law, as well as the extension of International Covenants to Macau.[96]

In the end, the Portuguese argument was that even though the Joint Declaration did not require the localisation of Macau laws with Portuguese origin, this would benefit Macau's legal modernisation and adaptation, and therefore Portugal would be willing to hold talks with China on plans for localisation. According to their point of view, the talks should always include experts from the Macau government and follow the Hong Kong model.[97]

The Chinese side expected to be consulted in advance or at least informed by the Portuguese on the elaboration of any new laws affecting the long-term interests of Macau citizens in case they contravened the Basic Law.[98] They wanted the Portuguese to submit drafts and reach consensus within the JLG before publishing localised laws in the Macau government bulletin.[99] The Chinese insisted that Portugal should submit all the legislation for approval to the JLG and that it remained binding after the handover. The Portuguese did not accept this principle.

However, the urge for discarding laws with colonial features forced the Portuguese to rapidly amend the less acceptable codes and laws.[100] The law reform consisted of re-approving obsolete Portuguese legal codes and adapting them to the local needs.[101] Priority was given to the major codes that regulated the main aspects Macau's inhabitants' lives: the criminal, the civil, and the commercial codes.[102] Several of these codes were outdated and had lost validity with the Macau Organic Law revision.[103] Another priority was the criminal procedure and civil procedure codes revision, and leaving Macau with what they believed to be an autonomous judicial organisation and efficient justice.[104]

Thus the Portuguese approach for updating Macau's legal system was to maintain untouched the Portuguese source of the Macau law while adapting it to local and regional realities.[105] There was permanent collaboration with the Chinese to guarantee that the judicial structure would remain unchanged in the subsequent fifty years.[106] The Chinese delegates were also very interested in this collaboration and rushed the Portuguese to finish the codes so that they would have time to make suggestions. Before producing a new law, the Portuguese would show the Chinese translation to their counterpart and negotiated any points of disagreement.

In 1990, based upon a proposal by Macau's Legislative Assembly, the Portuguese parliament consigned within the Macau Organic Law the judicial autonomy of the territory. The Base Law of the Macau Judicial Organisation ensured Macau's singularity and established the contents and limits of that autonomy.[107]

The majority of the Macau legislative powers that remained with the Portuguese Parliament were transferred to the Macau governor and the Macau Legislative Assembly. In the perception of the Portuguese political elite Macau got more advantages than Hong Kong in what refers to the question of the Legislative Assembly that was elected in Macau and not in Hong Kong. Thus, they consider that Macau Joint Declaration was more advanced than the one from Hong Kong because it included the issue of election and not only the nomination of representatives in the Legislative Assembly. A High Court of Justice was established in Macau granting the territory a high level of judicial autonomy.[108]

The Impact of Portuguese Politics upon the Localisation Process

The diffusion of power between the president and the prime minister allowed the existence of a presidential strategy for the Macau administration along with a governmental/prime ministerial strategy for the negotiations with China during the 1988–1999 period. This "parallel diplomacy" was particularly evident during the first years of the transition, as the president and the prime minister belonged to different political parties. With the political changes of the mid-1990s, the period of political cohabitation was replaced by one of socialist cooperation and there was a shift in the handling of the Macau issue. However, Portugal's double tutelage system did not have an apparent impact on the manner in which their delegation negotiated the three localisations in the JLG, as there was consensus among the Portuguese political elite regarding this topic.

The most controversial localisation was the civil service, as Portugal strongly rejected China's ethnic criterion for high posts in the administration. The Chinese constantly claimed the need for a civil service localisation plan, and that localisation should include Chinese represented in proportion to their population in the middle and high ranks of the civil service.[109] The Portuguese desire to remain a strong presence in the territory until the handover delayed the localisation of Chinese civil servants and the use of Chinese language. As a result, by 1999, Macau was left with a mediocre bureaucracy while unlikely to maintain much Portuguese cultural presence after the handover.[110] In negotiating the localisation of the Chinese language, Portugal secured the official status of Portuguese after 1999, which arguably should have been negotiated before the signature of the Joint Declaration. Portugal considered the law as the best guarantee for the maintenance of Macau's identity.

The Foreign Ministry defined two tasks for the Portuguese delegation in the JLG: to support the institutions created to protect the Portuguese presence in the Macau Special Administrative Region, and to avoid differences within the JLG becoming public.[111] This low profile strategy was mainly a consequence of the perception in the delegation that Portugal was negotiating from a weaker position, and the importance attributed to an honourable withdrawal from Macau to compensate for the traumatic decolonisation process of the mid-1970s.

Portuguese cooperation on Macau contrasted with the contentious Sino-British relations over Hong Kong.[112] Acquiescence with China, however, prevented Portugal from implementing further democratic reforms in Macau. The Portuguese sought, more than Macau's political autonomy from China, its economic autonomy from Zhuhai and Hong Kong.[113] The absence of a Portuguese common strategy for the negotiations diminished Portugal's negotiating power. We will see that this was most noticeable in the discussions of other delicate transition issues, analysed in detail in the next chapter.

4
Other Delicate Transition Issues

Covenants, Construction and Possible Corruption

This chapter focuses on three other sensitive issues of the transition: the inclusion in the Macau Basic Law of the provisions of the International Covenant on Civil and Political Rights as well as the International Covenant on Economic, Social and Cultural Rights; the construction of the Macau International Airport; and the Orient Foundation. These case studies represent examples of common Sino-Portuguese interests, a case of a predominantly Portuguese interest, and one of a predominantly Chinese interest.

The issue of the International Covenants highlights Portuguese weaknesses in the early Sino-Portuguese negotiations, especially the lack of foresight in negotiating the Joint Declaration. As we noted previously, the construction of the Macau International Airport was seen as vital to the economic development of the territory and to the maintenance of Macau's distinct identity.[1] The issue of the Orient Foundation demonstrates how the diffusion of power between the Portuguese president and the prime minister resulted in the absence of a common strategy and the loss of negotiating power in particular during the first years of the transition. As these issues were very sensitive in Portugal, this chapter was mainly based on restricted material gathered from interviews—some of which now is in the public domain.

The International Covenants

The UN adopted the International Covenant on Civil and Political Rights and the International Covenant on Economic, Social and Cultural Rights on 16 December 1966. Although these covenants were ratified by the Portuguese parliament in 1978, they were never published in the Official Bulletin of Macau. Thus, their applicability to Macau was unclear and there was no reference to them in the Sino-Portuguese Joint Declaration. In contrast, these covenants had been extended to Hong Kong when Britain signed them in 1976 and there was an express reference to them in the Sino-British Joint Declaration, and consequently in the Hong Kong Basic Law.[2]

Although the majority of Portuguese legal experts considered that the covenants were applicable to Macau because their clauses referred not only to the signatory states but also to territories under their jurisdiction, the Portuguese government wanted to dissipate any doubts and clarify this in the Joint Liaison Group (JLG).[3] The Chinese delegation considered the issue delicate and sensitive and wanted to keep it under maximum secrecy with views exchanged at a restricted level in the JLG's informal meetings.[4] The Portuguese were warned to be prudent and not present the issue to their parliament before agreement was reached.[5]

The Portuguese objective was to introduce clauses in Macau's Basic Law, identical to those in the Hong Kong Basic Law, which would be approved by the National Assembly of the PRC in March 1993.[6] Their arguments were that China had no grounds to treat Macau as secondary to Hong Kong and public opinion would resent it if that happened. Moreover, it was an opportunity for China to show openness regarding a problem that was closely observed by the international community. A benevolent attitude would bring China more prestige and would have a positive impact on its image. In addition, it would help the Portuguese to exert a moderating influence in international institutions such as the European Economic Community.[7]

The Portuguese wanted to find a formula on the applicability of the covenants to Macau and stressed that this did not conflict with Macau's political situation or the norms established in the Sino-Portuguese Joint Declaration. As Macau was not a case of decolonisation, the covenants' references to universal suffrage and to the right to self-determination did not apply, and therefore, did not clash with Macau's administrative system defined by the Sino-Portuguese Joint Declaration. In any event, universal suffrage had not been implemented fully in Macau under the Portuguese. Moreover, Portugal had not made the optional declaration, foreseen in Article 41 of the International Covenant on Civil and Political Rights, to accept the legitimacy of complaints presented by the member states of the Human Rights Committee.[8]

The Chinese position was that Hong Kong was a totally different case. The covenants were already in force there when the Sino-British Joint Declaration was signed. As a result, they were referred to in the agreement and in the Hong Kong Basic Law. In the Macau negotiations, the Portuguese did not make any reference to the covenants, so there was no reference to them in the draft of Macau's Basic Law.[9] Although the Portuguese argued that the difference between the two Joint Declarations was merely formal and not of substantive difference, the Chinese considered that there was no difference in policies but only a difference of local realities.[10] The British government had expressed various exclusions when ratifying the covenants, and the Portuguese government had not. Therefore, the applicability of the covenants to Macau depended on its publication in the Official Bulletin of Macau and on the promulgation of legislation in Macau establishing adequate reservations. These would have been absolutely vital in order to reach consensus within the JLG.[11] The Portuguese countered that there was no need to maintain the same exclusions that Britain had made regarding Hong Kong and proposed a generic safety clause to exclude the issues of self-determination and universal suffrage.[12]

By the Fourteenth JLG plenary meeting in July 1992, China agreed to the extension of the two covenants to Macau based upon certain conditions. Most of the contents of the covenants could be applied and corresponded to the needs of Macau's economic development and to the spirit of the Joint Declaration and did not contradict the Basic Law. However, Portugal stated that the clauses regarding the right to self-determination and universal suffrage did not apply to Macau.[13] Portugal also had to declare that the application of the covenants' clauses referring to civil rights and to liberties did not endanger the implementation of the Joint Declaration, corresponded to Macau's statute, and that Macau would elaborate specific legislation to the implementation of the clauses of the two covenants.[14]

In November 1992, during the JLG's Fifteenth Plenary meeting, the two sides formally confirmed agreement regarding the applicability to Macau of the International Covenant on Civil and Political Rights as well as the International Covenant on Economic, Social and Cultural Rights.[15] Macau Basic Law would include a clause stipulating that "the provisions of the International Covenants shall remain in force and shall be implemented through the laws of the Macau Special Administrative Region".[16]

It is puzzling that the Portuguese accepted the Chinese refusal to negotiate this issue during the Joint Declaration negotiations[17] and then raised it during the first years of the transition period and insisting upon its urgency due to the state of progress of the Basic Law. By overlooking this subject during the Joint Declaration talks, Portugal had risked China's refusal to consider it during the transition. China's willingness to exercise flexibility over the covenants made Portugal more vulnerable to Chinese pressure to raise issues that were not on the JLG agenda, such as the Orient Foundation. In the end, the Chinese were interested in extending the applicability of the covenants to Macau, and therefore, it was the first issue to be negotiated, and agreement was reached quickly in 1992.

The Macau International Airport

The proposal to construct the Macau International Airport is an example where the Portuguese negotiators were diplomatically astute and were able to exploit China's diplomatic weakness following the Tiananmen incident in 1989 to achieve important concessions. This was markedly different from the more dogmatic position of the British government, which did not refrain from criticising the actions of the Chinese government, regardless of the impact that this might have on Sino-British relations.[18]

The issue of the airport and the air traffic agreement was one with clear Portuguese interests. It was considered essential to guarantee Macau's autonomy and fit within the infrastructure-led approach adopted during the transition, which considered a better option to leave the territory with infrastructures rather than financial reserves. The Portuguese wanted to reach agreement so badly that they often suggested treating the issue at a higher level when no progress was made in the JLG. The Portuguese administration faced difficulties with the construction of the Macau International Airport from the very beginning. According to a member of the Portuguese delegation, during the two years of the airport negotiations they were never sure if the Chinese wanted the airport or not.

The Portuguese considered the construction of the Macau International Airport one of the more important and complex problems of the transition period.[19] Although the Chinese officials publicly supported the project, they constantly referred to technical difficulties in order to delay its construction and the conclusion of air traffic agreements. The Portuguese repeatedly argued that the difficulties raised by the Chinese had a negative impact on the planning of those projects, potentially raising doubts in the minds of investors. They said the airport would bring great prosperity to Macau while establishing conditions to aid the territory's autonomy, and if no airport was constructed prior to 2000, the Macau SAR would not be recognised as a genuinely autonomous entity and it would not be distinguishable from neighbouring Zhuhai.[20]

However, Zhuhai had already built its own domestic airport. Unlike Macau, where a complex system of piles and landfill had to be considered due to the lack of an available area, Zhuhai had enough vacant land for an airport, and therefore the cost of construction was much cheaper. Zhuhai put strong pressure on Beijing to have international status attributed to its airport and raised all kind of objections about the Macau plan, such as refusing to supply sand for the construction of the Macau airport and protesting against noise pollution from Macau flights affecting Zhuhai. The Portuguese negotiators informally asked the Chinese not to grant international status to the Zhuhai airport, but the Chinese never gave an answer; however, in the end the Zhuhai airport did not get international status.[21]

The construction of the Macau International Airport required China's authorisation for the use of air space as well as the extension of the annual limit of 20 hectares of granted land allowed by the Sino-Portuguese Joint Declaration.[22] As the Portuguese delegation in the Land Group was struggling to get an extension of this limit, the Tiananmen incident occurred in Beijing on 4 June 1989 and China came under criticism and censure from the Western world.

The Portuguese leadership decided to seize this opportunity to achieve a breakthrough in the JLG's negotiations. While the Sino-British JLG would not add anything substantial to Hong Kong, in Macau little infrastructure had been built and the Portuguese delegation in the JLG could not waste the few years left, otherwise the delays would be irremediable. During an informal meeting between the heads of the Chinese and Portuguese delegations to discuss Portugal's position regarding Tiananmen, China stated its willingness to make concessions over the airport if the Portuguese did not suspend the negotiations. The head of the Chinese side of the JLG, Ambassador Kang Jimin, said:

> If you agree to continue talks normally without suspending the JLG work, the Chinese party is ready to agree today to the concession of the land for the Macau airport.[23]

The head of the Portuguese side, Ambassador Pedro Catarino, accepted the proposal and made further demands: the next JLG meeting would still be on 31 July but would take place in Lisbon and not in Macau as expected, to avoid demonstrations that might be organised from Hong Kong; a more neutral wording would be used in the joint communiqué, mentioning that the meeting was held within a "spirit of openness" instead of the usual "spirit of cordiality" that suggested friendlier relations; the Chinese side had to retreat from the front line and to adopt a position of low profile and could not impose any conditions on the Portuguese Macau administration. After the meeting, the head of the Portuguese delegation of the Land Group obtained the formalization of China's concession of 194 hectares for the construction of the artificial island for the airport.[24]

The Portuguese believed that a visit by a Portuguese leader to Beijing after Tiananmen was a key negotiating advantage that Portugal should not waste, despite the potential criticism that it might raise among the international community. President Soares and Prime Minister Cavaco Silva carefully considered the issue in one of the rare occasions that they sat at the same table to discuss Macau.[25] The president and the prime minister were worried about their non-alignment with the Western position, as the European Union had decided that the presidents and prime ministers of the member states should not go to PRC in light of the Tiananmen incident.[26] Soares and Cavaco Silva received Governor Carlos Melancia in Lisbon expressly to consider his visit to Beijing that had been scheduled with the Chinese prime minister Li Peng. In the end, the three agreed to not postpone that meeting, concerning that Governor Melancia agenda proposed to solve transitional problems.[27]

In early October 1989, Carlos Melancia visited Beijing under the justification that the Macau transition period was already taking place and that it was the responsibility of the Portuguese state, and not the governor of Macau, to take position on the Tiananmen incident. The Chinese leaders were desperate to resume relations with the Western world and received Governor Melancia with the honours of a head of state—Melancia was the only governor of Macau to be received by Prime Minister Li Peng. During their meeting, Melancia tried to convince Li Peng of the advantages of the construction of the Macau International Airport in an attempt to achieve some progress over the airport issue.[28]

The following arguments were made. Melancia pointed out that the airport was a viable project. It could be used for direct flights to Taiwan which the PRC and Taiwan for political reasons were not able to have at the time. This would guarantee a minimum flow of traffic for the new airport. Second, the Macau airport could be used as a complementary airport to the region's other bigger airports, such as the Hong Kong airport, allowing a better service for air cargo and thus being highly beneficial to the region. Hong Kong International Airport had reached a saturation point and for security reasons did not allow night flights, whereas Macau could offer a 24-hour service. Further, as it was projected to be an international airport, the Macau airport could be used as a Chinese domestic airport after 1999 if China so wanted.[29] Most important, at least for the Portuguese and for Macau, the airport could guarantee Macau's autonomy. Governor Melancia argued that if the Chinese authorities did not help the Portuguese to achieve important infrastructural improvements that were needed in Macau, he would conclude that they were not interested in guaranteeing Macau's autonomy.[30]

The official ceremony for the beginning of the airport's construction took place in December 1989. However, many technical problems arose thereafter, mainly regarding noise pollution and the supply of sand for the landfill needed to build the airport.[31] Within one year further negotiations regarding the airport stalled in the JLG. Although reassuring that the JLG would remain the main place to deal with airport matters, the Portuguese authorities raised the issue at the highest diplomatic level to reinforce how important they felt the airport was and to show that it should be given special treatment.[32] The issue was considered most urgent for the Portuguese: they felt it was important for Macau that the airport was finished in early 1995, at least two years before the new Hong Kong airport, otherwise its profit and competitiveness could be jeopardised.[33]

The Portuguese asked the Chinese to adopt a positive attitude towards the airport on three different levels. At the political level, China should reiterate its support for the project. At the technical level, pending matters should be sorted out. Finally, a stronger engagement in the project was crucial at the financial level.[34] Although not vital in financial terms, a bigger Chinese involvement, however symbolic, would be an important political indicator and would have a positive psychological effect.[35] The investors in the airport feared a lack of Chinese support, agreeing that the PRC's open political endorsement was essential.[36]

After being discussed in many formal and informal meetings of the Land Group, by December 1991 the airport had become the most contentious issue in JLG meetings. Initial problems of noise pollution and sand supply for landfill persisted, as well as new doubts regarding the financial aspects from the Chinese. Prime Minister Li Peng commented on this directly to the new Macau governor, Rocha Vieira.[37] The governor had asked him two questions during his official visit to Beijing in November 1991: if the Chinese government would allow gambling in mainland China—this would reduce Macau's financial possibilities to implement the infrastructure-led strategy for the transition period, namely the construction of the airport; and if the Zhuhai airport, that was under construction, would become an international airport—which would affect Macau. According to Rocha Vieira:

> The answer on gambling was immediate and negative: there would be no gambling in China. As for the Zhuhai airport, Prime Minister Li Peng gave me no answer. It was two years before the answer came from China, Beijing. There was a divergence between Beijing, Guangzhou and Zhuhai. Zhuhai's authorities wanted the airport to be international and Beijing decided in favour of a regional airport, which was actually in Macau's interests. However, Prime Minister Li Peng was clear about the support China would give to the Macau airport. He mentioned certain conditions: it could not be used for military purposes, and the costs must not be allowed to spiral out of control. These issues were addressed without any kind of encoded language. The Chinese also understand open dialogue.[38]

The Chinese seemed particularly worried about the administration, control and finance of the airport—in particular which costs would the government of Macau support and who would be liable for the repayment of a possible loan.[39] The Chinese feared that financial expenses of the project would have an impact after 1999 and they were suspicious of the different consortiums working on the airport.[40]

The Portuguese argued that it would be very difficult for a single consortium to accept the complete building contract of such an immense project. The company in charge of the construction of the airport was CAM (*Companhia do Aeroporto de Macau*—Macau International Airport Company Limited), a private company founded in 1989 with participation of the government of Macau. After building the airport, CAM would be responsible for its management under a government concession. CAM would be controlled by the current government in Macau, and after 1999 by the Macau SAR government.[41] The management of the airport was defined in CAM's statutes, which stipulated that the government of Macau had the right of veto because it owned one-third of CAM's capital stock.[42] Owning one-third of the capital stocks it should support one-third of the costs and was responsible for over one-third of contracted loans.[43]

Another important shareholder of the company was STDM. The remaining financial shares were hold by mainland Chinese and local businesses and institutions. However, the Chinese authorities wanted the future Macau SAR government to be CAM's majority shareholder in order to have the legal right of total control over the airport. In 1992, the Macau administration only controlled 47 per cent of CAM and, with private investments, the Portuguese thought that it would be very difficult for them to get the majority of the capital stock. Meanwhile, the Chinese informally informed one member of the Macau Portuguese administration that one of the private companies that held 5 per cent of CAM was willing to sell its share. After buying this share the administration then held more than 50 per cent. The banks immediately lent CAM the money requested to finish the airport with the consent of the Macau administration and the financial problems were solved.[44]

In February 1992, Prime Minister Li Peng paid a visit to Lisbon, which both sides considered an important step in their bilateral relations. In his meeting with the Portuguese prime minister Cavaco Silva, Li stated that the Chinese government fully supported the airport project but highlighted some points of concern: the work of the airport should be concluded as soon as possible; the airport should be lucrative; and it should not leave the future Macau SAR in debt.[45]

Li Peng asked for definitive answers regarding various aspects of the project. First, the Chinese wanted a clear definition of the total cost and whether the Portuguese had found reliable financing sources. Second, Li Peng asked for a scientific decision on whether the works of the airport should use a system of piles for the foundation or landfill, taking into account the factors of cost, time, economic profitability and technical security. The Chinese premier also enquired about estimates of the project's economic profitability. A final concern regarded the management of the airport: how would the government of Macau control the airport?[46]

Work on the airport started in February 1992 before a decision was taken on whether piles or landfill would be used.[47] Initially the Portuguese side considered a hybrid project of piles and landfill, but later the use of piles of great diameter and depth was considered to bring technical difficulties and the use of landfill was preferred. Apart from being more desirable in technical terms, the use of the landfill alone would have been less costly, while the use of a hybrid system increased the cost of the project.[48] There were rumours that the Portuguese had preferred using piles because of a contract for a Portuguese firm whereas Zhuhai preferred landfill to gain the contract to supply the sand. In the end, the mayor of Zhuhai agreed to provide the sand for the airport runway and the smaller terminal area was built on piles.

There were also disagreements regarding air traffic. The Portuguese position was that the airport was a large project and it was important to inspire confidence in investors.[49] As the opening of the airport was expected by late 1993 or early 1994, air traffic agreements had to be made with all interested countries during early 1991.[50] Since the effects of these agreements went beyond 1999, the traffic documents would be submitted to the JLG for approval, so the Portuguese wanted agreement on a formula from the Chinese prior to negotiating those agreements.[51]

In March 1990, the Portuguese gave the Chinese side a project agreement on air traffic.[52] Technical problems regarding the airport project, namely potential noise pollution, were overcome in Beijing in 1991, but the Chinese side said it needed more time to study the Portuguese proposal on air traffic.[53] The Portuguese soon realised that air traffic agreements would only develop when other aspects of the airport plan were clarified.[54]

In the interim, the Macau administration made contacts with several countries to initiate talks on air traffic agreements—most importantly with the USA.[55] However, the head of the Chinese delegation was absolutely intransigent, saying that he had received clear instructions from Beijing that Macau could not negotiate agreements with third countries before accord was reached within the JLG. If the Portuguese proceeded to negotiate, they would have to face the consequences.[56] It was very complicated to pre-define a formula because it could affect aspects such as the sovereignty of air space.[57]

In reply, the Portuguese argued that exploratory talks would focus on private and commercial aspects, such as the conditions under which the airlines would work in Macau, and that this did not clash with the PRC's right of sovereignty. The control of airspace, which was China's exclusive right and other details including flight connections to the PRC, would not be negotiated.[58] Preliminary talks on air traffic agreements were vital to the physical and commercial success of the airport project. Besides, cancelling the talks with Washington would jeopardize the credibility of the government of Macau as well as the project.[59] The Portuguese also assured the PRC that the talks would not result in any compromise—the experts had no mandate nor authority to sign or to negotiate any agreement—and that a low profile would be assumed in contacts with the press.[60]

Showing some flexibility, the Chinese negotiators accepted the exploratory talks to assess airline interest in Macau, as long as talks were circumscribed to commercial and private aspects. They reiterated China's position that Macau should not negotiate nor sign air agreements with any country before Portugal and China agreed on the arrangement. Due to the urgency of the matter, the Portuguese wanted a joint working group to reach agreement on air traffic rights with airline companies as soon as possible, but the Chinese felt that conditions were not ripe for the constitution of such a group and argued that its absence did not affect progress.[61]

The Portuguese were extremely worried about delays imposed by the Chinese at a stage when the second phase of the construction had already started (landfill and construction of the runway). Although considering exploratory talks on the air traffic issue important, the Portuguese argued that there would be no progress until the airlines were informed about the traffic conditions under which they would operate. The airport could not open before the airlines knew their air traffic rights. CAM needed to have an idea about which airlines were interested, and the banks that financed the airport needed to have guarantees of profitability.[62]

For the Chinese, the need for a working group was related directly to the building of the airport, and China only gave the green light for the creation of the group when CAM signed the contract to build the runway and confirmed the method of building it.[63] Even then, the Chinese waited for complete clarification of the financial aspects before agreeing on the technical details for the working group, such as the composition of the Chinese delegation.[64] China feared that the costs of the airport would become a burden for the PRC after 1999 and that the government of the Macau Special Administrative Region would not be able to control the airport and air space if contracts were signed with private companies.

The Portuguese negotiators tried to reassure the Chinese that the financial framework of the airport was well defined and that it was vital to start to attract customers immediately before they decided to negotiate with other airports.[65] The president of CAM also warned that if the issue was not solved promptly, Macau would lose opportunities to Hong Kong.[66]

As the Portuguese believed that the construction of the Macau International Airport was one of the most important steps towards autonomy, they not only insisted on negotiating the issue at the JLG but also discussing it at a higher level. That Portugal broke alignment with other EEC countries to obtain Chinese concessions following the Tiananmen incident demonstrates that construction of the airport was a key objective in their plan for Macau.

Understanding this, China used the airport to obtain concessions on other issues—most notably the Orient Foundation. The Chinese delayed negotiations of the airport and air traffic agreements, using all kind of arguments. By November 1992, the Chinese started to relate the issue of the airport with the financial reserves that the Portuguese administration would leave in Macau after 1999.[67] The United Kingdom had agreed with China to leave financial reserves in Hong Kong, but Portugal insisted that the only reserves left in Macau would be the Land Fund, and they did not agree to discuss this issue.[68] In the end, the Macau International Airport finally opened for commercial operations in November 1995.

The Orient Foundation

The Chinese were suspicious of Portugal's financial management of Macau and their use of the resources of the Orient Foundation.[69] The Orient Foundation had been created in accordance with clause 21 of the gambling concession contract signed between the Macau administration and the STDM on 29 September 1986. The latter, a company headed by Stanley Ho, held the Macau gambling monopoly granted by the Macau government. In return an obliging STDM agreed to set aside sums of money for the creation of a foundation.[70]

At the time, Joaquim Pinto Machado, a university professor and political appointee having previously served as one of Mário Soares' campaign managers, took over as governor to implement the policies of President Soares. Pinto Machado was also Macau's first civil governor, marking a "demilitarisation of the government, which in Macau was equivalent to a change of regime".[71] In the end, he was alleged to not have the required political nature for the post of governor and faced a combination of events that impacted negatively on his authority.

As a consequence of Pinto Machado's loss of influence there was a decentralisation of the Macau administration leading to the under-secretaries gaining influence at the expense of the governor. As some of the under-secretaries had been appointed by President Soares and others had been chosen by Governor Pinto Machado, they were soon categorised as "the under-secretaries of the president" and "the under-secretaries of the governor", representing different factions and lobbies. Pinto Machado later regretted having accepted a hybrid team whose internal conflicts damaged his administration and forced him to resign after thirteen months.[72]

Pinto Machado also regretted not opposing the appointment of Carlos Monjardino, under-Secretary for economics, finances and tourism, as acting governor by President Soares. As we already noted, Monjardino was close to Soares. The institutionalisation of this "Acting Governor" role[73] created the image of a vice governor placed above the other under-secretaries, making him number two in the administration. As under-secretary for economics, finances and tourism, Monjardino was in charge of the gambling inspection and negotiated a ten-year gambling contract with the STDM in the name of the Macau government just before the signature of the Sino-Portuguese Joint Declaration. The contract obliged STDM to give the Macau government a certain amount of its profits that should be used in the interest of the territory. Monjardino suggested that the money was used to create an institution that would support research on East-West relations. When he returned to Portugal, President Soares asked him to create the foundation.[74] Thus, Monjardino became chairman of the Orient Foundation created from STDM casino profits, which was registered in Lisbon in 1988, including key people of the main Portuguese political parties.

In June 1991, the Chinese raised the Orient Foundation as an issue for the first time, referring to criticism that had appeared in the press regarding the use that the Foundation was making of its funds for private purposes and investment.[75] The sums the STDM attributed to the Foundation were significant: an initial fund of 400 million patacas— later changed to 312 million patacas; and from 1987 an annual contribution of the equivalent amount to 5 per cent of the STDM's annual net profit.[76] The Chinese claimed that the capital of the Foundation was supposed to be used in the interest of Macau, in activities that promoted Macau's economic development and social stability, or for the development of the Sino-Portuguese relations.[77]

The Orient Foundation soon became one of the most delicate topics of the JLG's meetings. The Portuguese delegation tried to keep this issue at an informal level and refused to include it in the agenda of the JLG's meetings. They noted that according to the Portuguese law, the Orient

Foundation was a private and independent institution that undertook public activities.[78] However, the Chinese refused to discuss the issue directly with Carlos Monjardino and insisted that the situation involving the Orient Foundation should be analysed in plenary meetings, even if the number of attendants was reduced to the members of the two delegations and the interpreters, avoiding the discussion of such a sensitive matter in front of technical staff and advisers. The Portuguese side, on the other hand, demanded that the issue of the International Covenants be treated in the plenary meetings.[79]

The Portuguese were well aware of the dubious nature of the Foundation's procedures, as Governor Pinto Machado acknowledged:

> its funds were one of the counterparts for the maintenance of the exclusive exploration of gambling. Therefore it was not a generous gift but a payment for a privilege obtained by a specific trading company. Thus, the Foundation could not be considered something private . . . and had to be for the use of Macau, in close relation and cooperation with Portugal.[80]

Although many Portuguese leaders were upset by this embarrassing situation created by the Orient Foundation, the official position was that it was a private organisation and did not depend on the Portuguese government.[81] Being a private association with its own regulations, the Foundation was outside the jurisdiction of the government, which had no right of intervention. Furthermore, the Foundation was constituted before the signature of the Joint Declaration, and therefore, could not be a subject of negotiation within the JLG.[82]

The Chinese refuted these arguments. First, the initial contract for the Orient Foundation was an act of the government of Macau that used its powers to transfer Macau's money to a private Portuguese institution against the interests of the Territory. The contract was between the STDM and the government of Macau—not Carlos Monjardino—and the money had belonged to the *Sociedade de Turismo e Diversões de Macau* and to the government.[83]

The STDM had agreed to offer funds to create a foundation as a means to get the monopoly for the gambling industry. The Portuguese could not argue that the Orient Foundation was created as a gift resulting from the STDM's free-will that had nothing to do with the gambling contract: those funds should be financial resources exclusively at the service of Macau. By artificially creating a private foundation, the Portuguese Macau administration renounced its power of control and was not defending the interests of Macau.[84]

Therefore, the Orient Foundation should not be considered a private institution and the government of Macau should have the right of inspection. The Chinese further argued they had the right of involvement in the issue because it affected Macau's long-term interests and the exit of Macau's money from the enclave was unacceptable.[85] Moreover, this practice did not correspond to the spirit of the Joint Declaration or to the interests of Macau's residents.[86] The Joint Declaration stated that the Macau SAR would use its financial resources for its own purposes, and this should be the guide for solution of the Orient Foundation matter.[87] Moreover, the gambling concession contract had been agreed on the eve of the signing of the Joint Declaration. While the paragraphs of the contract referring to the Orient Foundation did not define Macau as its area of action nor determined the Foundation's relationship with the government of Macau, the president of the Orient Foundation was at the time a representative of the government of Macau.

While the Chinese government only recognised the Macau administration in the Joint Declaration, the administration needed to reach consensus with China on such an important decision undertaken before that time.[88] The gambling contract was in force until 2001 and the Chinese claimed to have the right to interfere in contracts signed by the Macau government that went beyond 1999.[89] As such, the funding of the Orient Foundation was an unavoidable issue and the Chinese demanded serious consultation within the JLG in order to find a solution that was beneficial for Macau.[90]

As the Chinese negotiators did not drop the issue nor soften their position, but continued to question the legality of the acts of the Portuguese administration, the Portuguese delegation only had a couple of options: to wait for the Chinese to proceed to the next stage and accept the consequences, or to pre-empt the Chinese and present a Portuguese position on the Foundation.[91] Delays in taking a position, as the political party in charge of the negotiations was not connected with the personal interests involved in the Foundation, created the perception within the Chinese delegation that the Portuguese negotiators did not want to solve this issue in a responsible manner.[92]

For China, the key point was not to discuss whether it was a public or private foundation but to find out if the capital of the Foundation was being used in the interest of Macau, as most of the funds and investment capitals of the foundation were not in the territory.[93] The Chinese delegates questioned the Portuguese position that the original contract of the Orient Foundation was valid beyond 1999 as well as the terms of the contract, which they felt contained some illegalities.[94] To obtain Portugal's goodwill, the Chinese negotiators adopted some flexibility towards Portuguese interests such as the airport and the air traffic agreement while exerting mild pressure on issues they saw as important such as localisation and the Orient Foundation.[95]

The base of the dissension on the Orient Foundation was the STDM's contract.[96] By 1993, rumours in the press considered the Foundation as a financial source of the Socialist Party and the Portuguese President (Soares); these rumours were used by the Chinese politicians.[97] Most of the funds and investments of the Foundation were not in Macau but in Lisbon. China criticised the lack of transparency and suspected that the Orient Foundation funded the political campaign of the Socialist Party.[98] For China, this issue should be negotiated immediately to limit the amount of money being drained from Macau.[99] For a certain group of people in Portugal, the later the issue was negotiated the better, since the Orient Foundation was continuing to receive STDM contributions. In 1994–1995 Monjardino realised that the strategy of delaying the negotiations would not work much longer so he negotiated with the banks for an advance payment of STDM's contributions until 1996. Later, he tried to extend advanced payments through to 1999 but China reacted and declared that from 1 January 1996 the Orient Foundation would not receive any more money.[100]

The JLG never reached consensus on the Orient Foundation and the issue was only settled at a higher level during a meeting between President Soares and President Jiang Zemin in Beijing in April 1995. Before arriving to Beijing, Soares met Carlos Monjardino, Stanley Ho and the Portuguese ambassador in Beijing Duarte de Jesus in order to agree on a proposal to present to the Chinese president. According to Soares, the Chinese would only accept a solution that guaranteed that the Orient Foundation would no longer receive any money from Macau.[101] The Chinese officials finally accepted that the gambling contract would remain valid until 2001, as they were interested in maintaining the lucrative casino industry as a source of revenue for the future Macau SAR.

From January 1996 onwards, the annual contribution that the STDM must transfer to a foundation, was made instead to the Development and Co-operation Foundation of Macau (*Fundação para o Desenvolvimento e Cooperação de Macau*), which formally was inaugurated in May 1998.[102] However, to honour his engagements with Monjardino, Stanley Ho continued to give privately and at a non-official level, money to the Orient Foundation[103] arguably reducing the amount of money given to the Macau administration.[104]

The method of settlement of the Orient Foundation matter was the biggest concession made by the Portuguese during the transition period. The new foundation was created for China's benefit and not in the Portuguese interest since the contributions received from the STDM were to be used by the Chinese administration. This concession had consequences for Macau, which was left without any institution that assured a connection with Portugal. Some argue that if Lisbon had settled it earlier, it might have obtained a better agreement. Others say that the Portuguese could have used a Foundation settlement as a means to obtain concessions on other issues from an anxious China as the Portuguese were left without a financial card to play in the remaining negotiations.

Portugal, China, and the Transition Negotiations

At the time of the transfer of Macau to the People's Republic of China, the Portuguese government defined a strategy of accelerated economic and social development through infrastructure developments that were deemed essential to reinforce Macau's autonomy, such as an international airport. The Portuguese were particularly interested in the construction of an airport and took advantage of feelings of China's diplomatic weakness following the Tiananmen incident in order to gain important concessions. The fact that there was consensus amongst Portuguese and Macau elites on the importance of the construction of the airport led to one of the most successful results of the transition for Portugal. It suggests that, although being locked into a highly asymmetrical negotiation, Portugal might have obtained more concessions if there was strategic consensus among its political elite.

The strategy of the Portuguese government was to support the status quo of the Macau administration in order to guarantee the stability of the territory, as well as to hopefully avoid any potential crisis in their relations with China.[105] As a result of Lisbon's desire for a smooth transition and maximization of a Portuguese presence in Macau until the retrocession, their negotiators focused on the impact that solutions to different issues would have before 1999.

The first years of the transition were characterised by the existence of parallel Portuguese presidential and prime ministerial/governmental plans, which were the result of significant tensions between Social Democrat Prime Minister Cavaco Silva and Socialist President Soares. As a consequence, Portugal lost negotiating power on several delicate questions, in which the "parallel diplomacy" of the prime minister and president was very noticeable. Soares' new approach towards Macau after 1991 erased those tensions, leading to a more consensual attitude of the two Portuguese leaders. This was further enhanced with the change to a Socialist government in the mid-1990s (Figure 2), allowing cooperation for the solution of issues in which Socialist interests were prominent, such as the Orient Foundation.

The manner in which the Portuguese delegation negotiated the Orient Foundation reflected the constraints that Macau's double tutelage system (Figure 1) imposed for their negotiations. Initially the reaction of the Portuguese was to avoid and dismiss the issue and talk as little as possible about the Foundation, claiming that it was a useful non-profit organisation that spent most of its revenues in Macau, and that the activities that it developed in Portugal were related with Macau. The delays in agreeing to discuss and to take a position on the matter resulted in a hardening of the Chinese position and a loss of negotiating power for Portugal. During the JLG meetings, the Chinese delegation refused to negotiate on other issues prior to settlement of the Orient Foundation problem and used this vulnerability to obtain concessions.[106]

The Chinese suspicion that the Portuguese administration took Macau public funds also resulted in the intention of establishing a fiscal reserve for the future Special Administrative Region, similar to what happened in Hong Kong.[107] However, contrary to the Hong Kong agreement, the Macau Joint Declaration did not stipulate the need for a fiscal reserve and the Portuguese did not accept this. Portugal skilfully avoided the issue, arguing that Macau was backward and needed a large investment in infrastructure, which was not compatible with building up reserves.

A delicate issue that came to the fore on the eve of the handover was the establishment of a Chinese military force in Macau, which the Portuguese considered as an insult to their dignity. Unlike the Hong Kong Joint Declaration, the Macau agreement did not make specific reference to the entrance of Chinese military forces. Macau had a different system from Hong Kong with no Portuguese military forces in the territory since 1976, a consequence of the 25 April 1974 Portuguese Revolution.[108] Facing a Chinese decision of sending military forces to Macau a few days before the handover, President Jorge Sampaio threatened to not attend the ceremony.[109] This would harm China's desire to demonstrate to the international community and Taiwan that it could achieve a peaceful and smooth handover in Macau.

Being a very contentious issue, the entrance of Chinese forces into Macau was discussed through diplomatic channels between Beijing and Lisbon, not at the JLG. At the end of October 1999, a few weeks before the handover, President Jiang Zemin visited Portugal to insist on the presence of President Sampaio at the ceremony.[110] During the visit, Jiang declared to Sampaio China's right of defence over Macau included the establishment of military forces in the territory.[111] In the end there was a breakthrough. The Portuguese were able to control the entry of the troops before the exit of their president after the ceremony. In Hong Kong the Chinese military forces entered before the end of the British sovereignty.[112] To China's great relief, President Sampaio attended the handover ceremony.

5
A Final Assessment

Although in many ways the main actor in the Sino-Portuguese negotiations over Macau from 1986 to 1999 was the People's Republic of China, in essence this book analysed Portugal's foreign policy and how the Portuguese side dealt with the question of Macau. We found that the Portuguese approach towards the negotiations depended on the political parties and leaders that were in power. In general, poorly prepared diplomats through all Portuguese administrations and political constraints resulted in an inability to get the best benefits out of the negotiations for Macau and for Portugal. In some periods, divisions amongst Portuguese leaders and parties were noticeable and with this lack of a consensual strategy, the Chinese were able to control the pace of the negotiations.

There has been a scarcity of literature on the Sino-Portuguese negotiations. Although Macau did not prompt the same level of international concern and interest as Hong Kong, one would have expected that at least in Portugal there would have been more analysis on how the Portuguese conducted negotiations and on the Macau transition process itself. Contrary to the loss of their African colonies and Timor that still leaves marks in the Portuguese collective memory, Macau seemed to become unimportant after the handover. Perhaps this can be seen as the result of the low level of trauma connected with the transition to Chinese rule. It may also be a result of absorption of Macau into the Chinese national state, as with Goa into the Indian Union, both of which stand in contrast to the independent status of the former African colonies and East Timor.[1] The material used in this work—interviews with Portuguese officials involved in the negotiations and confidential documents previously unavailable to researchers—hopefully brings new perspectives.

The success of this "negotiated transition" is still being tested in the Macau Special Administrative Region up to 2049.[2] Portugal aimed at leaving Macau with consolidated institutions, a modern administration and a consistent juridical framework. As stated in the Joint Declaration, the rights, liberties and guarantees of the Macau people were codified in laws and by application of the main international covenants of rights.[3] Portugal's withdrawal from Macau in 1999 was not a case of decolonisation because Macau was not a colony *de jure* (although it was a colony *de facto*) and the inhabitants of the Territory were denied the right to self-determination. Rather the withdrawal was a case of retrocession, concluded through a process of negotiation with an existing state—the People's Republic of China. Contrary to the post-Second World War decolonisation movement, withdrawal from fragments of the empire in the 1980s and 1990s was inconceivable without the granting of civil rights to its inhabitants. In this new international context, China was willing to make concessions. Thus the separation between the rest of PRC and the Macau Special Administrative Region is not only economic but also political and constitutional—the Macau Basic Law is indeed a constitution—giving Macau a degree of autonomy, except in the areas of defence and foreign policy.

In Portugal, the Macau negotiations were perceived psychologically as part of the decolonisation process. The difference was that whereas African decolonisation took place in a very critical period for Portugal, the country, being a member of the European Community, was in a better position during the Macau negotiations. It would not accept for Macau less than Britain obtained for Hong Kong. The chief objective for the Portuguese government was to leave Macau with dignity to reduce the traumatic effects engendered by Portuguese Africa's decolonisation process.[4]

The Portuguese Strategy for the Macau Negotiations

We have seen that after the 1974 democratic revolution, the Portuguese state did not define a clear strategy for Macau, i.e. what Portugal wanted from Macau and for Macau. Probably because the new government wanted to have diplomatic relations with countries like the PRC, Portugal assumed international positions that seriously limited the possibilities of imposing a Portuguese strategic purpose for Macau upon China. This was the case with the Portuguese diplomatic communication of 6 January 1975, in which the Foreign Ministry stated that the government of the People's Republic of China was "the sole legitimate representative of the Chinese people" and that Taiwan was "an integral part" of Chinese territory, and that "Macau could be the object of negotiations when both governments considered it appropriate".[5] This declaration on the "One China Policy" was essential to grant the acceptance by the Chinese leaders to speak about Macau.

The Macau Organic Law and the Portuguese Constitution of 1976 reiterated the idea that Macau was "territory under Portuguese administration".[6] The Portuguese government made further concessions with the signature of the *Acta Secreta* in 1979, in exchange for the establishment of diplomatic relations with the PRC.[7] As a consequence, when the PRC decided to activate the process during President Ramalho Eanes' visit to Beijing in 1985, room for Portuguese negotiation over Macau was very limited. For Portugal, Macau's future had to be settled through negotiations that should not yield results inferior to the Hong Kong negotiations, and the starting date and conditions of the talks should be decided between the two countries.

Portugal's domestic political context and bureaucracy, however, had a direct and an indirect impact on the definition and implementation of their low-key and non-confrontational strategy. Their diplomacy was influenced largely by two factors: the aforementioned Portuguese bureaucratic inefficiency, noticeable at different stages of the negotiations, and the double tutelage system in relation to Macau. Although China sent several signals indicating that Macau would follow Hong Kong in the aftermath of the Sino-British negotiations in 1984, the Portuguese Foreign Ministry did not prepare a strategy for Macau. In 1985, after Portugal signed the joint communiqué with China agreeing to start talks on Macau in the near future, there was not a single diplomat fluent in Chinese and probably only one had studied deeply Macau's political background. The Portuguese admission to the European Economic Community in 1986 was an absorbing priority.

During the transition period after 1988, most of the diplomats that had gained some experience during the Sino-Portuguese negotiation process were given posts not related to Macau. The Portuguese delegation in the Joint Liaison Group changed membership at almost every meeting and this contributed to the long-standing absence in Lisbon of a pre-defined strategy for Macau. What strategy there was had a lot to do with the personality of the governor and the only common policy from recent governors seemed to be a plan for development of Macau's infrastructure and services.

Political changes in Lisbon also influenced Portugal's strategy during the negotiations. Both the prime minister and the president had powers over Macau, the so-called double tutelage, which could lead to the existence of two conflicting strategies within the Portuguese state. The policy of the Macau administration reflected presidential ideas and could change each time the president appointed a new governor, while the prime minister and the foreign minister defined the government's position for negotiations with China. During most of the negotiation period, the prime minister and the president belonged to different political parties and had different views, preventing at certain periods the definition of a single and coherent Portuguese negotiating strategy difficult. It would have been desirable for Portugal to present a united position towards the PRC. This would have meant cooperation between the president and the government, including the prime minister, in the definition and execution of a strategy as well as in the appointment and dismissal of Macau's governor.

In the 1986–1987 negotiations, the divisions were not so clear as in the transition period because Prime Minister Aníbal Cavaco Silva (PSD) did not want to get involved. According to Foreign Minister Pires de Miranda:

> The general terms of the negotiations were established with the agreement of the Prime Minister and the President of the Republic. And this was how we were always able to show a united front in our relations with the Chinese. There was only one Portuguese opinion.[8]

Macau was a very delicate issue for the prime minister, aware of the traumatic effects of the sensitive decolonisation in Africa and the Indonesian occupation of East Timor. This made him demand an honourable solution for Macau.[9] Being an economist, Cavaco Silva had probably concluded that Macau was a minor issue in his first years as prime minister, as Portugal had few commercial interests in Macau or in China. In any event, the prestige of the prime minister in Portugal came from domestic matters, and not foreign policy. Thus President Mário Soares (PS) tended to impose his plans over Cavaco Silva so that the existence of presidential "parallel diplomacy" was noticeable at a certain stage, when the objectives of the president were very different from the government regarding the handover date.

President Soares contributed significantly as he was involved in the whole process. In 1975, he was the foreign minister. The negotiations for the establishment of diplomatic relations and for the *Acta Secreta* in 1978 also were made under his government. The 1985 joint communiqué for initiating negotiations was signed by his ally and, in 1986, Soares took over as president and gave China the go ahead on negotiations. From 1988 to 1991 he continued to define Portuguese strategy. By 1991, corruption scandals regarding the airport, Governor Melancia, and the Orient Foundation were exposed, so President Soares changed his interventionist strategy and named Vasco Rocha Vieira—politically closer to Prime Minister Cavaco Silva than to himself—as governor, telling him to discuss matters with the prime minister. Thus from 1991 to 1995, the prime minister and diplomats of the Foreign Ministry conceived the strategy for the negotiations in which Rocha Vieira played a key role.

After 1995–1996, the Socialists, Prime Minister António Guterres and President Jorge Sampaio, coordinated their efforts and Foreign Minister Jaime Gama gained a strong role in Portugal's negotiating position. The attempt of Governor Rocha Vieira to keep his decision-making role in Macau caused many conflicts with Gama so the governor adopted a low profile.

Despite these divergences among the political elite, there were some commonalities throughout Portugal's approach to negotiation.[10] Extracting the maximum benefits from the Hong Kong model while adapting it to Macau was crucial to all negotiators. At the same time, pressing for a later handover date and for a different text from the Hong Kong agreement, particularly on the nationality issue, was another commonality.[11] Making sure the future Macau SAR would liaise directly with Beijing and not with Guangdong province was yet another.[12] Portugal also consistently wanted to preserve Macau's autonomy while maintaining a good relationship with China. Finally, Portuguese negotiation leaders all publicly agree that the Joint Declaration on the Macau Question was the best agreement possible at the time.

The Portuguese aim was to negotiate an orderly transfer of Macau with a reliable environment for progress and for Portuguese interests in the region through the Joint Liaison Group.[13] The Portuguese administration tried to adapt Macau's civil service and train local staff and to provide Macau with adequate institutions to guarantee its politico-administrative autonomy and the preservation of its identity. Both Portuguese and Chinese languages were given official status and bilingualism was attempted.[14]

Portuguese Negotiating Advantages

Portuguese officials perceived their key advantages in the negotiations with the PRC were that the Chinese authorities were not interested in taking unilateral action on Macau: both for international reasons and in order to avoid any adverse effect on their strategy for Taiwan. This was acknowledged by Jiang Zemin's speech at the handover ceremony:

> The Chinese Government has, in accordance with the great concept of "one country, two systems" initiated by Deng Xiaoping, successfully resolved the questions of Hong Kong and of Macau. This marks a significant progress made by the Chinese people in accomplishing the great task of national reunification. The implementation of the concept of "one country, two systems" in Hong Kong and Macau has played and will continue to play an important exemplary role for our eventual settlement of the Taiwan question. The Chinese Government and people are confident and capable of an early settlement of the Taiwan question and the complete national reunification.[15]

The PRC was concerned about its image and did not want the negotiations to end in failure. China's leaders wanted to show fair play and present an image that the PRC was acting sensibly. Although weaker and smaller, Portugal still had the ability to manipulate China's international image. China's criticisms of capitalist hegemony and third-world interventionism did not allow her to humiliate Portugal.[16] Given that Taiwan was their ultimate reunification goal, China had to make some concessions to Portugal in order to convince Taiwan of the viability of the "one country, two systems" formula. Portuguese officials were aware that Lisbon could not afford to lose influence over China's international image. At the same time they had to avoid Chinese negotiators taking advantage of their vulnerable issues such as the Orient Foundation's finances.

Although the Portuguese never threatened unilateral withdrawal at the table, they were aware that they had this veto. According to Minister of Foreign Affairs (1985–1987) Pires de Miranda:

> If the worse came to the worst, we could refuse to negotiate; it was the power of the weak. This attitude would clearly be very inconvenient for China and for us and it was never in fact taken. But we had this "back stop" and the Chinese were aware of our determination. I felt that we could not accept "surrender" but that we could live with "defeat".[17]

The Portuguese used it in private to irritate the Chinese negotiators and obtain concessions and made public the threat of unilateral withdrawal twice in the press: Governor Almeida e Costa in 1985, before the start of formal Sino-Portuguese negotiations and Carlos Monjardino, Macau under-secretary for economics, finances and tourism, in 1986, during the most contentious stage of the negotiations over the issue of the date of the handover.[18] Monjardino's statement, according to some negotiators, did not affect the negotiations because he was close to the president but not to the government and, therefore, not representative of the negotiating position, although President Soares had constantly been against the use of this threat.[19] However, others consider that it was a signal for the Chinese and certainly brought him personal advantages—control of the Orient Foundation. In any event, Monjardino's declaration led to the appearance of many articles on Portuguese colonialism in the Macau Chinese press.

Many Portuguese officials considered that unilateral withdrawal from Macau was a "non-admissible negotiating strategy". Portugal should never abandon the territory by its own decision as this would work against Portuguese interests similar to the abandonment of Timor in 1975. It would damage Portugal's international image, not China's.

Some even believed that a Portuguese withdrawal from Macau would not affect Taiwan. It would seem as if the Portuguese left Macau because they wanted to. Furthermore, an early entry of China into Macau would be a source of problems for the enclave and for Portugal.

There were also doubts among some Portuguese officials about the true intentions of China's threats to annex Macau whenever the Portuguese delegation said upsetting things. Most believed it was very unlikely that the Chinese would invade Macau but that there were many unpleasant things they could do inside the Territory such as causing incidents like the ones that occurred during the Cultural Revolution. The Chinese used other means of pressure when there were problems in the negotiations, including delaying negotiations with the Macau administration. As mentioned before, the negotiation of the air traffic agreement was long delayed due to the bigger issue of the airport.

Some Portuguese officials considered that Portugal obtained more negotiating advantages from the Hong Kong precedent despite the advantage the Chinese obtained from two years' experience negotiating with the British. First, the Portuguese side demanded for Macau the concessions that Britain obtained and they learned from mistakes in the negotiating tactics of the British. The Chinese leaders expected that Portugal, being a small power, would be happy to obtain the same deal as the United Kingdom. They underestimated the Portuguese determination to protect Macau specificities, which resulted in some public tensions and in a long gap between the first three plenary meetings and the last one.[20]

The fact that the UK confronted China while Portugal chose a cooperative strategy and was not so keen in announcing ruptures as the UK led China to use more flexible negotiating behaviour. The Portuguese believed that they had no power to enter into confrontation. Still, China wanted to give the image of treating the relatively big UK and small Portugal the same way—again because of Taiwan.

Some politicians and diplomats also have suggested that the Portuguese position was closer to China's than the British stance was. The British wanted Hong Kong to be independent from Beijing, while Portugal feared that China wanted to integrate Macau into Zhuhai and wanted Macau to have autonomy in relation to Guangzhou and Hong Kong. Thus the Portuguese felt Macau had to have a close and direct link to Beijing.[21]

Although the Macau and Hong Kong Joint Declarations were similar regarding the final results, the Portuguese and British strategies had different legal bases, levels of colonial power, and employed different methods. For the UK, the main objective was to maintain the capitalist system in Hong Kong, while for Portugal this economic aspect was already negotiated by the UK and only needed incorporation into the Macau agreement. Portugal seemed more interested in negotiating the continuity of its style of law and culture.

The UK and Portugal had different levels of power, and therefore, followed different tactics. The fact that the British had more negotiating power than the Portuguese became more evident during the transition period when the British used a confrontation strategy. Despite the different weight of the two territories, Portugal obtained the same advantages for Macau that the UK had obtained for Hong Kong. The Hong Kong agreement consolidated an already existent situation, while the Macau agreement introduced possibilities for economic development. The agreement for Macau considered special realities: questions of sovereignty[22] and nationality, retrocession date after Hong Kong, protection of economic and cultural interests, creation of a category of Portuguese citizens among Chinese nationals.[23] The Portuguese considered that they could negotiate a better deal for Macau than had the British for Hong Kong, although they had certain limits such as British pressure over the passport issue.[24]

Other factors that contributed to harmonious Sino-Portuguese negotiations included the absence of contention problems in their relations and that they generally negotiated in good faith and were serious in their proposals. Negotiations were also facilitated by the facts that Portugal had already declared in its Constitution that Macau was "territory under Portuguese administration" and gave it considerable autonomy in the Macau Organic Law, and that the Portuguese presence in Macau was very weak.[25]

Being part of the European Economic Community, Portugal and the UK represented doors for Chinese dialogue with Europe. Notwithstanding the Tiananmen incident the UK and Portugal kept normal relations with China because of the Hong Kong and Macau negotiations. Later, with the visit of Governor Melancia, a delegation of the Portuguese Air Force visited Beijing, breaking the EU decision of suspending military dialogue. The delegation was received with state honours, creating an atmosphere of sympathy which facilitated Sino-Portuguese negotiations—Portugal became China's best friend within the EU.[26] The good relationship between the Macau and the Hong Kong governments—despite the British pressure due to the nationality issue—was also positive for the negotiations:[27] the Portuguese negotiators and members of the Macau administration often met with the British in Hong Kong getting some inspiration at different stages of the negotiation and transition processes. Finally, in the late 1990s Macau experienced great economic prosperity, which facilitated the building of many infrastructure projects, further contributing to Macau's autonomy.

Negotiating Methods and Tactics

The Sino-Portuguese talks from 1986 to 1987 highlight the traditional Chinese style of negotiation. Portuguese officials were aware that the Chinese negotiators used specific methods of negotiation and pressure tactics. China's hand also was facilitated by the fact that negotiations took place in Beijing. The Portuguese tried to identify weaknesses in their methods and tactics and turn them to their advantage. They tried to reinforce their moral legitimacy by referring to "historical humiliations" and "unequal treaties" as well as show their public negotiating consensus in press releases. The Chinese manipulated documentation and the press to influence the negotiations, and insisted on an interpreter for symbolic reasons despite inaccuracies resulting from quick translation.[28]

The Portuguese quickly noticed that the Chinese negotiators prepared their positions in great detail. As a consequence, the Portuguese became more cautious and prudent. In addition, when a deficiency was found in such a carefully prepared position, the Chinese who had prepared that position lost face amongst his peers. Thus, the Chinese accepted the Portuguese tactic of hiding any dissension from their official public line. This brought some advantages for the Portuguese, as China had to obtain formulas sufficiently acceptable to produce a joint communiqué, so discussion focused on producing a consensual document and not a text wholly based upon Chinese positions.

The negotiations consistently followed Chinese prior declarations of principle. The Chinese negotiators would first seek agreement on general principles and only then discuss details.[29] They would not act without complete understanding of the true aims and the degree of flexibility of the Portuguese. When the Portuguese finally agreed on a particular issue, the Chinese then would try and seek additional advantages. Portuguese officials noticed that the Chinese used personal relations to obtain information. Chinese negotiators organised trips for the Portuguese delegation after the meetings during which they tried to obtain compromises or concessions on sensitive issues.

The most successful Chinese tactic was the use of deadlines as a form of pressure. After dragging out negotiations for a long time, the Chinese side suddenly would invoke some event as a deadline and insisted on the advantages for the Portuguese to accept the date, thus pressing them to take precipitated decisions. There were two major examples of this during the negotiations. First, the Chinese demanded that Macau must be reintegrated into China before the end of the twentieth century. Second, negotiation had to be concluded before April 1987, so that the agreement could be ratified in the National People's Congress and entered into force before the 13th Chinese Communist Party Congress in September 1987.

Towards the end of the negotiations, the Chinese team were in a delicate position due to their government's imposed deadlines. They had received very strict instructions that left them no alternative but to make concessions. The Chinese negotiators knew that there had to be a time difference between the Hong Kong and the Macau handovers, but pressed for a simultaneous handover. The Portuguese used the date issue to drag out the negotiations and to obtain concessions from the Chinese. Only in the last days of the negotiations did Portugal formally agree with the Chinese proposal. The date for the transfer of the administration was the biggest victory for the Portuguese, as alterations to the Hong Kong model were minimal.

Aware of these Chinese tactics, the Portuguese defined a strategy based on the "principle of the equality" of what China considered as "unequal treaties" should not be replaced by an agreement that was unequal for Portugal. Moreover, Portugal invoked the "principle of non-discrimination" from the beginning of the negotiations—Macau should obtain the same benefits as Hong Kong. From the second round onwards, Portugal invoked the "principle of the specificity"—the future situation of Macau should not be less advantageous than that of the Portuguese regime in the territory. The Portuguese felt that this resulted in advantages for the Macau agreement over that of Hong Kong.[30]

One of the reasons why the Sino-Portuguese negotiation process was less complicated and painful than the UK and China talks was the low professionalism of the Portuguese negotiators.[31] In the words of one of the Portuguese negotiators, the Portuguese preparation was "rushed and superficial".[32] In contrast, the Chinese delegates were very well prepared. While the Chinese delegation to the JLG only changed members when it was absolutely necessary and was based in Macau, the Portuguese delegation often changed and was located in Lisbon. The Chinese delegation had to do a great deal of consultation within their government before taking any position. This was a complex and sometimes long process, but they did not tell the Portuguese delegations in which stage of the process they were. The Portuguese delegation who tended to speak more during the process lost negotiating power. The Macau governor and the leader of the Portuguese JLG delegation needed to interact closely with each other. The governor negotiated issues that had implications for the future Macau SAR, whereas some of the issues negotiated by the JLG interfered with the Portuguese administration of Macau.

The Portuguese Foreign Ministry often rushed towards agreement, which was not always positive for their long-term position. When the JLG did not achieve results during meetings, the Portuguese delegation still wanted to show some progress at home, in an attempt of shaping the public opinion with a positive image of the retrocession process. Thus some Portuguese diplomats did not take firm positions and rushed to close dossiers fearing that China would suspend the negotiations without agreement. Portugal should have regarded lack of agreement as China's problem. It was China that was under time pressure, both before and after the Joint Declaration, and it was the Chinese who would be forced to make last-minute concessions.

Some weaknesses in the Macau Joint Declaration compared to that for Hong Kong came to have repercussions in negotiations during the transition period. The Macau Declaration merely mentioned that pensions paid to the civil servants that retire after 1999 cannot be lower to the amount paid prior to that date.[33] The Macau agreement made no reference to the applicability of the International Covenant on Civil and Political Rights or to the International Covenant on Economic, Social and Cultural Rights. There was no reference to military forces. Negotiations had also overlooked the official status of the Portuguese language after 1999.[34] All these matters required negotiation in the JLG that arguably could have been avoided.[35]

The low profile strategy adopted by the Portuguese officials to avoid conflict allowed the Chinese to define the agenda.[36] In the end, Portugal failed to protect their interests in a Portuguese presence in Macau. The local bureaucracy was left with few qualified people with experience of the Portuguese system as places were filled with civil servants trained by Beijing. The Macanese should have been supported more and given high posts in the administration prior to retrocession. Very few Portuguese chose to stay in the territory after 1999, the continuance of the Portuguese School[37] was not properly guaranteed, and the use of the Portuguese language continued to be a lost cause.

Asymmetrical Bargaining

The Sino-Portuguese negotiations on Macau's retrocession were asymmetrical with the PRC being the stronger player. For China, the negotiations largely were about recovery of national territory, which led their delegation to approach negotiations with a special sensitivity and rigidity. The Chinese government never accepted the "three-legged stool", and negotiations remained strictly bilateral as China knew Macau's opinion better than Portugal. Portuguese officials were aware that there were limits for the concessions they could obtain. One of their chief interests was the dignity of the negotiation process and an honourable withdrawal. For Portuguese leadership on the right it was absolutely vital to hide memories of the trauma that resulted from the hasty decolonisation in Africa.[38]

The Sino-Portuguese negotiations demonstrate how complex it is for a small, weak country with a tangled political bureaucracy to define strategy, aims and alternative scenarios when negotiating with a large and relatively strong state. For a small country, negotiations with a power require a lot of preparation in order to keep a good level of intervention during the talks. It also demands the understanding of the real intentions of the power so as to conclude whether an issue is really vital for the strong state, whether it is a question of principle that they consider non-negotiable or whether there is room for bargaining. Even in issues that were not vital, the Chinese made threats and, after concluding that the Portuguese continued to resist, they found solutions to save face.

For the Chinese negotiators, such an asymmetric negotiation also caused some concerns. As Portugal was a small country, they had to respect its dignity, as this would have a strong impact on China's international image and on Taiwan. The Portuguese had positions which conflicted internally as well as with the Chinese: the prime minister and the Foreign Ministry accepted the year 2000 while the president insisted on a later date for retrocession. The lack of a common strategy within the Portuguese state was extremely confusing to the Chinese officials who could not distinguish which of the two sides had more power. The Chinese often complained that they received "wrong signals".[39] Portugal had some negotiating cards and obtained concessions. For example, during the transition period, Portuguese negotiators obtained concessions on the construction of the airport, as well as to a certain degree on the nationality and localisation[40] although they could have done better on these last two issues.

Partly due to the long-standing debates over what Macau's sovereign status really was and partly due to a domestic context sensitive to decolonization, for the Portuguese government the handover was more about withdrawal from the last remain of the Empire than about Macau itself. Then again one could argue that Portugal had little legitimacy to negotiate in the name of the people of Macau. The Portuguese civil society was not involved on the Macau question and, contrary to Hong Kong, in Macau there was no debate of the Joint Declaration or consultation of the people who would be most affected by its outcome. Portuguese politicians had a permanent aim throughout the whole negotiation process: to create a positive perception in the public opinion regarding the retrocession of Macau. Thus, rather than being treated as a unique and almost unprecedented diplomatic situation, the Macau transition was mostly used for political purposes, with the various actors with a stake in this question often showing a total lack of coordination.

Notes

Introduction

1. Oran R. Young (ed.), *Bargaining: Formal Theories of Negotiation*, Urbana, University of Illinois Press, 1975, p. 398. Young treats asymmetries as neglected structural factors in bargaining situations.
2. William Mark Habeeb, *Power and Tactics in International Negotiation—How Weak Nations Bargain with Strong Nations*, London, Johns Hopkins University Press, 1988, p. 1.
3. Timo Kivimäki, "Distribution of Benefits in Bargaining between a Superpower and a Developing Country—A Study of Negotiation Processes between the United States and Indonesia," *Commentationes Scientiarum Socialium*, 45, 1993, p. 10.
4. Brigid Starkey, Mark A. Boyer and Jonathan Wilkenfeld, *Negotiating a Complex World*, Oxford, Rowman & Littlefield Publishers, 1999, pp. 37–38.
5. I. William Zartman, "Justice in Negotiation", in *International Comparative Studies of Negotiating Behavior*, International Research Center for Japanese Studies, Kyoto, March 1998, p. 15.
6. Herbert S. Yee, *Macau in Transition—From Colony to Autonomous Region*, London, Palgrave, 2001, p. 3.
7. Richard H. Solomon, *Chinese Political Negotiating Behavior, 1967–1984*, Santa Monica, RAND, 1995, p. 16.

Chapter 1 The Ambiguity over the Future of Macau

1. See Luis Filipe Barreto, "A Condição Histórico-Cultural de Macau (Séculos XVI e XVII)", *Guia do Museu*, Centro Científico e Cultural de Macau, 1999.
2. António Vasconcelos de Saldanha, *Estudos sobre as Relações Luso-Chinesas*, Lisbon, ISCSP and ICM, 1996, pp. 52–53.
3. See Barreto, *Guia do Museu*.
4. Saldanha, *Estudos sobre as Relações Luso-Chinesas*, pp. 17–23.
5. Wu Zhiliang, *Segredos da Sobrevivência—História Política de Macau*, Macau, Associação de Educação de Adultos de Macau, 1999, pp. 18–20.
6. Lourenço Maria da Conceição, *Macau entre Dois Tratados com a China, 1862–1887*, Macau, ICM, 1988, p. 175.

7. Moisés Silva Fernandes, *Sinopse de Macau nas Relações Luso-Chinesas, 1945–1995*, Lisbon, Fundação Oriente, 2000, p. 121.
8. Moisés Silva Fernandes, "Portugal, Macau e a China—confluência de interesses", *História*, New Series, Year 22, No. 21, January 2000, pp. 58 and 67.
9. Fernandes, "Portugal, Macau e a China", p. 67.
10. Boaventura de Sousa Santos and Conceição Gomes, *Macau, o Pequeníssimo Dragão*, Porto, Edições Afrontamento, 1998, p. 492.
11. For this paragraph see Wu Zhiliang, *Segredos da Sobrevivência*, Chapter 1; Fernando C. Oliveira, *500 Anos de Contactos Luso-Chineses*, Lisbon, Público and Fundação Oriente, 1998, Chapters 3, 4 and 5.
12. Oliveira, *500 Anos de Contactos*. See also George Bryan Souza, *The Survival of Empire: Portuguese Trade and Society in China and the South China Sea 1630–1754*, Cambridge University Press, 2004, pp. 56–58 and 85; and Sanjay Subrahmanyam, *The Portuguese Empire in Asia, 1500–1700: A Political and Economic History*, 2nd ed., Wiley-Blackwell, 2012, pp. 112 and 158–59.
13. There is some academic dispute about the date of the definitive settlement of the Portuguese in Macau. Dai Yixuan argues that both 1553 (presented by the Chinese sources) and 1557 (acknowledged by the Portuguese sources) are acceptable dates for the settlement of the Portuguese in Macau, since the first one refers to their first arrival in the enclave and the second concerns the building of the houses, as a sign of the permanent settlement. However, the Portuguese administration chose 1955 to celebrate the 400 years of the Portuguese settlement in Macau (the celebrations were cancelled by the PRC). Dai Yixuan, *Anotações Correctivas da Crónica de Folangji da História Oficial dos Ming*, Beijing, Editora de Ciências Sociais da China, 1984, p. 69, quoted in Wu, *Segredos da Sobrevivência*, p. 45; for this last paragraph, see pp. 45–47.
14. Francisco G. Pereira, *Portugal, a China e a "Questão de Macau"*, Macau, Instituto Português do Oriente, 1995, pp. 17–19.
15. Wu, *Segredos da Sobrevivência*, p. 74.
16. Arnaldo Gonçalves, "Macau, Timor and Portuguese India in the Context of Portugal's Recent Decolonization", in Stewart Lloyd-Jones and António Costa Pinto, *The Last Empire: Thirty Years of Portuguese Decolonization*, Bristol, Intellect, 2003, pp. 57–58.
17. Santos and Gomes, *Macau*, pp. 31–32.
18. Pereira, *Portugal, a China*, pp. 29–31, for the last paragraph.
19. Conceição, *Macau entre Dois Tratados*, p. 174.
20. Portuguese Ministry of Foreign Affairs, "Relações de Portugal com a China e situação em Macau" [Portugal-China relations and the situation in Macau], Informação de serviço [internal memorandum], Lisbon, 9 August 1976; Diplomatic Historical Archives—Ministry of Foreign Affairs, Lisbon.
21. Conceição, *Macau entre Dois Tratados*, pp. 45–46.
22. Jorge Noronha e Silveira, *Subsídios para a História do Direito Constitucional de Macau (1820–1974)*, Macau, IPO, p. 30, and Pereira, *Portugal A China*, p. 54.
23. Wu, *Segredos da Sobrevivência*, pp. 229 and 237–38.
24. Saldanha, *Estudos sobre as Relações Luso-Chinesas*, p. 21, and Pereira, *Portugal, a China*, p. 50.

25. Wu, *Segredos da Sobrevivência*, pp. 246 and 254–55.
26. Wu, *Segredos da Sobrevivência*, pp. 259–64.
27. The term "unequal treaties", used since the 1920s by the Kuomintang and by the PRC after 1949, was not the result of a doctrinal elaboration, but rather a general category in which China included all treaties and conventions containing, among others, "clauses relative to consular jurisdiction, unilateral clauses of most favoured nation, cessions or territorial leases", i.e. "all the treaties concluded by China over the 19th and early 20th centuries". Both Nationalist and Communist China maintained the position that all unequal treaties should be abolished. António Vasconcelos de Saldanha, "Some Aspects of the 'Macau Question' and Its Reflex in Sino-Portuguese Relations within the United Nations", *Portuguese Review of International and Community Institutions*, Lisbon, ISCSP, 1996, pp. 203–4 and 205–6.
28. Clarence B. Davis and Robert J. Gowen, "The British at Weihaiwei: A Case Study in the Irrationality of Empire", *Historian*, Fall 2000, Vol. 63, Issue 1, p. 87.
29. Edmund S. K. Fung, *The Diplomacy of Imperial Retreat: Britain's South China Policy, 1924–1931*, Hong Kong, Oxford University Press, 1991, p. 2.
30. Fung, *The Diplomacy of Imperial Retreat*, p. 14.
31. Zhang Yongjin, *China in the International System, 1918–20*, London, Macmillan, 1991, in William C. Kirby, "The Internationalization of China: Foreign Relations at Home and Abroad in the Republican Era", *The China Quarterly*, June 1997, Issue 150, p. 443.
32. Kirby, "The Internationalization of China".
33. Fung, *The Diplomacy of Imperial Retreat*, p. 30.
34. See Fung, *The Diplomacy of Imperial Retreat*, pp. 35–44.
35. Kirby, "The Internationalization of China", pp. 440–41.
36. Six years after the British leasehold of Weihaiwei the Colonial Office and the Foreign Office already debated its retrocession to China. The British found Weihaiwei to be militarily worthless and too poor to prosper economically. Thanks to its exceptional climate, it ended up being used mainly as a summer retreat for the British navy and expatriates. See for example N. J. Miners, Foreword to Pamela Atwell, *British Mandarins and Chinese Reformers: The British Administration of Weihaiwei (1898–1930) and the Territory's Return to the Chinese Rule*, Hong Kong, Oxford University Press, 1985, p. ix; Davis and Gowen, "The British at Weihaiwei", pp. 90–91; Julia C. Strauss, *Strong Institutions in Weak Polities: State Building in Republican China 1927–1940*, New York, Oxford University Press, 1998, p. 158.
37. N. J. Miners, Foreword to Atwell, *British Mandarins*, p. ix. One of the main reasons for the predisposition arose out of Britain's geo-political strategy at the time: Weihaiwei's lease agreement would sustain British supremacy over other foreign powers such as Russia through the creation of a naval base in the constituency. London was able to pull out an important trump card, making use of its hard power if required, when Russia occupied Port Arthur and Dairen and the Germans occupied Jiaozhou (Kiaochow) Bay, given that the UK had the naval base at Weihaiwei to fall back on. Although the lease had a date of expiry at the time of Russia's withdrawal from Port Arthur,

Britain was allowed to remain in Weihaiwei following Russia's upset in Port Arthur on the dawn of its devastating defeat to the Japanese in the Russo-Japanese War of 1904–1905. Miners, Foreword to Atwell, *British Mandarins*, pp. vii–x.
38. Strauss, *Strong Institutions in Weak Polities*, p. 160.
39. Kirby, "The Internationalization of China", pp. 440–41.
40. Saldanha, *Estudos sobre as Relações Luso-Chinesas*, p. 200.
41. "Exchange of Notes Between China and Portugal for the Relinquishment by Portugal of Its Rights Relating to the Consular Jurisdiction in China and the Adjustment of Certain Other Matters", Nanjing, 1 April 1947.
42. Wu, *Segredos da Sobrevivência*, pp. 305–311.
43. Fernandes, *Sinopse*, p. 45.
44. Fernandes, "Portugal, Macau e a China", p. 58.
45. Moisés Silva Fernandes, "Macau nas Relações Sino-Portuguesas, 1949–1979", *Administração*, no. 46, Vol. XII, 1999, pp. 998 and 1002.
46. Wu, *Segredos da Sobrevivência*, p. 313.
47. Fernandes, "Macau nas Relações Sino-Portuguesas", pp. 989–91, and *Sinopse*, p. xxii.
48. Fernandes, "Macau nas Relações Sino-Portuguesas", pp. 993–95 and 997.
49. Pedro José Lobo, chief of Macau Economic Services and one of the most powerful men in Macau, was greatly respected by the dictator, António Salazar. Pedro Lobo controlled the concession of the gold trade in Macau (the main source of Macau income in the 1950s and 1960s) along with his assessor Roque Choi, Y. C. Liang and Ho Yin, head of the Macau Chinese Chamber of Commerce and owner of the Tai Fung exchange office and the *Tái Chông Pou* daily newspaper. Among the members of the Chinese elite in Macau, which the PRC liked to call "red capitalist compatriots", the messengers favoured by China were O Lon, director of the Jinghu (Kiangvu) hospital, and Carlos Basto, attached-commissary of the Chinese maritime custom-house in the Lapa island, a Chinese speaker known as incorruptible. These intermediates were entrusted the most sensitive issues. For example, in 1949 Carlos Basto was chosen to transmit the PRC's intentions over Macau: the maintenance of the *status quo*. Shanghai would be invaded but not Macau. Fernandes, *Sinopse*, pp. xii–xvii; and conversation with Prof. Moisés Silva Fernandes, Lisbon, 18 and 20 December 2001.
50. Editorial published in the *People's Diary*, 8 March 1963, in Saldanha, "Some Aspects of the 'Macau Question'", pp. 196–97.
51. Silva Cunha, *O Ultramar, a Nação e o "25 de Abril"*, Coimbra, Atlântida Editora, 1977, p. 247.
52. *Rénmín rìbào*, 26 October 1955, in Moisés Silva Fernandes, "Macau nas Relações Sino-Portuguesas, 1949–1979", *Administração*, no. 46, Vol. XII, 1999, p. 1000.
53. Fernandes, *Sinopse*, pp. 247–48.
54. Portuguese Ministry of Foreign Affairs, "Relações de Portugal com a China".
55. *South China Morning Post*, 19 September 1963.
56. See José Pedro Castanheira, *Os 58 dias que abalaram Macau*, Publicações Dom Quixote, Lisboa, 1999.

57. *Jornal do Brasil*, 11 December 1966, in Fernandes, "Macau nas Relações Sino-Portuguesas", p. 1001.
58. Saldanha, "Some Aspects of the 'Macau Question'", pp. 169 and 176–77.
59. Nihal Jayawickrama, "The Right of Self-Determination", proceedings from a seminar on the Basic Law, held at the University of Hong Kong, 5 May 1990, p. 92.
60. Saldanha, "Some Aspects of the 'Macau Question'", pp. 199–200, 209–10 and 214–15, for the whole paragraph.
61. Ibid.
62. Saldanha, "Some Aspects of the 'Macau Question'", pp. 189–90 and 214.
63. See Gervase Clarence-Smith's classification of the three Portuguese empires in, *The Third Portuguese Empire 1825–1975*, Manchester, Manchester University Press, 1985, pp. 1–2 and 187. For Brazil see also ibid., p. 14.
64. António de Sousa Lara, *Colonização Moderna e Descolonização*, Lisbon, ISCSP, 2000, p. 14.
65. John Hargreaves, *Decolonization in Africa*, 2nd ed., London, Longman, 1996, p. xvii.
66. Franz Ansprenger, *The Dissolution of the Colonial Empires*, London, Routledge, 1989, p. 106.
67. Kenneth W. Thompson and Roy C. Macridis, "The Comparative Study of Foreign Policy", in Roy C. Macridis (ed.), *Foreign Policy in World Politics*, New Jersey, Prentice-Hall, Inc., Englewood Cliffs, 4th edition, 1972, p. 27.
68. Alice L. Conklin, *A Mission to Civilize—The Republican Idea of Empire in France and West Africa, 1895–1930*, Stanford, Stanford University Press, 1997, p. 1.
69. Muriel E. Chamberlain, *European Decolonisation in the Twentieth Century*, Longman Companions to History, London, Longman, 1998, p. 150.
70. Chamberlain, *European Decolonisation*, pp. 41–43.
71. Robert Jackson, *Quasi-States: Sovereignty, International Relations and the Third World*, Cambridge, Cambridge University Press, 1990, pp. 83–85.
72. Ansprenger, *The Dissolution of the Colonial Empires*, pp. 113–14.
73. Adriano Moreira, *Política Ultramarina*, Lisbon, Ministério do Ultramar, 1956, p. 295.
74. Clarence-Smith, *The Third Portuguese Empire*, p. 138.
75. John Darwin, *Britain and Decolonisation*, London, Macmillan, 1988, p. 334.
76. Ansprenger, *The Dissolution of the Colonial Empires*, p. 114, and Moreira, *Política Ultramarina*, pp. 271–75.
77. Darwin, *Britain and Decolonisation*, p. 334.
78. Robert Jackson, "The Weight of Ideas in Decolonization: Normative Change in International Relations", in Judith Goldstein and Robert Keohane, *Ideas and Foreign Policy*, Ithaca, Cornell University Press, 1993, p. 128.
79. Jackson, *Quasi-states*, pp. 83–85.
80. Jackson, *Quasi-states*, p. 124.
81. Henry S. Wilson, *African Decolonization*, London, Edward Arnold, 1994, p. 74.
82. Clarence-Smith, *The Third Portuguese Empire*, pp. vii and 15–16.
83. Eric Hobsbawm, *Age of Extremes*, London, Abacus, 1995, p. 221.

84. Franco Nogueira, *Terceiro Mundo*, 2nd ed., Lisbon, Ática, 1969, pp. 151 and 36–37.
85. Clarence-Smith, *The Third Portuguese Empire*, pp. 192–93.
86. Hargreaves, *Decolonization in Africa*, pp. 228–29.
87. Douglas Porch, *The Portuguese Armed Forces and the Revolution*, London, Croom Helm, 1977, pp. 12–13.
88. Clarence-Smith, *The Third Portuguese Empire*, pp. 192–93.
89. Hargreaves, *Decolonization in Africa*, p. 229.
90. Clarence-Smith, *The Third Portuguese Empire*, pp. vii and 15–16.
91. Anderson, "Portugal and the End of Ultra Colonialism", *New Left Review*, London, 1975, p. 72, in Porch, *The Portuguese Armed Forces*, p. 12.
92. Moreira, *Política Ultramarina*, pp. 35–36 and 69.
93. Nogueira, *Terceiro Mundo*, pp. 170 and 200.
94. Gilberto Freyre, *O Luso e o Trópico*, Lisbon, 1961, p. 13. Gilberto Freyre, *Portuguese Integration in the Tropics*, Lisbon, 1961, pp. 41 and 39. Henry S. Wilson, *African Decolonization*, London, Edward Arnold, 1994, p. ix, quotes Freyre in a similar vein: "Because the Portuguese were exceptional among European imperialists in being non-racist, their colonisation of tropical territories was characterized by racial egalitarianism in both legislation and informal human interaction."
95. Porch, *The Portuguese Armed Forces*, p. 21.
96. Cláudia Castelo, *"O Modo Português de Estar no Mundo": o Luso-Tropicalismo e a Ideologia Colonial Portuguesa (1933–1961)*, Edições Afrontamento, 1998, p. 89.
97. Ansprenger, *The Dissolution of the Colonial Empires*, p. 268.
98. Clarence-Smith, *The Third Portuguese Empire*, pp. 179–80.
99. See Castelo, *"O Modo Português"*, p.137; and Gerald J. Bender, *Angola under the Portuguese: The Myth and the Reality*, University of California Press, 1978, pp. xxiii–xxiv, 3 and 8–9.
100. Ansprenger, *The Dissolution of the Colonial Empires*, p. 268.
101. Letter of 8 Nov. 1956 (A/C.4/331, 20 Nov. 1956, para.2), quoted in Patricia Wohlgemuth, "The Portuguese Territories and the United Nations", *International Conciliation*, no. 545, Nov. 1963, pp. 9, 10.
102. Wohlgemuth, "The Portuguese Territories and the United Nations", p. 7.
103. General Assembly Official Records: 11th Session, 656th Plenary Meeting, 20 February 1957, paragraph 73.
104. R. F. Holland, *European Decolonization 1918–1981: An Introductory Survey*, London, Macmillan, 1985, p. 153.
105. Clarence-Smith, *The Third Portuguese Empire*, pp. 179 and 185.
106. Portuguese Ministry of Foreign Affairs, "Relações de Portugal com a China", and Fernandes, *Sinopse*, pp. 346–47.
107. Portuguese Ministry of Foreign Affairs, "Relações diplomáticas entre Portugal e a República Popular da China: passos para o seu estabelecimento" [Portugal-China diplomatic relations: steps for its resumption], Informação de Serviço [internal memorandum], Lisbon, 20 October 1975; Diplomatic Historical Archives—Ministry of Foreign Affairs, Lisbon.
108. *The New York Times*, 1 April 1975.

Notes to pages 24–28   121

109. "Macau Report Hotly Denied", *South China Morning Post* (3 February 1977) in Moisés Silva Fernandes, "Contextualização das negociações de Paris sobre a normalização das relações luso-chinesas, 1974–1979", *Negócios Estrangeiros*, no. 16, February 2010, pp. 77–78.
110. Garcia Leandro, *Macau nos Anos da Revolução Portuguesa—1974–1979*, Lisbon, Gradiva, 2011, pp. 21–22.
111. Moisés Silva Fernandes, "O comportamento português sobre a transição política e a integração regional de Macau na região do rio das Pérolas", *Administração / Xíngzhèng*, Vol. 10, no. 36, July 1997, p. 531.
112. See for example Ming K. Chan and Lo Shiu-hing, "Macao under Portuguese rule", in *Historical Dictionary of the Hong Kong SAR and the Macao SAR*, Lanham, Scarecrow Press, 2006, p. 283; Lo Shiu-hing, "Aspects of Political Development in Macao", *The China Quarterly*, no. 120, December 1989; Jonathan Porter, "A Question of Sovereignty", *China Perspectives*, 26, November/December 1999.
113. Chan and Lo, "Macao under Portuguese rule", p. 284; *Hong Kong Standard*, 10 June 1999; *Expresso*, caderno especial Macau 1, 25 November 1995, pp. 27–28.
114. Communication to the Press, Press Services of the Ministry of Foreign Affairs, Lisbon, 6 January 1975; Diplomatic Historical Archives—Ministry of Foreign Affairs, and *Diário de Notícias*, 9 January 1987.
115. Portuguese Ministry of Foreign Affairs, "Relações de Portugal com a China".
116. "China Welcomes Portuguese Government Statement: Yugoslav Report", TANJUG, Beijing, 13 January 1975, in *BBC Summary of World Broadcasts*, 15 January 1975, FE/4804/A1/1.
117. Fernandes, *Sinopse*, p. 340.
118. "Aerograma cifrado n°120 do embaixador de Portugal em Paris, António Coimbra Martins", Lisbon, 13 February 1975, PAA M. 1165; Diplomatic Historical Archives—Ministry of Foreign Affairs.
119. António Coimbra Martins, *Esperanças de Abril*, Lisbon, Perspectivas & Realidades, 1981, p. 433.
120. Portuguese Ministry of Foreign Affairs, "Relações diplomáticas".
121. Martins, *Esperanças de Abril*, p. 436.
122. Portuguese Ministry of Foreign Affairs, "Relações diplomáticas".
123. Macau Organic Law, Law no. 1/76, 17 February 1976. The Organic Law was confirmed in the Portuguese Constitution on the 25 April 1976.
124. Garcia Leandro, *Macau nos Anos da Revolução Portuguesa*, p. 23.
125. General Garcia Leandro, Macau governor from 1974 to 1979, interviewed in Lisbon, 25 July 2002.
126. Constitution of the Portuguese Republic, 1976, Article 306, and posterior constitutional revisions of 1982, 1989, 1992 and 1997, Article 292; and Macau Organic Law, Law no. 1/76, 17 February 1976, revised by Law no. 53/79 of 14 September 1979, Law no. 13/90 of 10 May 1990 and Law no. 23-A/96 of 29 July 1996.
127. Herbert Yee, *Macau in Transition: From Colony to Autonomous Region*, London, Palgrave, 2001, pp. 22–23.
128. Macau Organic Law, Law no. 23-A/96 of 29 July 1996, Article 7 and 20.

129. Macau Organic Law, Law no. 23-A/96 of 29 July 1996, Articles 25, 72 and 12.
130. This division of powers will be explained with further detail in the Double Tutelage section of this book.
131. Articles 5 and 306, *Constituição da República Portuguesa*, Coimbra, Atlântida Editora, 1976. In the new constitution, Portugal consisted of continental Portugal and the islands of the Azores and Madeira.
132. Garcia Leandro, "The Years of the Great Change 1874/1979", in Luís Filipe Barreto (ed.) *Proceedings of the Seminar Paths of Macau and of Portuguese-Chinese Relations (1974–1999)*, Lisbon, Centro Científico e Cultural de Macau, 2010, pp. 26–27.
133. All legislative and executive decisions that were not exclusive from Lisbon (Justice, Defense and External Relations) were then settled by Macau, which hold enormous legislative power. Subsequently questions that were not limited by the Constitution of the Republic were then responsibility of Macau. General Garcia Leandro, Macau governor from 1974 to 1979; interviewed in Lisbon, 28 June 2011.
134. John King Fairbank and Merle Goldman, *China: A New History*, Harvard, Belknap Press, 1998, pp. 404–5 and 407.
135. Fernandes, *Sinopse*, p. 350.
136. *Ponto Final*, 5 February, 1999.
137. Martins, *Esperanças de Abril*, p. 456.
138. Fernando Lima, *Macau: As Duas Transições*, Vol. 1, Macau, Fundação Macau, 1999, p. 533.
139. Martins, *Esperanças de Abril*, p. 456.
140. Martins, *Esperanças de Abril*, p. 434.
141. Fernandes, *Sinopse*, p. 359.
142. *Diário de Notícias*, 9 January 1987.
143. "Programa do IV Governo Constitucional" [Program of the 4th Constitutional Government], *Diário da Assembleia da República*, 2ª série, n°13, 5 December 1978, p. 227.
144. Martins, *Esperanças de Abril*, pp. 440–43.
145. Mota Pinto preferred to sound out the public first before moving ahead with the negotiations, provided a public vote of confidence was guaranteed.
146. "Comunicado Conjunto do Governo da República Popular da China e do Governo da República Portuguesa sobre o Estabelecimento de Relações Diplomáticas entre a China e Portugal" [Joint communiqué on the establishment of diplomatic relations between China and Portugal], Paris, 8 February 1979; Diplomatic Historical Archives—Ministry of Foreign Affairs, Lisbon.
147. Lima, *Macau*, p. 533.
148. Lima, *Macau*, p. 535.
149. "Chinese Foreign Minister Reports on Macau Accord to Fifth NPC Session", Xinhua News Agency, Beijing, 2 April 1987, in *BBC Summary of World Broadcasts*, 4 April 1987, FE/8534/C1/1–4.
150. *Expresso*, 10 January 1987.
151. Lima, *Macau*, p. 535.

152. "Acta das Conversações sobre a Questão de Macau" [Minutes of Conversations on the Macau Question], Paris, 8 February 1979; Diplomatic Historical Archives—Ministry of Foreign Affairs, Lisbon, paragraph 1.
153. *Expresso*, 10 January 1987.
154. *Diário de Notícias*, 26 and 31 December 1986 and 4 January 1987.
155. *Expresso*, 10 January 1987.
156. Fernandes, *Sinopse*, p. 411.
157. Moisés Silva Fernandes, "O comportamento português sobre a transição política e a integração regional de Macau na região do rio das Pérolas", *Administração / Xíngzhèng*, Vol.10, No. 36, July 1997, p. 212.
158. *Diário de Notícias*, 26 December 1986.
159. *Diário de Notícias*, 3 January 1987.
160. *Diário de Notícias*, 4 January 1987.
161. Fernandes, "O comportamento português", p. 212.
162. *Diário de Notícias*, 9 January 1987.
163. "As Relações entre Portugal e a RPC: Análise da Estratégia Portuguesa, 1975–1978" [Portugal-PRC relations: analysis of the Portuguese strategy, 1975–1978], GEP/DE/1/78; Diplomatic Historical Archives—Ministry of Foreign Affairs, Lisbon, pp. 112–14.

Chapter 2 Negotiations for the Sino-Portuguese Joint Declaration on Macau

1. Moisés Silva Fernandes, *Sinopse de Macau nas Relações Luso-Chinesas, 1945–1995*, Lisbon, Fundação Oriente, 2000, pp. 381 and 385.
2. Herbert Yee, *Macau in Transition: From Colony to Autonomous Region*, London, Palgrave, 2001, p. 3.
3. Francisco G. Pereira, *Portugal, a China e a "Questão de Macau"*, Macau, Instituto Português do Oriente, 1995, pp. 11 and 20.
4. Yee, *Macau in Transition*, pp. 3–5.
5. The British wanted to change what was their colonial structure of authority, namely the system of appointing the members of the Legislative Assembly—they wanted them to become elected. In Macau, a percentage of those members were already elected during Portuguese rule, being expectable to maintain it in the Joint Declaration.
6. Boaventura de Sousa Santos and Conceição Gomes, *Macau, o Pequeníssimo Dragão*, Porto, Edições Afrontamento, 1998, p. 492.
7. Conclusions drawn by information provided during interviews to Portuguese diplomats involved in the process. The date of 19 December was agreed during an official lunch in Beijing during the last negotiation round, in which Zhou Nan said that the last day of the year would be acceptable for the Chinese but he acknowledged that New Year's Eve was an important date for the Portuguese so he suggested five days earlier. As someone said that Christmas was even more important, later Zhou Nan would come up with the suggestion of 20 December.
8. Gerald Segal, *The Fate of Hong Kong*, London, Simon & Schuster, 1993, pp. 10–11.

9. Segal, *The Fate of Hong Kong*, pp. 14–15.
10. Jayawickrama, "The Right of Self-Determination", p. 90.
11. Peter Wesley-Smith, *Unequal Treaty 1898–1997*, Revised Edition, Hong Kong, Oxford University Press, 1998, p. 58.
12. Steve Tsang, *Hong Kong, An Appointment with China*, London, I. B. Tauris, 1997, pp. 7–11.
13. Jayawickrama, "The Right of Self-Determination", p. 90.
14. Wesley-Smith, *Unequal Treaty*, pp. 272 and 229–231.
15. Tsang, *Hong Kong*, pp. 33–34, 53–54, 62–63, 71 and 79 for the whole paragraph.
16. Willem van Kemenade, *China, Hong Kong, Taiwan, Inc.*, London, Abacus, 1999, p. 75.
17. Percy Cradock, *Experiences of China*, London, John Murray, 1999, pp. 177–78 and 162.
18. Pereira, *Portugal e China*, p. 70.
19. Cradock, *Experiences of China*, pp. 163, 166–67 and 169 for the whole paragraph.
20. Cradock, *Experiences of China*, pp. 169–71. See Robert Cottrell, *The End of Hong Kong: The Secret Diplomacy of Imperial Retreat*, London, John Murray, 1993.
21. Fernandes, *Sinopse*, p. 381.
22. Wesley-Smith, *Unequal Treaty*, p. 4 and Jermain T. M. Lam, "Sino-British Relations over Hong Kong during the Final Phase of Political Transition", *International Studies*, 34, 4, 1997, p. 427.
23. Cradock, *Experiences of China*, p. 162.
24. Lam, "Sino-British Relations", p. 427.
25. Wesley-Smith, *Unequal Treaty*, pp. 3, 4 and 298.
26. Georg Ress, "The Hong Kong Agreement and Its Impact on International Law", in Jürgen Domes and Shaw Yu-ming (eds.), *Hong Kong, A Chinese and International Concern*, Boulder, Westview Press, 1988, p. 133.
27. Cradock, *Experiences of China*, pp. 172–73.
28. Jean-Luc Domenach, "Hong Kong: O Fim de Uma Colónia", *Política Internacional*, no. 14, vol. 1, Spring–Summer 1997, p. 12.
29. Kemenade, *China, Hong Kong, Taiwan*, p. 77.
30. Kemenade, *China, Hong Kong, Taiwan*, pp. 77–78.
31. Cradock, *Experiences of China*, pp. 183–86.
32. The Standing Committee of the Sixth NPC Congress endorsed the Joint Declaration on 14 November and the British Parliament approved it in early December.
33. According to *Beijing Review*, 24 December 1984, after the agreement was signed and sealed, Zhao praised Thatcher's notable "vision and statesmanship" during the Sino-British negotiations and "significant and praiseworthy contribution to the satisfactory settlement of the Hong Kong question".
34. "Deng Xiaoping Says Macau Problem Can Be 'Kept Aside'", *Wen Wei Po*, Hong Kong, 7 October 1984, in *BBC Summary of World Broadcasts*, 10 October 1984, FE/7770/A3/2 and 3.

35. Jaime Gama, *Política Externa Portuguesa, 1983–1985*, Lisbon, Ministry of Foreign Affairs, 1985, pp. 291–92.
36. Fernandes, *Sinopse*, p. 399.
37. Fernandes, *Sinopse*, p. 401.
38. Gama, *Política Externa Portuguesa*, pp. 291–92.
39. Ambassador António Costa Lobo, Portuguese ambassador in Beijing from 1982 to 1985; interviewed in Lisbon, 7 August 2002.
40. "Chinese Foreign Minister Reports on Macau Accord to Fifth NPC Session", Xinhua News Agency, Beijing, 2 April 1987, in *BBC Summary of World Broadcasts*, 4 April 1987, FE/8534/C1/1–4.
41. *Expresso*, 30 August 1986.
42. Ambassador António Costa Lobo, interviewed in Lisbon, 7 August 2002.
43. *Expresso*, 30 August 1986, for the last paragraph.
44. "China and Portugal Agree to Discuss Macau", Xinhua News Agency, Beijing, 23 May 1985, in *BBC Summary of World Broadcasts*, 24 May 1985, FE/7959/A1/1–2.
45. *Jornal de Notícias*, 24 May 1985.
46. "Acta do Conselho de Estado" [Proceedings of the Portuguese Council of State], no. 9, 17 June 1985, Archives of the Presidency of the Portuguese Republic, Lisbon.
47. For the whole paragraph see: Aníbal Cavaco Silva, *Autobiografia Política*, Lisbon, Temas e Debates, 2002, pp. 203–4.
48. Silva, *Autobiografia Política*, p. 205.
49. *South China Morning Post*, 6 January 1986.
50. Silva, *Autobiografia Política*, p. 205.
51. Silva, *Autobiografia Política*, pp. 205–6.
52. "Relatório das Negociações e Acordo Luso-Chinês sobre Macau" [Report of the Negotiations and Sino-Portuguese agreement on Macau], Informação de Serviço [internal memorandum], Ministry of Foreign Affairs, Lisbon, 29 June 1987, paragraph 6.
53. Silva, *Autobiografia Política*, p. 206.
54. Pedro Pires de Miranda, *Política Externa Portuguesa, 1985–1987*, Lisbon, Ministry of Foreign Affairs, 1987, pp. 192–93.
55. Fernandes, *Sinopse*, p. 410.
56. *Far Eastern Economic Review*, 22 August 1985.
57. "Relatório das Negociações e Acordo Luso-Chinês sobre Macau", paragraph 4, and Pedro Pires de Miranda, "The Joint Declaration Negotiations", in Luís Filipe Barreto (ed.), *Proceedings of the Seminar Paths of Macau and of Portuguese-Chinese Relations (1974–1999)*, Lisbon, Centro Científico e Cultural de Macau, 2010, p. 72.
58. "Relatório das Negociações e Acordo Luso-Chinês sobre Macau", paragraph 5.
59. Silva, *Autobiografia Política*, pp. 206–7.
60. Silva, *Autobiografia Política*, p. 207.
61. Silva, *Autobiografia Política*, p. 207. The details included: a longer transition period, maintenance of the Portuguese administration during the

transition, guarantee of an unchanged system and maintenance of rights and liberties for a fifty-year period after the handover.
62. Fernandes, *Sinopse*, pp. 411 and 414.
63. "Chinese Foreign Minister Reports on Macau Accord to Fifth NPC Session", Xinhua News Agency, Beijing, 2 April 1987, in *BBC Summary of World Broadcasts*, 4 April 1987, FE/8534/C1/1–4.
64. Miranda, "The Joint Declaration Negotiations", pp. 74–75, and Silva, *Autobiografia Política*, p. 206.
65. Chang Jaw-ling, "Settlement of the Macao Issue: Distinctive Features of Beijing's Negotiating Behavior", *Case Western Reserve Journal of International Law*, Vol. 20, No. 1, Winter 1988, pp. 267–69.
66. *Expresso*, 22 November 1986.
67. See Silva, *Autobiografia Política*, p. 207.
68. *Expresso*, 22 November 1986.
69. Silva, *Autobiografia Política*, p. 208.
70. Fernandes, *Sinopse*, p. 401.
71. Miranda, "The Joint Declaration Negotiations", pp. 74–75.
72. Silva, *Autobiografia Política*, pp. 208–9.
73. Silva, *Autobiografia Política*, pp. 208–9, for the whole paragraph.
74. Silva, *Autobiografia Política*, p. 209.
75. *Expresso*, 22 November 1986. The threats apparently originated with Zhou Nan during the meeting with Pires de Miranda (confirmed by interviews with people involved in the process).
76. *Diário de* Notícas, 10 January 1987. The Ministry declared that negotiations were held in an environment of mutual respect.
77. Silva, *Autobiografia Política*, pp. 209–10.
78. Zhou Nan's visit to Porto was under a much more relaxed atmosphere than his meetings in Lisbon. For details see Miranda, "The Joint Declaration Negotiations".
79. *O Tempo*, 8 January 1987 and "China Optimistic about Quick Solution of Macau Issue", Lisbon, Xinhua, 23 November 1986, in *BBC Summary of World Broadcasts*, 25 November 1986, FE/8425/A1/2.
80. Silva, *Autobiografia Política*, pp. 209–10.
81. "China Seeks Return of Macau Before 2000", Beijing, 31 December 1986, in *BBC Summary of World Broadcasts*, 1 January 1987, FE/8454/i.
82. *Diário de Notícias*, 28 December 1986.
83. *O Tempo*, 8 January 1987.
84. Miranda, "The Joint Declaration Negotiations", p. 74.
85. Silva, *Autobiografia Política*, p. 210.
86. See Pedro Catarino, "Macau Seen from Four Angles at Four Different Moments in Its History: From Macau, Hong Kong, Lisbon, and Beijing", in Barreto (ed.), *Proceedings*, pp. 89–108.
87. As mentioned in Chapter 1, there is lack of clarity about Portuguese arrival and settlement in Macau and thus the use of 1553 or 1557 as an official "starting date" for the Portuguese presence.
88. *Far Eastern Economic Review*, 25 September 1986.
89. Pedro Catarino, "Macau Seen from Four Angles", pp. 103–4.

90. Silva, *Autobiografia Política*, p. 211. Fernandes, *Sinopse*, p. 418.
91. President Eanes declared that the *Acta* remained in the archives of the prime minister's office while Cavaco Silva stated that it had been misplaced. *Expresso*, 10 January 1987.
92. Fernandes, "Contextualização das negociações", p. 112.
93. *Diário de Notícias*, 7 January 1987.
94. *Diário de Notícias*, 9 January 1987. For a closer analysis of the mentioned documents see previous sections.
95. *Expresso*, 10 January 1987 and *Diário de Notícias*, 9 January 1987.
96. *Diário de Notícias*, 9 January 1987.
97. Silva, *Autobiografia Política*, p. 212.
98. Silva, *Autobiografia Política*, pp. 211–12 and 215.
99. Fernandes, *Sinopse*, p. 420.
100. *Diário de Notícias*, 26 January 1987.
101. *Diário de Notícias*, 30 January 1987.
102. Silva, *Autobiografia Política*, p. 215.
103. *Diário de Notícias*, 20 March 1987.
104. Portuguese Nationality Law of 1981 (Law 37/81).
105. Nationality Law of the People's Republic of China—China Law No. 71, 10 September 1980, article 3rd.
106. "Relatório das Negociações", paragraphs 47–50.
107. "Relatório das Negociações", paragraphs 50–52.
108. "Relatório das Negociações", paragraphs 50–52.
109. Silva, *Autobiografia Política*, p. 208.
110. Silva, *Autobiografia Política*, p. 216 and Vieira, "Macau and the Future", p. 147.
111. "Relatório das Negociações", paragraph 116.
112. Chang, "Settlement of the Macao Issue", p. 264.
113. Silva, *Autobiografia Política*, p. 208.
114. Silva, *Autobiografia Política*, p. 216.
115. Miranda, "The Joint Declaration Negotiations", p. 75.
116. The memorandum signed with the Macau Joint Declaration did not refer to the descendants of those with Portuguese nationality. The alteration in the Portuguese Nationality Law of 1981 (Law 37/81) predicted *jus sanguinis*: children of Portuguese passport's holders were Portuguese and had the right to hold Portuguese passports (Law 25/1994).
117. Silva, *Autobiografia Política*, pp. 216–17.
118. Silva, *Autobiografia Política*, pp. 217–18.
119. "Chinese Foreign Minister Reports on Macau Accord to Fifth NPC Session", Xinhua News Agency, Beijing, 2 April 1987, in *BBC Summary of World Broadcasts*, 4 April 1987, FE/8534/C1/1–4. The text of the agreement was made public on the same day.
120. With the exception of two: the president of the Legislative Assembly, Carlos d'Assumção, and Henrique de Senna Fernandes, Macanese lawyer and writer. Governor Pinto Machado was invited in his capacity as adviser to the Portuguese State Council while Carlos Monjardino and Mário Cordeiro, under-Secretaries in Macau, were nominal guests of the Portuguese government (Fernandes, *Sinopse*, p. 429).

121. "Joint Declaration of the Government of the People's Republic of China and the Government of the Republic of Portugal on the Question of Macau", Beijing, 13 April 1987, paragraph 2.
122. *Diário de Notícias*, 26 March 1987 for the paragraph.
123. *Diário de Notícias*, 26 March 1987.
124. The censure motion was allegedly caused by a controversy regarding the government cancelation of a visit of a parliamentary delegation to the Soviet Union with a call at Estonia, at a time in which democratic parliaments did not pay official visits to Soviet states. With little perspectives of increasing its electoral capital in a future legislative election, the PRD wanted to increase its limited political influence in the parliament. Maritheresa Frain, "O PSD como partido dominante em Portugal", *Análise Social*, 4th Issue, vol. xxxi (138), p. 990. See also *Expresso*, 4 April 1987 and *Diário de Notícias*, 3 April 1987.
125. Silva, *Autobiografia Política*, p. 218.
126. *Expresso*, 17 April 1987.
127. *Diário de Notícias*, 9 March 1987.
128. *Diário de Notícias*, 11 April 1987.
129. *Diário de Notícias*, 28 December 1986. See also *Diário de Notícias*, 28 January 1987.
130. *Diário de Notícias*, 11 April 1987.
131. *Diário de Notícias*, 11 April 1987.
132. *Diário de Notícias*, 11 April 1987. According to Cavaco Silva (*Autobiografia Política*, p. 215), 20 December 1999 was an acceptable date for Portugal, with a transition period of thirteen years and with the transfer of the administration two and a half years after the Hong Kong's handover. According to *Diário de Notícias* (20 March 1987), Macau Governor Pinto Machado agreed that 1999 was compatible with the necessary adjustments to be made for safeguarding the interests of the people of Macau during the transfer of administration. Pires de Miranda also shared this opinion: Miranda, "The Joint Declaration Negotiations", p. 75.
133. Silva, *Autobiografia Política*, p. 217.
134. Miranda, *Política Externa Portuguesa*, p. 162.
135. *Diário de Notícias*, 27 March 1987.
136. Silva, *Autobiografia Política*, p. 220.
137. *Beijing Review*, 13 April 1987. "Chinese Foreign Minister Reports on Macau Accord to Fifth NPC Session", Xinhua News Agency, Beijing, 2 April 1987, in *BBC Summary of World Broadcasts*, 4 April 1987, FE/8534/C1/1–4.
138. "Chinese Foreign Minister Reports on Macau Accord to Fifth NPC Session", Xinhua News Agency.
139. Silva, *Autobiografia Política*, p. 221.
140. *Beijing Review*, 13 April 1987.
141. As previous Governor Garcia Leandro noted, referring to the drafting of the Organic Law in 1976: "The process of the new Organic Law was followed with interest by the Government of Hong Kong, but not only. In particular the question of the Legislative Assembly (two thirds of which elected and not chaired by the governor) . . . In the case of the Assembly,

it was an innovative and far-reaching experience, since in Hong Kong such situation did not exist, being all members of the Legislative Council appointed or carrying out their duties by right. Moreover, in both Hong Kong and London, some entities with political responsibilities and citizens on a personal level defended the existence of a semi-elected Legislative Council, arguing that local government would not be possible for several reasons, but mainly because China would not accept it. The experience in Macau has come to put in doubt this thesis. . . . Almost in the end of his administration in Hong Kong, Governor Chris Patten made a great effort towards democratization of the legislative and decision making, being registered known historical difficulties. In Macau the matter was solved 20 years before." Leandro, "The Years of the Great Change", p. 95.

Chapter 3　The Transition Period and the Problems of "Localisation"

1. Ambassador José Manuel Duarte de Jesus, Portuguese Ambassador in Beijing from 1992 to 1997; interviewed in Lisbon, 3 June 2011.
2. Pedro Vieira, *Todos os Portos a que Cheguei*, Lisbon, Gradiva, 2010, p. 227.
3. The post of under-secretary for the transition was created by Governor Melancia and abolished by Governor Rocha Vieira. In the Rocha Vieira administration it was mainly the under-secretary for justice that handled the issues of the transition, arguably leading to some delays in the localization of the Law.
4. The heads were Simões Coelho (1988–1989) and Pedro Catarino (1990–1992); the under-secretary was João de Deus Ramos. Catarino, "Macau Seen from Four Angles", pp. 95–101.
5. *Ponto Final*, 28 May 1999.
6. Having re-established the Socialist Party in Portugal in 1973, Soares was prime minister from 1976 to 1978, negotiating the resumption of Portuguese-Chinese bilateral relations, and from 1983 to 1985, in a governing coalition with the PSD.
7. It was widely believed that unlike Carlos Melancia, seen as "the man of the President", Rocha Vieira was appointed under the umbrella of a PS/PSD cohabitation period, suggesting greater political impartiality. See Vasco Rocha Vieira, "Macau and the Future", pp. 139–40.
8. See Vieira, *Todos os Portos*, pp. 261–68 and Vieira, "Macau and the Future", p. 139.
9. See António Ramalho Eanes in the "Preface" of Vieira, *Todos os Portos*, p. 25.
10. As mentioned in Chapter 2, Gama signed the joint communiqué for the launch of Sino-Portuguese negotiations in 1985.
11. Jorge Sampaio, *Portugueses*, Vol. IV, Imprensa Nacional-Casa da Moeda, Lisbon, 2000, p. 403.
12. Pedro Vieira, *Todos os Portos*, p. 265. See also Leandro, "The Years of the Great Change", pp. 40–41.
13. Mário Soares, *Intervenções 4*, Imprensa Nacional-Casa da Moeda, Lisbon, 1990, p. 406.
14. See: Carlos Melancia, "The Challenges of Transition", pp. 109–22.

15. Pedro Vieira, *Todos os Portos*, p. 191 and Vieira, "Macau and the Future", pp. 126–27.
16. Soares, *Intervenções 3*, p. 29.
17. Soares, *Intervenções 4*, p. 405.
18. Mário Soares, "Macau: Uma Responsabilidade Histórica—Discurso de Sua Excelência o Presidente da República Dr. Mário Soares", Missão de Macau em Lisboa, Lisbon, 22 May 1990, p. 10.
19. Soares, *Intervenções 8*, Imprensa Nacional-Casa da Moeda, Lisbon, 1994, p. 77.
20. Soares, "Macau", pp. 3–4.
21. Soares, "Macau", p. 5 and Soares, *Intervenções 5*, Imprensa Nacional-Casa da Moeda, Lisbon, 1991, p. 440.
22. Soares, "Macau", pp. 6–8.
23. Vieira, "Macau and the Future", 126.
24. Governor Rocha Vieira's speech in the Portuguese State Council meeting, Lisbon, 15 April 1997.
25. Governor Rocha Vieira's speech in the Portuguese State Council meeting, Lisbon, 15 April 1997, and Vieira, "Macau and the Future", p. 134.
26. Vieira, "Macau and the Future", p. 134.
27. Vieira, "Macau and the Future", p. 134, and Vieira, *Todos os Portos*, pp. 323–24.
28. Vieira, *Todos os Portos*, pp. 323–24.
29. Sampaio, *Portugueses*, Vol. IV, p. 433.
30. Sampaio, *Portugueses*, Vol. I, Imprensa Nacional-Casa da Moeda, 1997, p. 347 and Vol. IV, pp. 404 and 414.
31. "Joint Declaration . . . on the Question of Macau", Annex II, Section I.
32. Pedro Catarino, "Grupo de Ligação Conjunto Luso-Chinês" [Sino-Portuguese Joint Liaison Group], Informação de Serviço [internal memorandum], Ministry of Foreign Affairs, Lisbon, 11 April 1990, p. 2.
33. "Joint Declaration . . . on the Question of Macau", Annex II, Section I.
34. During the transition period Joint Liaison Group's meetings took place alternatively between Lisbon, Beijing and Macau. Whenever negotiations at the JLG stalled, alternative meetings were allowed for on a rotating basis, with the view to turn to bilateral diplomacy as a means against which a solution would be sought. The general rule for the Portuguese would be to seek directly resolution for divergent views with representatives of the Chinese government. The Chinese on the other hand seemingly saw the meetings in Lisbon and Macau as a means with which to exert pressure on Portuguese authorities, swaying the negotiations in a specific direction in their interest.
35. Catarino, "Macau Seen from Four Angles", pp. 100–5. According to one observer, the Chinese delegation received instructions from the Macau Office in the Foreign Ministry, from the Macau Office in the State Council, from the president and from the prime minister. They did not have an interlocutor, but had to consult all these elements that sometimes had divergent opinions.
36. "Joint Declaration . . . on the Question of Macau", Annex II, Section II, paragraph 2.

37. Ribeiro Gomes, "Funções do Grupo de Terras" [Functions of the Land Group], Office of the Under-Secretary for Public Works and Housing, Macau, 10 February 1988, pp. 3–4.
38. "Joint Declaration . . . on the Question of Macau", Annex II, Section II, paragraph 3.
39. "Joint Declaration . . . on the Question of Macau", Annex II, Section II.
40. "Funções do Grupo de Terras; Sua interferência no processo de concessão de terrenos" [Functions of the Land Group; Its interference in the process of concession of land], Sino-Portuguese Land Group, 14 June 1988, pp. 3–4.
41. Catarino, "Grupo de Ligação Conjunto", p. 2.
42. Yee, *Macau in Transition*, p. 41.
43. For the whole paragraph, Yee, *Macau in Transition*, p. 42.
44. Yee, *Macau in Transition*, p. 41.
45. Lo Shiu Hing, *Political Development in Macau*, Hong Kong, The Chinese University Press, 1995, p. 166.
46. Yee, *Macau in Transition*, pp. 55 and 49.
47. *Tribuna de Macau*, 14 December 1991. Lo, *Political Development in Macau*, p. 156.
48. Yee, *Macau in Transition*, p. 42.
49. "A Questão da Localização na Administração" [The localisation question in the administration], Memorandum, Governor's Office, Macau Government, p. 5.
50. "Joint Declaration . . . on the Question of Macau", Annex I, paragraphs V and VI.
51. Lo, *Political Development in Macau*, p. 164.
52. Meeting of the Joint Working Group on the Three Big Issues, Macau, 10 July 1991.
53. Yee, *Macau in Transition*, pp. 42–46 and 52. Yee points out that, prior to 1989 the administration did not recognize degrees from non-Portuguese language universities.
54. "Localização de Quadros e Generalização do Uso da Língua Chinesa na Administração—Balanço dos Trabalhos Realizados em 1994" [Localisation of the civil service and use of the Chinese language in the administration—balance of the works undertaken in 1994], Speech of the Under-Secretary for Administration, Education, and Youth Affairs, Macau Government, C.A.T., 24 February 1995, p. 6.
55. Lo, *Political Development in Macau*, pp. 156 and 158.
56. Formerly known as the University of East Asia.
57. Yee, *Macau in Transition*, p. 52.
58. Decree no. 39/93/M, Macau, 26 July 1993.
59. Yee, *Macau in Transition*, p. 47.
60. "Integração" [Integration], Serviço de Informação e Administração Pública, Macau Government, no date (perhaps 1991).
61. Vieira, "Macau and the Future", p. 135.
62. Decree no. 357/93, Lisbon, 14 October 1993, in "Localização de Quadros e Generalização do Uso da Língua Chinesa", p. 20. In February 1994, the

Macau government issued a decree authorising civil servants to take early retirement or to leave the civil service by paying a financial compensation with the transfer of responsibilities to the CGA.
63. Decree no. 14/94/M, Macau, 23 February 1994, in "Localização de Quadros e Generalização do Uso da Língua Chinesa", pp. 20–22.
64. Vieira, "Macau and the Future", p. 136.
65. Lo, *Political Development in Macau*, p. 156.
66. Luís Crucho de Almeida, "Competência para Legislar sobre o Estatuto da Língua Chinesa em Macau" [Competence to legislate the status of the Chinese language in Macau], Informação de Serviço [internal memorandum], Ministry of Foreign Affairs, Lisbon, 7 August 1991, p. 3.
67. In July 1991, the draft of the Macau Basic Law included the following paragraph in Chapter I, Article 9: "Besides the Chinese language, the Portuguese language can be used in the administrative, legislative and judicial bodies of the Macau Special Administrative Region. The Portuguese language is also an official language." In "Acta de conversa na 10ª reunião do GLC sobre o estatuto da língua chinesa e língua portuguesa em Macau" [Minutes of talks on the 10th JLG meeting on the status of the Chinese language and Portuguese language in Macau], Macau, 12 April 1991.
68. Decree no. 455/91, *Diário da República* [The Official Journal], Lisbon. I Série A, n.º 301, 2º suplemento, 31 December 1991.
69. In February 1992, the governor created a Linguistics Commission (*Comissão de Acompanhamento da Situação Linguística de Macau*), an organ of direct support to the governor, presided by the governor and composed by other twenty-three elements from within and outside the administration, to monitor the official use of the Chinese language and to discuss the problems resulting of the linguistic situation of Macau. Despatch no. 16/GM/92, *Official Bulletin of Macau*, no. 8, 24 February 1992. The governor also asked the Chinese Affairs Bureau (*Direcção dos Serviços de Assuntos Chineses*) to propose measures to the enlargement of the use of the Chinese language in the public services of the administration, facilitating the access of the majority of the population to the administrative system. Despatch no. 106/GM/91, *Official Bulletin of Macau*, 27 May 1991.
70. "Reunião Informal do Grupo de Trabalho sobre as Três Grandes Questões" [Preparation of the Meeting of the Joint Working Group on the Three Big Issues], to take place on 10 June 1991.
71. Despatches no. 46/GM/94 and 47/GM/94, *Official Bulletin of Macau— Series I*, 30 May 1994 and 25 July 1994, and Decree no. 174/94/M, *Official Bulletin of Macau—Series I*, 8 August 1994. The teams assessed the linguistic needs for training in the civil service and created special scholarships for training and professional improvement.
72. No author (perhaps Eduardo Cabrita), no name, Legal Translation Bureau, Macau Government, no date (perhaps 1991), p. 5.
73. "Joint Declaration . . . on the Question of Macau", paragraph 2 (5).
74. Yee, *Macau in Transition*, p. 58.
75. Yee, *Macau in Transition*, p. 57.

76. "Oficialização da Língua Chinesa" [Official use of the Chinese language], Legal Translation Bureau, Macau Government, 1991 and Eduardo Cabrita, "Oficialização da Língua Chinesa no Âmbito do Processo Legislativo" [Official use of the Chinese language within the legislative process], Legal Translation Bureau, Macau Government, 4 June 1991, p. 3.
77. The sources in the previous note observe that the criteria for the solution to possible divergences of interpretation between Portuguese and Chinese versions of text were inadequate.
78. Cabrita, "Oficialização da Língua Chinesa", p. 4.
79. No author (perhaps Eduardo Cabrita), no name, Legal Translation Bureau, Macau Government, no date (perhaps 1991), pp. 3 and 6–7.
80. Decree no. 11/89/M, 20 February 1989, in Cabrita, "Oficialização da Língua Chinesa", p. 4.
81. No author (perhaps Eduardo Cabrita), no name, Legal Translation Bureau, Macau Government, no date (perhaps 1991), pp. 9–10.
82. Cabrita, "Oficialização da Língua Chinesa", p. 8.
83. Cabrita, "Oficialização da Língua Chinesa", p. 33. Sampaio, *Portugueses*, Vol. I, pp. 359–62 note that the magistrates were gradually localized to work in synchrony with the community that they served.
84. According to Eduardo Cabrita, "Nível de Localização do G.T.J.", Memorandum, Legal Translation Bureau, Macau Government, 3 September 1991, the Legal Translation Bureau aimed at "creating conditions for the existence of official versions in the Chinese language of the normative acts in force invoked with the same rigour and juridical security of the versions in Portuguese language". No author (perhaps Eduardo Cabrita), no name, Legal Translation Bureau, Macau Government, no date (perhaps 1991), p. 17 notes that in 1991, the GTJ had seven translation teams, each composed of a jurist with Portuguese training, a jurist of Chinese training, an interpreter-translator and a scholar.
85. Macau had a District Court with appeal to the High Court of Justice in Lisbon.
86. No author (perhaps Eduardo Cabrita), no name, Legal Translation Bureau, Macau Government, no date (perhaps 1991), p. 19. These included the Constitution of the Portuguese Republic, the Macau Organic Law, the Law of the Bases of the Judicial Organisation of Macau, and the five "major codes".
87. Sampaio, *Portugueses*, Vol. IV, p. 404. Portuguese laws either were enacted specifically for Macau or were national laws extended to Macau through publication in the Official Bulletin of Macau. According to Yee, *Macau in Transition*, p. 59, so-called local laws were created by Macau's bodies with legislative authority such as the Legislature Assembly or the governor.
88. "Joint Declaration . . . on the Question of Macau", no. 2 (4).
89. Cabrita, "Oficialização da Língua Chinesa no Âmbito do Processo Legislativo", p. 17.
90. Members of the juridical department of Xinhua News Agency privately repeated to the coordinator of the Macau Legal Affairs Bureau that the Chinese interpretation of "laws in force in Macau" only referred to the

legal laws that emanated from the bodies of the territory. In Jorge Oliveira and Luis Melo, "Da 'Localização das Leis' à Definição de uma Estratégia Conjunta entre Portugal e a RPC quanto à Continuidade do Ordenamento Jurídico de Macau" [From the 'Localization of the Law' to the definition of a common strategy between Portugal and the PRC on the continuity of Macau's juridical organisation], Legal Affairs Bureau, Macau Government, no date (perhaps 1991), pp. 4–5.
91. For the whole paragraph, Oliveira and Melo, "Da 'Localização das Leis'", p. 32.
92. According to Annex I, Paragraph II, of the Sino-British Joint Declaration, "After the establishment of the Hong Kong Special Administrative Region, the laws previously in force in Hong Kong (i.e. the common law, rules of equity, ordinances, subordinate legislation and customary law) shall be maintained, save for whatever therein may contravene the Basic Law or subject to any amendment by the Hong Kong Special Administrative Region legislature."
93. Oliveira and Melo, "Da 'Localização das Leis'", pp. 30 and 37–40.
94. No author (perhaps Eduardo Cabrita), no name, Legal Translation Bureau, Macau Government, no date (perhaps 1991), pp. 36–37. According to Oliveira and Melo ("Da 'Localização das Leis'", pp. 7–9) for the Portuguese authorities preservative of Portuguese law in Macau was an objective of "the highest priority".
95. Oliveira and Melo, "Da 'Localização das Leis'", pp. 14 and 35–36.
96. Sampaio, *Portugueses*, Vol. I, pp. 352–53, 359–62. For the extension of the International Covenants to Macau see Chapter 5.
97. Oliveira and Melo, "Da 'Localização das Leis'", pp. 52–55.
98. Meeting of the Joint Working Group on the Three Big Issues, Macau, 10 July 1991.
99. *China Daily*, 28 December 1994.
100. *O Comércio de Macau*, 31 August 1991.
101. The most relevant legislation was inserted in specific legal codes, namely the "major codes".
102. Macedo Almeida, "Localização das Leis—Informação tendo em vista a preparação da 11ª reunião plenária do GLC" [Localisation of the Law— Information to prepare the 11th JLG plenary meeting], Office of the Under-Secretary for Justice, Macau Government, 1 July 1991.
103. *Ou Mun*, 30 September 1991. For example, according *O Comércio de Macau*, 31 August 1991, while the Portuguese criminal code of 1982 had already been revised several times, in Macau the criminal code in force dated from 1886 and its limitations had been surpassed by the production of detached legislation since the 1970s.
104. Almeida, "Localização das Leis", 1 July 1991.
105. The aim of the Portuguese negotiators was that the laws would remain in force after the handover, contrary to what happened in Hong Kong. Teresa Silva and Carlos Dias (cords.), *Direito e Justiça em Macau*, Office of the Under-Secretary for Justice, Editora Livros do Oriente, Macau, 1999, p. 11.
106. Sampaio, *Portugueses*, Vol. IV, pp. 405 and 427–28.

Notes to pages 82–87   135

107. Law no. 112/91, 29 August 1991, Lisbon.
108. For the whole paragraph, Sampaio, *Portugueses*, Vol. I, p. 359–62, p. 351.
109. "As Quatro Grandes Preocupações da Parte Chinesa Relativamente ao Processo de Localização dos Quadros".
110. Lo, *Political Development in Macau*, p. 161 and Richard Louis Edmonds and Herbert S. Yee, "Macau: From Portuguese Autonomous Territory to Chinese Special Administrative Region", *The China Quarterly*, no. 160, December 1999, p. 813.
111. "Relatório das Negociações e Acordo Luso-Chinês sobre Macau", paragraph 120. In paragraph 129 it is pointed out that the Portuguese feared that the settlement of sensitive issues through diplomatic channels could affect the Sino-Portuguese bilateral relations.
112. Lo, *Political Development in Macau*, p. 251.
113. According to Lo, *Political Development in Macau*, p. 249, this explains the infrastructure driven strategy of the Macau administration during the transition period.

Chapter 4   Other Delicate Transition Issues

1. Sampaio, *Portugueses*, Vol. IV, pp. 424 and 442.
2. Meeting of the heads of the JLG's delegations, Macau, 26 November 1991, p. 8.
3. Proceedings of JLG's 12th plenary meeting, Macau, 2–4 December 1991, p. 31. "Reunião com o Senhor Embaixador Nunes Portela" [meeting with Ambassador Nunes Portela], Letter from the Under-Secretary for Justice to the Governor, Macau Government, 29 October 1991.
4. Informal meeting of the heads of the JLG's delegations, Macau, 22 February 1992, p. 1.
5. Proceedings of JLG's 13th plenary meeting, Lisbon, 16–19 March 1992, p. 6.
6. Vasco, "Macau and the Future", p. 145.
7. Meeting of the heads of the JLG's delegations, Macau, 26 November 1991, pp. 8–9.
8. According to Article 41 of the International Covenant on Civil and Political Rights, http://www2.ohchr.org/english/law/ccpr.htm#art41 accessed on 24 November 2010, "A State Party to the present Covenant may at any time declare under this article that it recognizes the competence of the Committee to receive and consider communications to the effect that a State Party claims that another State Party is not fulfilling its obligations under the present Covenant. Communications under this article may be received and considered only if submitted by a State Party which has made a declaration recognizing in regard to itself the competence of the Committee. No communication shall be received by the Committee if it concerns a State Party which has not made such a declaration."
9. Proceedings of JLG's 12th plenary meeting, Macau, 2–4 December 1991, p. 32.
10. Proceedings of JLG's 13th plenary meeting, Lisbon, 16–19 March 1992, p. 5.

11. Pedro Catarino, "JLG's 13th Plenary Meeting, Lisbon, 16–19 March 1992", Informação de Serviço [internal memorandum], Ministry of Foreign Affairs, Lisbon, 27 April 1992, p. 5.
12. Informal meeting of the heads of the JLG's delegations, Macau, 6 July 1992, p. 2.
13. International Covenant on Economic, Social and Cultural Rights, Article 1, Part I; International Covenant on Civil and Political Rights, Article 25.
14. Pedro Catarino, "JLG's 14th Plenary Meeting, Macau, 6–8 July 1992", Informação de Serviço [internal memorandum], Ministry of Foreign Affairs, Lisbon, 20 August 1992, p. 6 for the whole paragraph.
15. Press Release on JLG's 15th Plenary Meeting, Beijing, 12 November 1992.
16. Basic Law of the Macau Special Administrative Region, chapter III, paragraph 40.
17. The Chinese side did not accept to include in the Joint Declaration memoranda the applicability to Macau of the International Covenants.
18. Lo, *Political Development in Macau*, p. 24.
19. Informal meeting of the heads of the JLG's delegations, Macau, 21 June 1991, p. 4.
20. Proceedings of JLG's 9th plenary meeting, Lisbon, 3 December 1990, pp. 2–3.
21. Carlos Melancia, "The Challenges of Transition", in Luís Filipe Barreto (ed.), *Proceedings of the Seminar Paths of Macau and of Portuguese-Chinese Relations (1974–1999)*, Lisbon, Centro Científico e Cultural de Macau, 2010, pp. 111 and 117 for the whole paragraph. See also Vieira, *Todos os Portos*, p. 208.
22. Catarino, "Macau Seen from Four Angles", p. 101.
23. Quoted in Catarino, "Macau Seen from Four Angles", p. 101.
24. Melancia, "The Challenges of Transition", p. 116.
25. Melancia, "The Challenges of Transition", p. 116.
26. Catarino, "Macau Seen from Four Angles", p. 100.
27. Interview with Engineer Carlos Melancia, Macau Governor from July 1987 to April 1991; Lisbon, 30 July 2002 and Melancia, "The Challenges of Transition", p. 116.
28. Melancia, "The Challenges of Transition", p. 116
29. CAM, "Macau International Airport, presenting the project to the JLG", Companhia do Aeroporto de Macau [Macau International Airport Company Limited] Macau, 6 July 1992, p. 1. For Melancia's arguments see Melancia, "The Challenges of Transition", pp. 115–17.
30. Melancia, "The Challenges of Transition", p. 117. See also Vieira, *Todos os Portos*, pp. 203 and 207.
31. Letter from Pedro Catarino to Luis Vasconcelos, Ministry of Foreign Affairs, Lisbon, 11 December 1990, p. 3. See also Vieira, *Todos os Portos*, pp. 205–7.
32. Informal meeting of the heads of the JLG's delegations, Macau, 4 September 1991, p. 2.
33. Informal meeting of the heads of the JLG's delegations, Beijing, 10 September 1991, pp. 6–7.
34. Letter from the Under-Secretary for Justice to the Governor, 25 September 1991, p. 3.

35. Pedro Catarino, "JLG's 11th Plenary Meeting, Beijing, 10–13 September 1991", Informação de Serviço [internal memorandum], Ministry of Foreign Affairs, Lisbon, 23 September 1991, p. 9.
36. Informal meeting of the heads of the JLG's delegations, Beijing, 10 September 1991, p. 5.
37. Pedro Catarino, "JLG's 12th Plenary Meeting", Macau, 2–4 December 1991, Informação de Serviço [internal memorandum], Ministry of Foreign Affairs, Lisbon, 17 December 1991, p. 13. See also Vieira, *Todos os Portos*, pp. 205–7.
38. Vieira, "Macau and the Future", pp. 160–61.
39. Informal meeting of the heads of the JLG's delegations, Macau, 18 June 1991, pp. 7–8.
40. Catarino, "JLG's 12th Plenary Meeting", p. 14.
41. Informal meeting of the heads of the JLG's delegations, Macau, 21 June 1991, pp. 5–6.
42. Oliveira and Melo, "Da 'Localização das Leis'", p. 3.
43. Informal meeting of the heads of the JLG's delegations, Macau, 21 June 1991, pp. 5–6.
44. For a detailed account of the final financial shares of the Macau International Airport see Vieira, *Todos os Portos*, p. 210.
45. Informal meeting of the heads of the JLG's delegations, Macau, 19 February 1992, p. 7.
46. Informal meeting of the heads of the JLG's delegations, Macau, 19 February 1992, p. 7.
47. Informal meeting of the heads of the JLG's delegations, Macau, 19 February 1992, p. 8 and Melancia, "The Challenges of Transition", p. 115.
48. Informal meeting of the heads of the JLG's delegations, Macau, 22 February 1992, pp. 2–4.
49. Proceedings of JLG's 10th plenary meeting, Macau, 10 April 1991, p. 1.
50. Proceedings of JLG's 9th plenary meeting, Lisbon, 4 December 1990, p. 3.
51. Proceedings of JLG's 10th plenary meeting, p. 2.
52. Proceedings of JLG's 7th plenary meeting, Beijing, 16 May 1990, p. 9.
53. Proceedings of JLG's 10th plenary meeting, p. 3.
54. Pedro Catarino, "JLG's 12th Plenary Meeting", p. 6.
55. Proceedings of JLG's 10th plenary meeting, p. 2.
56. Informal meeting of the heads of the JLG's delegations, Macau, 21 June 1991, p. 11.
57. Proceedings of JLG's 11th plenary meeting, Macau, p. 10.
58. Informal meeting of the heads of the JLG's delegations, Macau, 21 June 1991, p. 10.
59. Informal meeting of the heads of the JLG's delegations, Macau, 22 June 1991, pp. 1–2.
60. Proceedings of JLG's 11th plenary meeting, p. 11.
61. Proceedings of JLG's 12th plenary meeting, pp. 22 and 24.
62. Proceedings of JLG's 12th plenary meeting, pp. 21 and 23.
63. Proceedings of JLG's 13th plenary meeting, Lisbon, 16–19 March 1992, pp. 8–9.

64. Pedro Catarino, "JLG's 14th Plenary Meeting, Macau, 6–8 July 1992", Informação de Serviço [internal memorandum], Ministry of Foreign Affairs, Lisbon, 20 August 1992, p. 3.
65. Proceedings of JLG's 14th plenary meeting, Macau, 7 July 1992, p. 3.
66. Informal meeting of the heads of the JLG's delegations, Macau, 6 July 1992, p. 4.
67. Andresen Guimarães, "Macau Airport", note, JLG and LG Portuguese Representation in Macau, 6 November 1992, p. 2.
68. The issue of possible financial reserves after the handover worried Cavaco Silva and Jaime Gama. Both wanted to talk with Ambassador Duarte Jesus about this issue and there was also a meeting with the economist Vítor Pessoa, concluding that the Macau obligations before the handover would not be inherited by Portugal. Ambassador José Manuel Duarte de Jesus, Portuguese Ambassador in Beijing from 1992 to 1997; interviewed in Lisbon, 3 June 2011.
69. Lo, *Political Development in Macau*, p. 27.
70. Proceedings of JLG's 12th plenary meeting, p. 25.
71. Declarations of Carlos Monjardino to the *Expresso*, 29 March 1991.
72. *Expresso*, 29 March 1991.
73. Before, the acting governor was a momentary choice and all the undersecretaries had the same statute.
74. António Alçada Baptista, "Os primeiros dez anos da Fundação Oriente: a criação da Fundação", *Fundação Oriente: 10 anos—1988–1998*, Lisbon, Orient Foundation, 1998, pp. 15–17. According to the foundation website: "The Orient Foundation was created on 18 March 1988 and is a non-profit-making private law organisation with established legal status . . . recognised as being of public utility in Portugal by a declaration in the supplement to Diário da República [The Official Journal], Lisbon, n°. 10, II Série, 6 March 1989, and in Macau by Decree Law n°. 16/89/M, 8 March, published in the Boletim Oficial de Macau, No. 10", http://www.foriente.pt.
75. Informal meeting of the heads of the JLG's delegations, Macau, 18 June 1991, p. 7.
76. In 1989 this amount changed to 1.6 per cent of STDM's gross revenue. Proceedings of JLG's 12th plenary meeting, Macau, p. 25. In 1988 the Orient Foundation had a capital of 300 million patacas—the equivalent to 37 million US dollars—and the annual contributions of STDM exceeded 200 million patacas. In Yee, *Macau in Transition*, note 45, p. 173.
77. Informal meeting of the heads of the JLG's delegations, Macau, 21 February 1992, p. 8.
78. Informal meeting of the heads of the JLG's delegations, Macau, 21 February 1992, pp. 7–8.
79. Informal meeting of the heads of the JLG's delegations, Lisbon, 16 March 1992, p. 1.
80. Declarations of Governor Pinto Machado to the *Expresso*, 22 August 1987.
81. Informal meeting of the heads of the JLG's delegations, Macau, 22 June 1991, pp. 5–6. See also Vieira, "Macau and the Future", p. 140.

82. Letter of the Under-Secretary for Justice to the Governor, "Preparation of JLG's 12th Plenary Meeting", Macau, 27 November 1991, p. 3.
83. Proceedings of JLG's 12th plenary meeting, p. 25, and Informal meeting of the heads of the JLG's delegations, Macau, 21 February 1992, p. 8.
84. Meeting restricted to the members of the JLG's delegations, Macau, 7 July 1992, p. 2.
85. Proceedings of JLG's 12th plenary meeting, p. 25, and Informal meeting of the heads of the JLG's delegations, Macau, 21 February 1992, p. 8.
86. Informal meeting of the heads of the JLG's delegations, Beijing, 10 September 1991, p. 2.
87. Meeting restricted to the members of the JLG's delegations, Macau, 7 July 1992, p. 5.
88. Ibid., p. 2.
89. Informal meeting of the heads of the JLG's delegations, Macau, 22 June 1991, pp. 5–6.
90. Meeting restricted to the members of the JLG's delegations, Macau, 7 July 1992, p. 5.
91. Ambassador Pedro Catarino to the Portuguese Ministry of Foreign Affairs, Telegram no. 459, 1st part, Macau, 12 July 1992.
92. Meeting restricted to the members of the JLG's delegations, Macau, 11 November 1992, pp. 1–3.
93. Informal meeting of the heads of the JLG's delegations, Macau, 21 February 1992, pp. 7–8.
94. Informal meeting of the heads of the JLG's delegations, Beijing, 10 September 1991, pp. 2–3.
95. Pedro Catarino, "JLG's 11th Plenary Meeting, Beijing, 10–13 September 1991", Informação de Serviço [internal memorandum], Ministry of Foreign Affairs, Lisbon, 23 September 1991, pp. 8–10.
96. Lo, *Political Development in Macau*, p. 50, note 42.
97. Baptista, "Os primeiros dez anos", p.18.
98. Yee, *Macau in Transition*, pp. 27–28.
99. Vieira, "Macau and the Future", p. 140.
100. See Vieira, "Macau and the Future", pp. 142–43.
101. Ambassador José Manuel Duarte de Jesus, Portuguese Ambassador in Beijing from 1992 to 1997; interviewed in Lisbon, 3 June 2011.
102. Yee, *Macau in Transition*, p. 12. The Development and Co-operation Foundation of Macau financed the creation of the Jorge Álvares Foundation in Portugal (*Fundação Jorge Álvares*), to be headed by Governor Rocha Vieira after the handover. This led to an incident which destroyed Social Democrat Rocha Vieira's political ambitions in Portugal, as he was accused of intending to use the Jorge Álvares Foundation for his own interests, and as Socialist President Sampaio (PS) and Foreign Minister Jaime Gama (PS) delayed the process of legalizing the Foundation. For the two contentious views see: João Gabriel, *Confidencial: A Década de Sampaio em Belém*, Prime Books, 2007, pp. 318–19; and António Ramalho Eanes in the "Preface" of Vieira, *Todos os Portos*, p. 2 and Vieira, *Todos os Portos*, pp. 283–88.
103. Lo, *Political Development in Macau*, p. 49, note 42.

104. Vieira, "Macau and the Future", pp. 140–43 and 157.
105. Sampaio, *Portugueses*, Vol. IV, pp. 438 and 442.
106. Gabriel, *Confidencial*, p. 317.
107. Lo, *Political Development in Macau*, p. 28.
108. Vieira, *Todos os Portos*, p. 333.
109. Gabriel, *Confidencial*, p. 321.
110. Gabriel, *Confidencial*, p. 321.
111. *Diário de Notícias*, 27 October 1999.
112. Gabriel, *Confidencial*, p. 321. For a detailed account of this issue see Vieira, *Todos os Portos*, pp. 333–49.

Chapter 5   A Final Assessment

1. Conversation with Prof. Richard Louis Edmonds, Coimbra, 18 November 2010.
2. António Santana Carlos, "Macau—O Modelo da Transição", *A Presença Portuguesa no Pacífico—Forum Macau*, Lisbon, ISCSP, 1999, p. 174.
3. Sampaio, *Portugueses*, Vol. IV, p. 434.
4. About the importance of dignity, see, for example, Miranda, "The Joint Declaration Negotiations", p. 68.
5. Communication to the Press, Press Services of the Ministry of Foreign Affairs, Lisbon, 6 January 1975; Diplomatic Historical Archives—Ministry of Foreign Affairs, Lisbon.
6. Articles 5 and 306, *Constitution of the Portuguese Republic*, Coimbra, Atlântida Editora, 1976.
7. See paragraph one of the *Acta* in Chapter 1: "Macau is part of Chinese territory and will be returned to China . . . when both Governments consider appropriate." "Acta das Conversações sobre a Questão de Macau".
8. Miranda, "The Joint Declaration Negotiations", p. 72.
9. Silva, *Autobiografia Política*, pp. 203–4.
10. These points were confirmed by interviews with people involved in the process.
11. For the Portuguese elite perception of the differences between Macau and Hong Kong see, for example, Miranda, "The Joint Declaration Negotiations", p. 73 and Vieira, "Macau and the Future", p.127.
12. Vasco, "Macau and the Future", p. 134.
13. Catarino, "Grupo de Ligação Conjunto", p. 2.
14. Sampaio, *Portugueses*, Vol. IV, p. 444.
15. Jiang Zemin, "Speech at the Official Handover Ceremony—20/12/1999", *Macau Focus*, Handover Issue, vol. I, no. 1, March 2000, pp. 75–76.
16. João de Deus Ramos, "As Relações Luso-Chinesas e a Declaração Conjunta de 1987", *A Presença Portuguesa no Pacífico—Forum Macau*, Lisbon, ISCSP, 1999, p. 153.
17. Miranda, "The Joint Declaration Negotiations", p. 73.
18. *Far Eastern Economic Review*, 22 August 1985 and 25 September 1986. See Chapter 2 of this book.

19. Ambassador José Manuel Duarte de Jesus, Portuguese Ambassador in Beijing from 1992 to 1997; interviewed in Lisbon, 3 June 2011.
20. Ramos, "As Relações Luso-Chinesas", p. 152.
21. See, for example, Miranda, "The Joint Declaration Negotiations", pp. 74–75.
22. Portugal accepted not having sovereignty over Macau since early stages of the settlement.
23. "Relatório das Negociações e Acordo Luso-Chinês sobre Macau", paragraphs 111–14.
24. See, for example, Vieira, "Macau and the Future", p. 147.
25. Carlos, "Macau", p. 162.
26. Ambassador José Manuel Duarte de Jesus, interviewed in Lisbon, 3 June 2011.
27. Vieira, "Macau and the Future", p. 133.
28. "Relatório das Negociações e Acordo Luso-Chinês sobre Macau", paragraphs 23–32 and 37–38.
29. Lucian W. Pye, *Chinese Negotiating Style: Commercial Approaches and Cultural Principles*, New York, Quorum Books, 1992, p. 51.
30. "Relatório das Negociações e Acordo Luso-Chinês sobre Macau", paragraphs 33–36.
31. Catarino, "Macau Seen from Four Angles", p. 94.
32. Ramos, "As Relações Luso-Chinesas", p. 152.
33. Carlos, "Macau", p. 165.
34. Catarino, "Macau Seen from Four Angles", p. 104.
35. Carlos, "Macau", p. 171.
36. Santos and Gomes, *Macau*, p. 492.
37. For more information on the solution found for the Portuguese School, kindly see Vieira, "Macau and the Future", pp. 157–58.
38. *Expresso*, 30 August 1986. Miranda, "The Joint Declaration Negotiations", p. 68.
39. Ambassador Octávio Neto Valério, Portuguese Ambassador in Beijing from 1985 to 1989 and advisor of the Portuguese delegation in the negotiations with China; interviewed in Lisbon, 1 August 2002.
40. Herbert S. Yee, *Macau in Transition: From Colony to Autonomous Region*, London, Palgrave, 2001, p. 154.

Bibliography

Primary Sources

Unpublished material

Interviews

Engineer Carlos Melancia, Macau Governor from July 1987 to April 1991; interviewed in Lisbon, 30 July 2002.
Ambassador António Costa Lobo, Portuguese Ambassador in Beijing from 1982 to 1985; interviewed in Lisbon, 7 August 2002.
Ambassador José Manuel Duarte de Jesus, Portuguese Ambassador in Beijing from 1992 to 1997; interviewed in Lisbon, 3 June 2011.
Ambassador Octávio Neto Valério, Portuguese Ambassador in Beijing from 1985 to 1989 and advisor of the Portuguese delegation in the negotiations with China; interviewed in Lisbon, 1 August 2002.
General Garcia Leandro, Macau Governor from 1974 to 1979; interviewed in Lisbon, 25 July 2002 and 28 June 2011.
Prof. Moisés da Silva Fernandes, professor of the University of Lisbon; conversation in Lisbon, 18 and 20 December 2001.
Prof. Richard Louis Edmonds, Macau Expert; conversation in Coimbra, 18 November 2010.

Documents

"Acta do Conselho de Estado" [Proceedings of the Portuguese Council of State], no. 9, 17 June 1985, Archives of the Presidency of the Portuguese Republic, Lisbon.
"Acta de conversa na 10ª reunião do GLC sobre o estatuto da língua chinesa e língua portuguesa em Macau" [Minutes of talks on the 10th JLG meeting on the status of the Chinese language and Portuguese language in Macau], Macau, 12 April 1991.
Almeida, Luís Crucho de, "Competência para Legislar sobre o Estatuto da Língua Chinesa em Macau" [Competence to legislate the status of the Chinese language in Macau], Informação de Serviço [internal memorandum], Ministry of Foreign Affairs, Lisbon, 7 August 1991.

Almeida, Macedo, "Localização das Leis—Informação tendo em vista a preparação da 11ª reunião plenária do GLC" [Localisation of the Law—Information to prepare the 11th JLG plenary meeting], Office of the Under-Secretary for Justice, Macau Government, 1 July 1991.

Ambassador Pedro Catarino to the Portuguese Ministry of Foreign Affairs, Telegram no. 459, 1st part, Macau, 12 July 1992.

"As Quatro Grandes Preocupações da Parte Chinesa Relativamente ao Processo de Localização dos Quadros" [The big four Chinese preoccupations regarding the localisation of the civil service], Serviço de Informação e Administração Pública, Macau Government.

"A Questão da Localização na Administração" [The localization question in the Administration], Memorandum, Governor's Office, Macau Government.

"As Relações entre Portugal e a RPC: Análise da Estratégia Portuguesa, 1975–1978" [Relations between Portugal and the PRC: Analysis of the Portuguese Strategy, 1975–1978], GEP/DE/1/78; Diplomatic Historical Archives—Ministry of Foreign Affairs, Lisbon.

Cabrita, Eduardo, "Nível de Localização do G.T.J.", Memorandum, Legal Translation Bureau, Macau Government, 3 September 1991.

Cabrita, Eduardo, "Oficialização da Língua Chinesa no Âmbito do Processo Legislativo" [Official use of the Chinese language within the legislative process], Legal Translation Bureau, Macau Government, 4 June 1991.

CAM, "Macau International Airport, presenting the project to the JLG", Companhia do Aeroporto de Macau [Macau International Airport Company Limited], Macau, 6 July 1992.

Catarino, Pedro, "Grupo de Ligação Conjunto Luso-Chinês" [Sino-Portuguese Joint Liaison Group], Informação de Serviço [internal memorandum], Ministry of Foreign Affairs, Lisbon, 11 April 1990.

Catarino, Pedro, "JLG's 11th Plenary Meeting, Beijing, 10–13 September 1991", Informação de Serviço [internal memorandum], Ministry of Foreign Affairs, Lisbon, 23 September 1991.

Catarino, Pedro, "JLG's 12th Plenary Meeting, Macau, 2–4 December 1991", Informação de Serviço [internal memorandum], Ministry of Foreign Affairs, Lisbon, 17 December 1991.

Catarino, Pedro, "JLG's 13th Plenary Meeting, Lisbon, 16–19 March 1992", Informação de Serviço [internal memorandum], Ministry of Foreign Affairs, Lisbon, 27 April 1992.

Catarino, Pedro, "JLG's 14th Plenary Meeting, Macau, 6–8 July 1992", Informação de Serviço [internal memorandum], Ministry of Foreign Affairs, Lisbon, 20 August 1992.

"Exchange of Notes between China and Portugal for the Relinquishment by Portugal of its Rights Relating to the Consular Jurisdiction in China and the Adjustment of Certain Other Matters", Nanjing, 1 April 1947.

"Funções do Grupo de Terras; Sua interferência no processo de concessão de terrenos" [Functions of the Land Group; Its interference in the process of concession of land], Sino-Portuguese Land Group, 14 June 1988.

Bibliography   145

Gomes, Ribeiro, "Funções do Grupo de Terras" [Functions of the Land Group], Office of the Under-Secretary for Public Works and Housing, Macau, 10 February 1988.
Guimarães, Andresen, "Macau Airport", note, JLG and LG Portuguese Representation in Macau, 6 November 1992.
Informal meeting of the heads of the JLG's delegations, Beijing, 10 September 1991.
Informal meeting of the heads of the JLG's delegations, Lisbon, 16 March 1992.
Informal meeting of the heads of the JLG's delegations, Macau, 18 June 1991.
Informal meeting of the heads of the JLG's delegations, Macau, 21 June 1991.
Informal meeting of the heads of the JLG's delegations, Macau, 22 June 1991.
Informal meeting of the heads of the JLG's delegations, Macau, 4 September 1991.
Informal meeting of the heads of the JLG's delegations, Macau, 19 February 1992.
Informal meeting of the heads of the JLG's delegations, Macau, 21 February 1992.
Informal meeting of the heads of the JLG's delegations, Macau, 22 February 1992.
Informal meeting of the heads of the JLG's delegations, Macau, 6 July 1992.
"Informal meeting of the heads of the Portuguese and Chinese delegations of the JLG regarding the integration of Macau civil servants in Portugal's civil service", Portuguese Representation to the JLG and LG in Macau, 3 September 1991.
"Integração" [Integration], Serviço de Informação e Administração Pública, Macau Government, no date (perhaps 1991).
Letter from Pedro Catarino to Luis Vasconcelos, Ministry of Foreign Affairs, Lisbon, 11 December 1990.
Letter from the Under-Secretary for Justice to the Governor, 25 September 1991.
Letter from the Under-Secretary for Justice to the Governor, "Preparation of JLG's 12th Plenary Meeting", Macau, 27 November 1991.
"Localização de Quadros e Generalização do Uso da Língua Chinesa na Administração—Balanço dos Trabalhos Realizados em 1994" [Localisation of the civil service and use of the Chinese language in the administration—balance of the works undertaken in 1994], Speech of the Under-Secretary for Administration, Education, and Youth Affairs, Macau Government, C.A.T., 24 February 1995.
Meeting of the heads of the JLG's delegations, Macau, 26 November 1991.
Meeting of the Joint Working Group on the Three Big Issues, Macau, 10 July 1991.
Meeting restricted to the members of the JLG's delegations, Macau, 7 July 1992.
Meeting restricted to the members of the JLG's delegations, Macau, 11 November 1992.
No author (perhaps Eduardo Cabrita), no name, Legal Translation Bureau, Macau Government, no date (perhaps 1991).
"Oficialização da Língua Chinesa" [Official use of the Chinese language], Legal Translation Bureau, Macau Government, 1991.

Oliveira, Jorge and Luis Melo, "Da 'Localização das Leis' à Definição de uma Estratégia Conjunta entre Portugal e a RPC quanto à Continuidade do Ordenamento Jurídico de Macau" [From the 'Localization of the Law' to the definition of a common strategy between Portugal and the PRC on the continuity of Macau's juridical organisation], Legal Affairs Bureau, Macau Government, no date (perhaps 1991).
Proceedings of JLG's 7th plenary meeting, Beijing, 16 May 1990.
Proceedings of JLG's 9th plenary meeting, Lisbon, 3 December 1990.
Proceedings of JLG's 9th plenary meeting, Lisbon, 4 December 1990.
Proceedings of JLG's 10th plenary meeting, Macau, 10 April 1991.
Proceedings of JLG's 11th plenary meeting, Macau, 11 September 1991.
Proceedings of JLG's 12th plenary meeting, Macau, 2–4 December 1991.
Proceedings of JLG's 13th plenary meeting, Lisbon, 16–19 March 1992.
Proceedings of JLG's 14th plenary meeting, Macau, 7 July 1992.
Governor Rocha Vieira's speech in the Portuguese State Council meeting, Lisbon, 15 April 1997.
"Relações diplomáticas entre Portugal e a República Popular da China: passos para o seu estabelecimento" [Portugal-China diplomatic relations: steps for its resumption], Informação de Serviço [internal memorandum], Lisbon, 20 October 1975; Diplomatic Historical Archives—Ministry of Foreign Affairs.
"Relações de Portugal com a China e situação em Macau" [Portugal-China relations and the situation in Macau], Informação de Serviço [internal memorandum], Lisbon, 9 August 1976; Diplomatic Historical Archives—Ministry of Foreign Affairs.
"Relatório das Negociações e Acordo Luso-Chinês sobre Macau" [Report of the negotiations and Sino-Portuguese agreement on Macau], Informação de Serviço [internal memorandum], Ministry of Foreign Affairs, Lisbon, 29 June 1987.
"Reunião com o Senhor Embaixador Nunes Portela" [meeting with Ambassador Nunes Portela], Letter from the Under-Secretary for Justice to the Governor, Macau Government, 29 October 1991.
"Reunião Informal do Grupo de Trabalho sobre as Três Grandes Questões" [Preparation of the Meeting of the Joint Working Group on the Three Big Issues], to take place on 10 June 1991.

Published Material

Government documents

"Acta das Conversações sobre a Questão de Macau", Paris, 8 February 1979; Diplomatic Historical Archives—Ministry of Foreign Affairs, Lisbon.
Basic Law of the Hong Kong Special Administrative Region.
Basic Law of the Macau Special Administrative Region.
Constitution of the Portuguese Republic.
Diário da República [The Official Journal], Lisbon.
International Covenant on Civil and Political Rights.

International Covenant on Economic, Social and Cultural Rights.
Joint Declaration of the Government of the People's Republic of China and the Government of the Republic of Portugal on the Question of Macau, Beijing, 13 April 1987.
Joint Declaration of the Government of the People's Republic of China and the Government of the United Kingdom of Great Britain and Northern Ireland on the Question of Hong Kong, Beijing, 19 December 1984.
Macau Organic Law.
Nationality Law of the People's Republic of China—China Law No. 71, 10 September 1980.
Nationality Law of the Portuguese Republic—Law 37/81, 1981.
Official Bulletin of Macau.

Memoirs and Official Speeches

Baptista, António Alçada, "Os primeiros dez anos da Fundação Oriente: a criação da Fundação", *Fundação Oriente: 10 anos—1988-1998*, Lisbon, Orient Foundation, 1998.
Catarino, Pedro, "Macau Seen from Four Angles at Four Different Moments in Its History: From Macau, Hong Kong, Lisbon, and Beijing", in Luís Filipe Barreto (ed.) *Proceedings of the Seminar Paths of Macau and of Portuguese-Chinese Relations (1974-1999)*, Lisbon, Centro Científico e Cultural de Macau, 2010, pp. 89-108.
Gabriel, João, *Confidencial: A Década de Sampaio em Belém*, Prime Books, 2007.
Gama, Jaime, *Política Externa Portuguesa, 1983-1985*, Lisbon, Ministry of Foreign Affairs, 1985.
Howe, Geoffrey, *Conflict of Loyalty*, London, Pan Books, 1995.
Jiang, Zemin, "Speech at the Official Handover Ceremony—20/12/1999", *Macau Focus*, Handover Issue, vol. I, no. 1, March 2000.
Leandro, Garcia, "The Years of the Great Change 1974/1979", in Luís Filipe Barreto (ed.) *Proceedings of the Seminar Paths of Macau and of Portuguese-Chinese Relations (1974-1999)*, Lisbon, Centro Científico e Cultural de Macau, 2010, pp. 19-42.
———. *Macau nos Anos da Revolução Portuguesa—1974-1979*, Lisbon, Gradiva, 2011.
Machado, Joaquim Pinto, "The Governance of the Territory during the Luso-Chinese Talks on the 'Question of Macau'", in Luís Filipe Barreto (ed.) *Proceedings of the Seminar Paths of Macau and of Portuguese-Chinese Relations (1974-1999)*, Lisbon: Centro Científico e Cultural de Macau, 2010, pp. 43-65.
Martins, António Coimbra, *Esperanças de Abril*, Lisbon, Perspectivas & Realidades, 1981.
Melancia, Carlos, "The Challenges of Transition", in Luís Filipe Barreto (ed.) *Proceedings of the Seminar Paths of Macau and of Portuguese-Chinese Relations (1974-1999)*, Lisbon: Centro Científico e Cultural de Macau, 2010, pp. 109-22.
Miranda, Pedro Pires de, *Política Externa Portuguesa, 1985-1987*, Lisbon, Ministry of Foreign Affairs, 1987.

———. "The Joint Declaration Negotiations", in Luís Filipe Barreto (ed.) *Proceedings of the Seminar Paths of Macau and of Portuguese-Chinese Relations (1974–1999)*, Lisbon, Centro Científico e Cultural de Macau, 2010, pp. 67–75.
Moreira, Adriano, *Política Ultramarina*, Lisbon, Ministério do Ultramar, 1956.
Nogueira, Franco, *Terceiro Mundo*, 2nd ed., Lisbon, Ática, 1969.
Patten, Chris, *East and West*, London, Pan Books, 1999.
Sampaio, Jorge, *Portugueses*, Vol. I, Lisbon, Imprensa Nacional-Casa da Moeda, 1997.
———. *Portugueses*, Vol. IV, Lisbon, Imprensa Nacional-Casa da Moeda, 2000.
Silva, Aníbal Cavaco, *Autobiografia Política*, Vol. I, Lisbon, Temas e Debates, 2002.
———. *Autobiografia Política*, Vol. II, Lisbon, Temas e Debates, 2004.
Silva, Teresa e Dias, Carlos (cords.), *Direito e Justiça em Macau*, Office of the Under-Secretary for Justice, Macau, Editora Livros do Oriente, 1999.
Soares, Mário, *Intervenções 3*, Lisbon, Imprensa Nacional-Casa da Moeda, 1989.
———. *Intervenções 4*, Lisbon, Imprensa Nacional-Casa da Moeda, 1990.
———. "Macau: Uma Responsabilidade Histórica—Discurso de Sua Excelência o Presidente da República Dr. Mário Soares", Missão de Macau, Lisbon, 22 May 1990.
———. *Intervenções 5*, Lisbon, Imprensa Nacional-Casa da Moeda, 1991.
———. *Intervenções 8*, Lisbon, Imprensa Nacional-Casa da Moeda, 1994.
Vieira, Pedro, *Todos os Portos a que Cheguei*, Lisbon, Gradiva, 2010.
Vieira, Vasco Rocha, "Macau and the Future", in Luís Filipe Barreto (ed.) *Proceedings of the Seminar Paths of Macau and of Portuguese-Chinese Relations (1974–1999)*, Lisbon, Centro Científico e Cultural de Macau, 2010, pp. 123–62.

Press

BBC Summary of World Broadcasts (London)
Beijing Review (Beijing)
Diário de Notícias (Lisbon)
Expresso (Lisbon)
Far Eastern Economic Review (Hong Kong)
Hong Kong Standard (Hong Kong)
Jornal de Notícias (Lisbon)
The New York Times (New York)
O Comércio de Macau (Macau)
O Tempo (Lisbon)
Ponto Final (Macau)
Semanário (Lisbon)
South China Morning Post (Hong Kong)
Tribuna de Macau (Macau)

Secondary Works

Books

A Presença Portuguesa no Pacífico—Forum Macau, Lisbon, ISCSP, 1999.

Ansprenger, Franz, *The Dissolution of the Colonial Empires*, London, Routledge, 1989.
Atwell, Pamela, *British Mandarins and Chinese Reformers: The British Administration of Weihaiwei (1898–1930) and the Territory's Return to the Chinese Rule*, Hong Kong, Oxford University Press, 1985.
Bender, Gerald J., *Angola under the Portuguese: The Myth and the Reality*, University of California Press, 1978.
Berridge, G. R., *Diplomacy: Theory and Practice*, second ed., London, Palgrave, 2002.
Castanheira, José Pedro, *Macau: Os Últimos Cem Dias do Império*, Lisbon, Publicações Dom Quixote e Livros do Oriente, 2000.
———. *Os 58 dias que abalaram Macau*, Lisboa, Publicações Dom Quixote, 1999.
Castelo, Cláudia, *"O Modo Português de Estar no Mundo": o Luso-Tropicalismo e a Ideologia Colonial Portuguesa (1933–1961)*, Edições Afrontamento, 1998.
Chamberlain, Muriel E., *European Decolonisation in the Twentieth Century*, Longman Companions to History, London, Longman, 1998.
Chan, Ming K. and Lo Shiu-hing, *Historical Dictionary of the Hong Kong SAR and the Macao SAR*, Lanham, Scarecrow Press, 2006
Clarence-Smith, Gervase, *The Third Portuguese Empire 1825–1975*, Manchester, Manchester University Press, 1985.
Cohen, Raymond, *Negotiating Across Cultures: Communication Obstacles in International Diplomacy*, Washington, United States Institute of Peace Press, 1995.
Conceição, Lourenço Maria da, *Macau entre Dois Tratados com a China, 1862–1887*, Macau, ICM, 1988.
Conklin, Alice L., *A Mission to Civilize—The Republican Idea of Empire in France and West Africa, 1895–1930*, Stanford, Stanford University Press, 1997.
Cottrell, Robert, *The End of Hong Kong: The Secret Diplomacy of Imperial Retreat*, London, John Murray, 1993.
Cradock, Percy, *Experiences of China*, London, John Murray, 1999.
Cunha, Silva, *O Ultramar, a Nação e o "25 de Abril"*, Coimbra, Atlântida Editora, 1977.
Darwin, John, *Britain and Decolonisation*, London, Macmillan, 1988.
Edmonds, Richard Louis, (compiler), *Macau*, Vol. 105, Oxford, Clio Press, 1989.
Fairbank, John King, and Merle Goldman, *China: A New History*, Harvard, Belknap Press, 1998.
Fernandes, Moisés Silva, *Sinopse de Macau nas Relações Luso-Chinesas—1945–1995*, Lisbon, Fundação Oriente, 2000.
Fok Fai Cheong, *Estudos sobre a Instalação dos Portugueses em Macau*, Lisbon, Gradiva, 1996.
Freyre, Gilberto, *O Luso e o Trópico*, Lisbon, 1961.
Fung, Edmund S. K., *The Diplomacy of Imperial Retreat: Britain's South China Policy, 1924–1931*, Hong Kong, Oxford University Press, 1991.
Goh, Bee Chen, *Negotiating with the Chinese*, Aldershot, Dartmouth, 1996.
Habeeb, William Mark, *Power and Tactics in International Negotiation—How Weak Nations Bargain with Strong Nations*, London, Johns Hopkins University Press, 1988.

Hargreaves, John, *Decolonization in Africa*, 2nd ed., London, Longman, 1996.
Hobsbawm, Eric, *Age of Extremes*, London, Abacus, 1995.
Holland, R. F., *European Decolonization 1918–1981: An Introductory Survey*, London, Macmillan, 1985.
Jackson, Robert, *Quasi-States: Sovereignty, International Relations and the Third World*, Cambridge, Cambridge University Press, 1990.
Kemenade, Willem Van, *China, Hong Kong, Taiwan, Inc.*, London, Abacus, 1999.
Lara, António de Sousa, *Colonização Moderna e Descolonização*, Lisbon, ISCSP, 2000.
Lima, Fernando, *Macau: As Duas Transições*, Vol. 1 and 2, Macau, Fundação Macau, 1999.
Lo, Shiu Hing, *Political Development in Macau*, Hong Kong, The Chinese University Press, 1995.
Merrills, *International Dispute Settlement*, London, Sweet & Maxwell, 1984.
Oliveira, Fernando C., *500 Anos de Contactos Luso-Chineses*, Lisbon, Público and Fundação Oriente, 1998.
Pereira, Francisco G., *Portugal A China e a "Questão de Macau"*, Macau, Instituto Português do Oriente, 1995.
Porch, Douglas, *The Portuguese Armed Forces and the Revolution*, London, Croom Helm, 1977.
Pye, Lucian W., *Chinese Negotiating Style: Commercial Approaches and Cultural Principles*, New York, Quorum Books, 1992.
Saldanha, António Vasconcelos de, *Estudos sobre as Relações Luso-Chinesas*, Lisbon, ISCSP and ICM, 1996.
Santos, Boaventura de S. and Gomes Conceição, *Macau—O Pequeníssimo Dragão*, Porto, Edições Afrontamento, 1998.
Segal, Gerald, *The Fate of Hong Kong*, London, Simon & Schuster, 1993.
Silveira, Jorge Noronha, *Subsídios para a História do Direito Constitucional de Macau (1820–1974)*, Macau, IPO.
Solomon, Richard H., *Chinese Political Negotiating Behavior, 1967–1984*, Santa Monica, Rand, 1995.
Souza, George Bryan, *The Survival of Empire: Portuguese Trade and Society in China and the South China Sea 1630–1754*, Cambridge University Press, 2004.
Starkey, Brigid, Mark A. Boyer and Jonathan Wilkenfeld, *Negotiating a Complex World*, Oxford, Rowman & Littlefield Publishers, 1999.
Stein, Janice Gross (ed.) *Getting to the Table*, The Processes of International Prenegotiation, Baltimore, The Johns Hopkins University Press, 1989.
Strauss, Julia C., *Strong Institutions in Weak Polities: State Building in Republican China 1927–1940*, New York, Oxford University Press, 1998.
Subrahmanyam, Sanjay, *The Portuguese Empire in Asia, 1500–1700: A Political and Economic History*, 2nd ed., Wiley-Blackwell, 2012.
Tsang, Steve, *Hong Kong, An Appointment with China*, London, I. B. Tauris, 1997.
Wesley-Smith, Peter, *Unequal Treaty 1898–1997*, Revised Edition, Hong Kong, Oxford University Press, 1998.
Wilson, Henry S., *African Decolonization*, London, Edward Arnold, 1994.
Wu Zhiliang, *Segredos da Sobrevivência—História Política de Macau*, Macau, Associação de Educação de Adultos de Macau, 1999.

Yee, Herbert S., *Macau in Transition: From Colony to Autonomous Region*, London, Palgrave, 2001.
Young, Oran R. (ed.) *Bargaining: Formal Theories of Negotiation*, Urbana, University of Illinois Press, 1975.
Zartman, I. William and Maureen R. Berman, *The Practical Negotiator*, New Haven, Yale University Press, 1982.

Articles

Barreto, Luis Filipe, "A Condição Histórico-Cultural de Macau (Séculos XVI e XVII)", *Guia do Museu*, Centro Científico e Cultural de Macau, 1999.
Berton, Peter, "Culture-Communication-Negotiation: Japan, China and the Soviet Union/Russia", *International Comparative Studies of Negotiating Behavior*, Kyoto, International Research Center for Japanese Studies, March 1998.
Chang, Jaw-ling, "Settlement of the Macao Issue: Distinctive Features of Beijing's Negotiating Behavior", *Case Western Reserve Journal of International Law*, vol. 20, no. 1, Winter 1988.
Davis, Clarence B. and Robert J. Gowen, "The British at Weihaiwei: A Case Study in the Irrationality of Empire", *Historian*, Fall 2000, vol. 63, issue 1.
Domenach, Jean-Luc, "Hong Kong: O Fim de Uma Colónia", *Política Internacional*, no. 14, vol. 1, Spring–Summer 1997.
Edmonds, Richard Louis, and Herbert S. Yee, "Macau: From Portuguese Autonomous Territory to Chinese Special Administrative Region", *The China Quarterly*, no. 160, December 1999.
Faure, Guy Olivier, "Cultural Aspects of International Negotiation", *International Comparative Studies of Negotiating Behavior*, Kyoto, International Research Center for Japanese Studies, March 1998.
Fernandes, Moisés Silva, "O comportamento português sobre a transição política e a integração regional de Macau na região do rio das Pérolas", *Administração*, vol. 10, no. 36, July 1997.
———. "Enquadramento das Relações Luso-Chinesas entre 1949 e 1966", *Administração*, vol. 11, no. 40, June 1998.
———. "Macau nas Relações Sino-Portuguesas, 1949–1979", *Administração*, no. 46, vol. 12, 1999.
———. "Macau e os Reflexos do Maoísmo, 1949–1979", *Encontros*, no. 5, 1st Semester 2000.
———. "Portugal, Macau e a China—Confluência de Interesses", *História*, New Series, Year 22, No. 21, January 2000.
———. "A iniciativa gorada de Franco Nogueira para o estabelecimento de relações diplomáticas entre Portugal e a China Continental em 1964", *Administração*, vol. 15, no. 56, June 2002.
———. "A Normalização das Relações Luso-Chinesas e a Questão da Retrocessão de Macau à China Continental, 1974–1979", *Administração*, vol. 16, no. 61, September 2003.
———. "Contextualização das negociações de Paris sobre a normalização das relações luso-chinesas, 1974–1979", *Negócios Estrangeiros*, no. 16, February 2010.

Frain, Maritheresa, "O PSD como partido dominante em Portugal", *Análise Social*, 4th Issue, vol. xxxi (138).
Gonçalves, Arnaldo, "Macau, Timor and Portuguese India in the Context of Portugal's Recent Decolonization", in Stewart Lloyd-Jones and António Costa Pinto, *The Last Empire: Thirty Years of Portuguese Decolonization*, Bristol, Intellect, 2003.
Jackson, Robert, "The Weight of Ideas in Decolonization: Normative Change in International Relations", in Judith Goldstein and Robert Keohane, *Ideas and Foreign Policy*, Ithaca, Cornell University Press, 1993.
Jayawickrama, Nihal, "The Right of Self-Determination", proceedings from a seminar on the Basic Law, held at the University of Hong Kong, 5 May 1990.
Kirby, William C., "The Internationalisation of China: Foreign Relations at Home and Abroad in the Republican Era", *The China Quarterly*, June 1997, Issue 150.
Kivimäki, Timo, "Distribution of Benefits in Bargaining between a Superpower and a Developing Country—A Study of Negotiation Processes between the United States and Indonesia", *Commentationes Scientiarum Socialium*, 45, 1993.
Lam, Jermain T. M., "Sino-British Relations over Hong Kong during the Final Phase of Political Transition", *International Studies*, 34, 4, 1997.
Lo Shiu-hing, "Aspects of Political Development in Macao", *The China Quarterly*, no. 120, December 1989.
Porter, Jonathan, "A Question of Sovereignty", *China Perspectives*, 26, November/ December 1999.
Ress, Georg, "The Hong Kong Agreement and Its Impact on International Law", in Domes Jürgen and Shaw Yu-ming (eds.) Hong Kong, *A Chinese and International Concern*, Boulder, Westview Press, 1988.
Saldanha, António Vasconcelos de, "Some Aspects of the 'Macau Question' and its Reflex in Sino-Portuguese Relations within the United Nations", *Portuguese Review of International and Community Institutions*, Lisbon, ISCSP, 1996.
Thompson, Kenneth W. and Roy C. Macridis, "The Comparative Study of Foreign Policy", in Roy C. Macridis (ed.) *Foreign Policy in World Politics*, New Jersey, Prentice-Hall, Englewood Cliffs, 4th edition, 1972.
Wohlgemuth, Patricia, "The Portuguese Territories and the United Nations", *International Conciliation*, no. 545, November 1963.
Zartman, I. William, "The Political Analysis of Negotiation: How Who Gets What and When", *World Politics*, 26, April 1974, p. 385.
——. "Negotiation as a Joint Decision-Making Process", *Journal of Conflict Resolution*, vol. 21, no. 4, December 1977.
——. "Justice in Negotiation", *International Comparative Studies of Negotiating Behavior*, International Research Center for Japanese Studies, Kyoto, March 1998.

Index

Acta Secreta (Secret Memorandum)/
  Acta das Conversações (Minutes of
  Conversations),
  content, 32, 140n7
  impact for Hong Kong, 41
  in Sino-Portuguese negotiations,
    37, 43, 48, 61
  making it public, 31
  negotiation of, 8, 34–35, 45,
    105–106
  source of embarrassment/
    Portuguese disagreements,
    32–33, 54
Acto Colonial (Colonial Act), 20, 23
Amaral, Joaquim Ferreira do, 7, 11
Ascensão, João 48

Banco Nacional Ultramarino, 53, 57
Barroso, José Manuel Durão, 66
Beijing (*see also* China), 9, 12, 39,
  64–65, 88–91, 93, 99, 105, 107,
  109–111, 113
  Sino-Portuguese talks in, 43–51, 53,
    55, 57–61, 105, 111

Caetano, Marcelo, 23
Caixa Geral de Aposentações, 77
Carnation Revolution, 1
Carvalho, José Manuel Nobre de, 16
Catarino, Pedro, 66, 89, 129n4
China (*see also* Beijing, People's
  Republic of China, Macau, joint
  communiqué, *Acta Secreta*),

negotiations with UK, 4, 38–42, 46,
  61, 105, 109
relationship with Portugal in the
  1970s, 25, 29, 43
sovereignty over Hong Kong and
  Macau, 37–38, 41
Chinese Communist Party, 2
  Central Committee, 3
  Congress, 49, 112
Coelho, Simões, 129n4
colonialism,
  anti-, 20, 24, 34
  European models, 19–20
  neo-, 21
  Portuguese, 1, 8, 17, 21–22, 26–27,
    108
colonial war, 21, 23, 32
Constitution of the People's Republic
  of China (Chinese Constitution),
  3
Constitution of the Portuguese
  Republic (Portuguese
  Constitution), 8, 11, 28, 30,
  46, 54–55, 105, 110, 122n131,
  122n133
Convention of Peace and Friendship,
  39, 41
Cordeiro, Mário, 127n120
Costa, Alfredo Nobre da, 30
Costa, Vasco Almeida e, 43, 47, 108
Council of the Revolution
  (Portuguese), 27
Cultural Revolution (Chinese), 15, 28

Decolonization, 9,
  United Nations Special Committee on, 17,
  Portuguese, 24, 32, 104, 114
Deng, Xiaoping, 28, 37, 41, 60, 107, 124n34

Eanes, António Ramalho, 33, 43–45, 50, 54, 59, 105, 127n91
Estado Novo (New State), 19, 21–23
Estatuto Orgânico de Macau (Macau Organic Law), 8, 27–28, 54, 75, 79–82, 105, 110, 121n123
Evans, Richard, 42

Falklands War, 42
Ferreira, José Medeiros, 29
First World War, 12
Freyre, Gilberto, 22, 120n94

Gama, Jaime, 45, 66, 68, 107, 129n10, 138n68, 139n102
Gaspar, Carlos, 47, 49
Geneva Conference, 14
Granting of Independence to Colonial Countries and Peoples, 20
Guangdong, 16, 107
Guangzhou, 12, 91, 109
Guimarães, Andresen, 66
Guterres, António, 66–68, 107

Handover,
  Hong Kong, 2–3, 5, 39, 55, 57, 81, 112, 128n132
  Macau, 2–4, 39, 48–49, 51–52, 63, 66, 68, 71, 73, 75–78, 81–83, 101, 103, 106–108, 112, 114, 126n61, 134n105, 138n68, 139n102,
Han, Kehua, 29–32
Hankou, 12–13
Han, Zhaokang, 49
Hong Kong (*see also* handover, Joint Declaration on Hong Kong, retrocession, transition), 70

airport, 90–91, 95
colonial history, 12–13, 39–40
comparison with Macau, 4–5, 9, 14, 37–39, 46, 50, 53, 58, 59–60, 61, 83–87, 89, 101, 103, 109–110, 112–114
impact on Macau, 2–3, 8, 11, 31, 42–45, 47–48, 50, 55–56, 61, 72, 80–82, 104–105, 107, 112
in China's policy for national reunification (including Taiwan) 16–17, 24–25, 34, 37, 41, 107
Hong Kong and Macau Office, 48, 64
Hong Kong Basic Law, 86, 134n92
Hong Kong Special Administrative Region (*see also* Hong Kong), 134n92
Horta, Basílio, 30
Ho, Stanley, 95, 99

International Covenant on Civil and Political Rights, 4, 85–87, 113, 135n8
International Covenant on Economic, Social and Cultural Rights, 4, 85, 87, 113

Jesus, José Henriques de, 47, 49
Jesus, José Manuel Duarte de, 99, 138n68
Jiang, Zemin, 99, 101, 107
Jinjiang, 12
Jiujiang, 12
joint communiqué,
  on the resumption of Sino-Portuguese diplomatic relations, 8, 29–31, 34, 54
  for initiating Sino-Portuguese Joint Declaration negotiations, 44–45, 54, 105–106, 129n10
  during the Sino-Portuguese Joint Declaration negotiations, 55, 89, 111
Joint Declaration on Hong Kong (Sino-British), 42, 60–61, 81, 86, 101, 109, 124n32, 134n92

Joint Declaration on Macau (Sino-
   Portuguese) (*see also* China,
   Portugal, joint communiqué),
   107
  annexes, 39, 48–49, 61, 72, 74,
   127n116
  Chinese concerns, 49, 113
  content and wording, 7, 79, 81
  comparison with Joint Declaration
   on Hong Kong, 109, 113–114
  implementation of, 64, 70–74, 76,
   80, 82–83, 85–87, 89, 98, 101,
   104, 136n17
  negotiations of, 50, 69
  signing of, 58–60, 63
  time period (before the, during
   the, after the) 4, 7, 63, 78, 83,
   96–97
Joint Liaison Group (Sino-
   Portuguese), 4, 39, 50, 53, 57, 64,
   72, 86, 105, 107, 130n34

Ke, Zhaisuo, 48
Ke, Zhengping, 48
Korean War, 8, 15, 40
Kowloon Peninsula, 39

Land Fund, 95
Land Group, 4, 64, 72, 74–75, 89, 91
Leal Senado (Loyal Senate), 10
Leandro, José Garcia, 24, 28, 128n141
Legal Translation Bureau, 80, 91–92,
   133n84
Li, Peng, 90–92
Lisbon (*see also* Portugal), 29–30, 37,
   55, 59, 64, 69,
  Orient Foundation in, 96, 99
  Portuguese delegation of the Joint
   Liaison Group based in, 72–73,
   112
  Sino-Portuguese (possible)
   meetings in, 43, 50–51, 53,
   89–90, 92
Lisbon Protocol (1887), 7, 11, 15
Li, Xiannian, 43, 45, 60
Lorena, Nuno, 47
Lusotropicology, 22

Macau (*see also Acta Secreta*, handover,
   Joint Declaration on, retrocession, transition, International
   Covenant, Land Group, Macau
   Basic Law, Macau International
   Airport)
  civil service, 76–78
  in Portuguese decolonization,
   24–25
  legal reforms, 80–82
  political system, 8, 27, 51, 66
  use of Chinese, 79–80, 83
Macau Basic Law, 4, 78, 85, 87, 104,
   132n67
Macau International Airport, 4, 70,
   75, 85, 88–92, 94, 95
Macau Special Administrative Region
   (*see* Macau)
Machado, Joaquim Pinto, 33, 51, 69,
   95–97, 127n120, 128n132
MacLehose, Murray, 41
Mao, Zedong, 25
Martins, António Coimbra, 27, 30–32,
   54
Medina, Rui, 47–48, 58
Melancia, Carlos, 65–67, 69–70, 90,
   106, 110, 129n3, 129n7
Memorandum of Understanding
   on the Portuguese and Chinese
   languages status (1991), 78
Ming dynasty, 10, 11, 15
Miranda, Pedro Pires de, 46, 51,
   54–55, 60, 106, 108, 126n75,
   128n132
Monjardino, Carlos, 53, 96–97, 99,
   108, 127n120
Moreira, Adriano, 33

Nogueira, Alberto Franco, 21–22
North Atlantic Treaty Organisation,
   14

"one country, two systems", 1–2, 37,
   41, 44, 49, 71, 107–108
Opium War, 11, 39
Organization of African Unity, 26

Orient Foundation (*Fundação Oriente*), 4, 53, 67, 69, 78, 85, 87, 95–101, 106, 108, 138n74, 138n76

Partido Renovador Democrático (PRD—Democratic Renewal Party), 59
Partido Social Democrata (PSD—Social Democrat Party), 1, 33, 45, 67
Partido Socialista (PS—Socialist Party), 1, 29, 33, 53, 67–68, 99, 129n6
People's Republic of China (PRC, *see also* China), 1, 30–33, 58,100, 103–104
Pinheiro, João de Deus, 66
Pinto, Carlos Mota, 30, 31, 33, 54, 122n145
Porta do Cerco (Barrier Gate), 10, 15
Portugal (*see also* Lisbon, Macau, *Acta Secreta*, decolonization, joint communiqué), 24–27, 43–45, 47–48, 50–51, 57, 63–66, 68–69, 78, 89–90
  aims for the negotiations, 5, 103–104, 106–107
  consular jurisdiction, 12, 14, 117n27
  negotiation cards/strategy, 20, 38, 72–73, 100–101, 104–106, 108–112
Portuguese-speaking countries, 2
Providências Régias (Regal Providences), 11

Ramos, João de Deus, 47, 49, 129n4
retrocession, 12–13
  concept, 9
  of Hong Kong, 9, 37–38, 41–42, 50, 117n36
  of Macau, 1, 3, 9, 16, 31, 34, 37–38, 43, 45, 50–52, 54–56, 58, 61, 70, 100, 104,110, 113–114
Ritto, Jorge, 66

Salazar, António Oliveira, 14, 16, 19, 22–23, 25, 118n49
Sampaio, Jorge, 66–68, 71, 101, 107
Santos, António Almeida, 24

Second Convention of Beijing, 41
Second World War, 19–20, 42, 104
Shandong, 13
Shanghai, 12–13
Shao, Tianren, 48
Silva, Aníbal Cavaco, 33, 45–49,51–52, 54–60, 66–68, 89, 92, 100, 106, 127n91, 128n132, 138n68
Soares, Eduardo Azevedo, 55
Soares, Mário, 29–30, 33, 45–47, 49, 51–55, 59, 61, 66–68, 70, 95, 99–100, 106, 108, 129n6
Special Committee on Decolonization, 17
State Council,
  Chinese, 48
  Portuguese, 33, 45, 54, 57, 59, 71, 127n120, 130n35

Taipa Island, 16
Taiwan, 1–2, 5, 16–17, 25–26, 31–32, 34, 37, 41, 43, 52, 90, 101, 104, 107–109, 114
Thatcher, Margaret, 42
Tiananmen (incident), 4, 63, 88–90, 95, 100, 110
Tianjin, 12, 39
transition (period),
  Hong Kong, 4, 110,
  Macau, 8, 28, 39, 50, 55, 60–61, 63–64, 66, 69–70, 72, 74–75, 78, 87–88, 90–91, 99, 105–106, 110, 113–114, 125n61, 128n132, 130n34, 135n113
Treaty of Friendship and Trade, 7, 11–12
Treaty of Humen, 39
Treaty of Nanjing, 11–12, 39, 41
Treaty of Tianjin, 39

"unequal treaties", 12
United Kingdom, 4, 42, 46, 95, 109
United Nations, 17, 23, 34, 47–48, 75
  General Assembly Declaration on the Granting of Independence to Colonial Countries and Peoples, 20

Valério, Octávio Neto, 48
Vieira, Vasco Rocha, 67–71, 78, 91,
  106–107, 129n3, 129n7, 139n102

Weihaiwei, 13, 117n36, 117n37
Wu, Xueqian, 31, 43, 45, 60

Xiamen, 12–13
Xinhua News Agency, 29, 133n90

Yangzi valley, 12

Zeng, Tao, 27, 29
Zhao, Jihua, 48–49
Zhao, Ziyang, 42, 44, 50, 60, 63
Zhou, Enlai, 25
Zhou, Nan, 42, 46, 48–53, 58, 60,
  123n7, 126n75, 126n78
Zhuhai
  airport, 88–89, 91, 93
  Macau's autonomy from, 80, 84,
    88, 109
  Special Economic Zone, 50
Zhu, Hua, 48
Zhu (Pearl) River, 9–10, 70–71

www.ingramcontent.com/pod-product-compliance
Ingram Content Group UK Ltd.
Pitfield, Milton Keynes, MK11 3LW, UK
UKHW041914140426
5217IPUK00011B/143/J